AFRICA UNDER NEOLIBERALISM

The period since the 1980s has seen sustained pressure on Africa's political elite to anchor the continent's development strategies in neoliberalism in exchange for vitally needed development assistance. Rafts of policies and programmes have come to underpin the relationship between continental governments and the donor communities of the West and particularly their institutions of global governance – the International Financial Institutions. Over time, these policies and programmes have sought to transform the authority and capacity of the state to effect social, political and economic change, while opening up the domestic space for transnational capital and ideas. The outcome is a continent now more open to international capital, export-oriented and liberal in its political governance. Has neoliberalism finally arrested underdevelopment in Africa?

Bringing together leading researchers and analysts to examine key questions from a multidisciplinary perspective, this book involves a fundamental departure from orthodox analysis which often predicates colonialism as the referent object. Here, three decades of neoliberalism with its complex social and economic philosophy are given primacy. With the changed focus, an elucidation of the relationship between global development and local changes is examined through a myriad of pressing contemporary issues to offer a critical multidisciplinary appraisal of challenge and change in Africa over the past three decades.

Nana Poku is Research Professor of Health Economics at the Health Economics and AIDS Research Division (HEARD) at the University of KwaZulu-Natal, South Africa. He was formerly Executive Director, United Nations Commission on HIV/AIDS and Governance in Africa (2003–05) and Director of Operational Research, World Bank AIDS Treatment Acceleration Programme (2004–06).

Jim Whitman is Professorial Fellow and Co-Director of the HEARD PhD Programme, University of KwaZulu-Natal, South Africa, and General Editor of the Palgrave *Global Issues* series.

Contemporary African Politics Series

1 **Ethnicity, Democracy and Citizenship in Africa**
Political Marginalisation of Kenya's Nubians
Samantha Balaton-Chrimes

2 **African Youth Cultures in a Globalized World**
Challenges, Agency and Resistance
Edited by Paul Ugor, Lord Mawuko-Yevugah

3 **State, Land and Democracy in Southern Africa**
Edited by Arrigo Pallotti and Corrado Tornimbeni

4 **Reinventing Development**
Aid Reform and Technologies of Governance in Ghana
Lord Mawuko-Yevugah

5 **The Horn of Africa Since the 1960s**
Local and International Politics Intertwined
Edited by Aleksi Ylnen and Jan Zahorik

6 **Politics, Public Policy and Social Protection in Africa**
Evidence from Cash Transfer Programmes
Edited by Nicholas Awortwi and E. Remi Aiyede

7 **Africa's Checkered Democracy**
Institutions, Participation and Accountability
Edited by Said Adejumobi

8 **Africa Under Neoliberalism**
Edited by Nana Poku and Jim Whitman

AFRICA UNDER NEOLIBERALISM

Edited by
Nana Poku and
Jim Whitman

LONDON AND NEW YORK

First published 2018
by Routledge
2 Park Square, Milton Park, Abingdon, Oxon OX14 4RN

and by Routledge
711 Third Avenue, New York, NY 10017

Routledge is an imprint of the Taylor & Francis Group, an informa business

© 2018 selection and editorial matter, Nana Poku and Jim Whitman; individual chapters, the contributors

The right of Nana Poku and Jim Whitman to be identified as the authors of the editorial matter, and of the authors for their individual chapters, has been asserted in accordance with sections 77 and 78 of the Copyright, Designs and Patents Act 1988.

All rights reserved. No part of this book may be reprinted or reproduced or utilized in any form or by any electronic, mechanical, or other means, now known or hereafter invented, including photocopying and recording, or in any information storage or retrieval system, without permission in writing from the publishers.

Trademark notice: Product or corporate names may be trademarks or registered trademarks, and are used only for identification and explanation without intent to infringe.

British Library Cataloguing in Publication Data
A catalogue record for this book is available from the British Library

Library of Congress Cataloging in Publication Data
A catalog record for this book has been requested

ISBN: 978-1-4724-2570-6 (hbk)
ISBN: 978-1-4724-2573-7 (pbk)
ISBN: 978-1-315-56596-5 (ebk)

Typeset in Bembo
by Wearset Ltd, Boldon, Tyne and Wear

CONTENTS

List of figures	vii
List of tables	viii
Notes on contributors	ix
Acknowledgments	xii
List of abbreviations and acronyms	xiii

1 Africa under neoliberalism   1
Nana Poku and Jim Whitman

2 Neoliberalism and economic growth in contemporary Africa   23
Augustin Kwasi Fosu and Eric Kehinde Ogunleye

3 As the global commodity super-cycle ends, Africans
continue uprising against 'Africa rising'   48
Patrick Bond

4 Neoliberalism, urbanization and change in Africa   61
Pádraig Carmody and Francis Owusu

5 From urban crisis to political opportunity:
African slums   76
Jeffrey W. Paller

6 The poverty of 'poverty reduction': the case of
African cotton   95
Adam Sneyd

vi Contents

7 Water, water everywhere but not a drop to drink
   (except for a price)   115
   Larry A. Swatuk

8 Autocrats and activists: human rights, democracy and the
   neoliberal paradox in Nigeria   136
   Bonny Ibhawoh and Lekan Akinosho

9 Neoliberalism and alternative forms of citizenship   151
   Amy S. Patterson

Index   173

FIGURES

2.1	Real per capita GDP annual growth, Africa vs. world (1961–2012)	31
2.2	Terms of trade index (1963–2011), sub-Saharan Africa	32
2.3	Evolution of syndrome-free (SF) regime, SSA (1960–2000)	37
2.4	Ghana's real GDP and real per capita GDP growth (per cent) (1961–2014)	38
2.5	Ghana's GDP per capita vs. SSA median (constant 2005 US$) (1960–2014)	39
3.1	Polanyi's 'double movement' in the West, with socio-ecological uprisings anticipated	49
7.1	Share of commodities in total exports	120
7.2	Global commodity index	122

TABLES

2.1	Growth decomposition for sub-Saharan Africa	33
2.2	Per capita GDP growth (annual percentage) for SSA countries between 1961 and 2014, five-year averages (per cent)	34
3.1	Africa's relative labour militancy according to World Economic Forum Competitiveness rankings for 140 countries	56
7.1	GDP growth per capita (current US$) and change in GDP composition 1996–2014	120
7.2	Percentage of labour force in agriculture and classic dependency X/M profile	121
7.3	Exports (X) as a percentage of GDP over time and relative value	121
7.4	Surface water resources in the sub-regions of Africa	127
7.5	Milestones and targets of the African Water Vision for 2025	128
7.6	Consumption as percentage of total household income	130
7.7	Selected country access to improved sanitation and improved water supply	130

CONTRIBUTORS

Lekan Akinosho is a political historian, writer and researcher on issues of human rights, civil society and democracy in Africa. He holds a Bachelor's degree in History from the University of Ibadan, Nigeria and two Masters degrees from Brock University and the University of Waterloo, Canada. He has worked as a journalist, and with pro-democracy organizations that shaped the process of democratization in Nigeria after prolonged military rule.

Patrick Bond is Professor of Political Economy at the University of the Witwatersrand in Johannesburg. Recent books include *BRICS: An Anti-Capitalist Critique* (co-edited, 2016) and *Elite Transition* (3rd edn, 2014). He directed the University of KwaZulu-Natal Centre for Civil Society from 2004–16.

Pádraig Carmody teaches Geography at Trinity College, University of Dublin, where he did his undergraduate and Masters work. His PhD is from the University of Minnesota in the US, where after graduation he also taught at the University of Vermont. At TCD, he co-directs the TCD-UCD Masters in Development Practice. His research centres on the political economy of globalization in Africa and he has published in journals such as *European Journal of Development Research*, *Review of African Political Economy*, *Economic Geography* and *World Development*.

Augustin Kwasi Fosu is Professor, ISSER, University of Ghana; Extraordinary Professor, University of Pretoria, South Africa; Visiting Professor of Economics, Aalto University, Finland; and CSAE Research Associate, University of Oxford, UK. Previously he was Deputy Director, UNU-WIDER, Helsinki; Senior Policy Advisor/Chief Economist, UN-ECA, Addis Ababa; and Director of Research, AERC, Nairobi. He holds a PhD in Economics from Northwestern University, USA.

x Contributors

Bonny Ibhawoh is a Professor of Global Human Rights History, and Peace and Conflict Studies at McMaster University, Canada. He has taught in universities in Nigeria, the United Kingdom, the United States and Canada. He is the author of several books on African history, human rights and peace and conflict studies, including *Imperialism and Human Rights* and *Imperial Justice: Africans in Empire's Court.*

Eric Kehinde Ogunleye, PhD, is currently serving as a Technical Adviser (Policy and Planning) to Nigeria's Honourable Minister of Budget and National Planning. He is widely published on development, macroeconomic and trade issues.

Francis Owusu is Professor and Chair of the Department of Community and Regional Planning at Iowa State University. He holds a PhD in Geography from the University of Minnesota. He teaches courses on international development, world cities and globalization, economic and urban planning, and planning methods. His research focus includes development policy, public sector reforms and capacity building, as well as urban development and livelihood issues, and has published extensively on these topics. He has consulted for several international development agencies, including the World Bank, Partnership for African Social and Governance Research (PASGR), Africa Capacity Building Foundation (ACBF) and National Science Foundation (NSF). He chaired the Africa Specialty Group of the Association of American Geographers from 2005 to 2008.

Jeffrey W. Paller is Assistant Professor of Politics at the University of San Francisco. He was previously a postdoctoral research fellow at the Earth Institute at Columbia University, working with the Center for Sustainable Urban Development. He was written extensively on African urban issues.

Amy S. Patterson is a Professor of Politics at the University of the South, Tennessee, USA. She is editor of *The African State and the AIDS Crisis*, and author of *The Politics of AIDS in Africa*, *The Church and AIDS in Africa*, *Africa in Global Health Governance* (2017), and *Dependent Agency in the Global Health Regime* (with Emma-Louise Anderson, 2016). She has published articles on AIDS, civil society, religion and gender in Africa in *Africa Today*, *Journal of Modern African Studies*, *Canadian Journal of African Studies*, *African Journal of AIDS Research, Global Public Health, Contemporary Politics*, *African Affairs* and *African Studies Review*. She teaches courses on international relations, African politics, global health and development, the politics of AIDS and democratization.

Nana Poku is Research Professor of Health Economics at the Health Economics and AIDS Research Division (HEARD) at the University of KwaZulu-Natal. He was formerly Executive Director, United Nations Commission on HIV/AIDS and Governance in Africa (2003–05) and Director of Operational Research, World Bank AIDS Treatment Acceleration Programme (2004–06).

Adam Sneyd is an Associate Professor in the Department of Political Science and the International Development Studies programme at the University of Guelph. His research focuses on the global politics of commodities, and emphasizes food, resource and development challenges particularly in African contexts. He has published solely authored academic books on the politics of cotton in the Polity Press *Resources Series* and Palgrave Macmillan's *International Political Economy Series*. Adam is currently conducting research on the politics of responsibility in Cameroon's commodity sector.

Larry A. Swatuk is Professor and Director of the Master of Development programme in the School of Environment, Enterprise and Development, University of Waterloo. His latest book is *Water in Southern Africa* (UKZN Press).

Jim Whitman is Professorial Fellow and Co-Director of the HEARD PhD Programme, University of KwaZulu-Natal and General Editor of the Palgrave *Global Issues* series.

ACKNOWLEDGMENTS

We would like to thank all of the contributors for their enthusiasm and responsiveness and for the kind of tolerance that edited book projects usually entail.

Chapter 4 was originally published as: Pádraig Carmody and Francis Owusu. 2016. Neoliberalism, Urbanization and Change in Africa: the Political Economy of Heterotopias. *Journal of African Development* (2016) 18:18: 61–73. We are grateful to the African Finance and Economic Association for permission to reprint it.

Chapter 6 was originally published as: Adam Sneyd. 2015. The Poverty of 'Poverty Reduction': The Case of African Cotton. *Third World Quarterly* 36(1): 55–74. We are grateful to Taylor & Francis Group for permission to reprint it.

Figure 3.1 originally appeared in Michael Burawoy, 'Marxism After Polanyi', in Michelle Williams and Vishwas Satgar (eds), *Marzisms in the 21st Century: Crisis, Critique and Struggle* (Johannesburg: Wits Press, 2013). We are grateful to Wits Press for permission to reprint it.

ABBREVIATIONS AND ACRONYMS

AAACP	All African Agricultural Commodities Programme
ACA	African Cotton Association
ACP	African, Caribbean and Pacific Group of States
ACTIF	African Cotton and Textile Industries Federation
ADMARC	Agricultural and Development Marketing Corporation
AERC	African Economic Research Consortium
AG	Action Group
ANC	African National Congress
AProCA	African Cotton Producers Association
AU	African Union
BCI	Better Cotton Initiative
BRICS	Brazil, Russia, India, China, South Africa
BWI	Bretton Woods Institutions
CAADP	Comprehensive Africa Agriculture Development Programme
CBO	Community-Based Organization
CD	Campaign for Democracy
CDHR	Committee for the Defence of Human Rights
CEEAC	Communauté Économique des États de l'Afrique Centrale
CEMAC	Communauté Économique et Monétaire de l'Afrique Centrale
CLO	Civil Liberties Organization
CmiA	Cotton Made in Africa
CODESRIA	Council for the Development of Social Science Research in Africa
COMESA	Common Market for Eastern and Southern Africa
COS-Coton	Comité d'orientation et de suivi du Partenariat UE-Afrique sur le coton
CPR	Constitutional Rights Projects
CSR	Corporate Social Responsibility

xiv Abbreviations and acronyms

ECA	Economic Commission for Africa
ECOWAS	Economic Community of West African States
ERP	Economic Recovery Programme
ESAF	Enhanced Structural Adjustment Facility
EU	European Union
FAL	Final Act of Lagos
FAO	Food and Agriculture Organization
FDI	Foreign Direct Investment
GDP	Gross Domestic Product
Ha	Hectare
HDI	Human Development Index
HIPC	Heavily Indebted Poor Countries
ICAC	International Cotton Advisory Committee
ICTSD	International Centre for Trade and Sustainable Development
IFF	Illicit Financial Flows
IMF	International Monetary Fund
ING	Interim National Government
ITC	International Trade Centre
IWRM	Integrated Water Resources Management
LFF	Licit Financial Flows
LPA	Lagos Plan of Action
MOSOP	Movement for the Survival of Ogoni People
NANS	National Association of Nigerian Students
NBA	Nigeria Bar Association
NCF	National Consultative Forum
NCNC	National Council of Nigerian Citizens
NEPAD	New Economic Partnership for Economic Development
NGO	Nongovernmental Organization
NMA	Nigeria Medical Association
NNAASP	New Asian-African Strategic Partnership
NPC	Northern People's Congress
NUJ	Nigerian Union of Journalists
NUPENG	National Union of Petroleum and Natural Gas Workers Union
OAU	Organization of African Unity
OECD	Organization for Economic Cooperation and Development
OFDI	Overseas Foreign Direct Investment
PACRM	EU–Africa Partnership on Cotton
PAMSCAD	Program of Action to Mitigate the Social Cost of Adjustment
PPCP	Public–Private–Community Partnership
PPP	Public–Private Partnership
PRC	Provisional Ruling Council
SADC	Southern African Development Community
SAP	Structural Adjustment Programme
SDG	Sustainable Development Goals

SEZ	Special Economic Zone
SF	Syndrome-Free
SNC	Sovereign National Conference
SOE	State-Owned Enterprise
SSA	Sub-Saharan Africa
TFP	Total Factor Productivity
TNC	Transnational Corporation
ToT	Terms of Trade
UEMOA	L'Union Économique et Monétaire Ouest-Africaine
UK	United Kingdom
UN	United Nations
UNCTAD	United Nations Conference on Trade and Development
UNDP	United Nations Development Programme
UNECA	United Nations Economic Commission for Africa
US	United States
US$	US Dollar
WC	Washington Consensus
WIN	Women in Nigeria
WTO	World Trade Organization

1

AFRICA UNDER NEOLIBERALISM

Nana Poku and Jim Whitman

The expansion and consolidation of neoliberalism

Neoliberalism is now both everywhere and nowhere. In political discourse and in academic literature, the visibility of 'neoliberalism' as a primary term in International Political Economy has shrunk very considerably[1] while, at the same time, it has taken adjectival form in research fields as diverse as conservation, criminal justice, urban studies, health care reform, higher education and party politics. The puzzling diffusion of the term can be accounted for in part by the remarkably wide and often imprecise ways in which it has been deployed. Indeed, one research project which examined the literature over a 14-year span concluded that 'the term is often undefined; it is employed unevenly across ideological divides; and it is used to characterize an excessively broad variety of phenomena' (Boas and Gans-Morse 2009, 161). Yet 'neoliberalism' is still frequently invoked in ways that signal both its embeddedness and its decades-long, pervasive effects, often as shorthand to depict – and frequently, to castigate – the inequities of capitalism.

'Neoliberalism' has resisted definitional consensus for many other reasons: its complex history; the involvement of a multitude of both state and non-state actors; shifting, highly adaptable purposes; and varying forms and degrees of political and financial expression. It is not monolithic; unilinear; irresistible; unambiguously good or bad; and in terms of its far-reaching effects, not easy to comprehend from a single viewpoint – socio-political, economic or institutional. But although 'neoliberalism' lacks precision, it has after all taken explicit ideological and programmatic forms; and there are sufficient commonalities between its varieties and phases to make the term meaningful and its history coherent. For our purposes, we can characterize as neoliberal the philosophical and political determination to give primacy to free markets over state-led regulatory regimes for business and trade; and over forms of tax-generated public subsidies. So neoliberalism is concerned essentially with the configuration and re-configuration of relational qualities, particularly between states, citizens and markets (Jones 2012; Burgin 2012). Neoliberal initiatives most often take the form of deregulation and privatization initiatives, as conditional loans in response to financial crises, as 'corrective' austerity measures or as a domestic political determination that formerly state-owned, directed or subsidized sectors will perform more efficiently and to the greater good if obliged to operate in a competitive market.

Much like the wider, enabling dynamics propelling globalization, there is no directing power for neoliberalism writ large, no grand strategic, unified purpose beyond a loosening of restraints on the largely private accumulation of wealth. One needs no recourse to conspiratorial or mono-causal imaginings: the dynamics involved are generated from common (and increasingly networked) interests in re-framing state–market relationships and exploiting opportunities for wealth transference and/or accumulation. In addition to the familiar instruments of neoliberalism – capital controls, the opening up of domestic markets and the shrinking of the state, particularly through curbs on fiscal deficits and the accumulation of debt – there are also politico-financial arrangements such as tax competition, offshore tax havens, forms of inward investment, complex investment vehicles and the ease and speed with which capital can be moved around the world, all of which facilitate neoliberal initiatives, even in the absence of philosophically explicit neoliberalist ideals.

Over decades, the accretion and institutionalization of neoliberal values has been pervasive, both nationally and internationally, constraining and shaping socio-political expectation as much as the institutions of governance. Throughout much of the developed world – and in the US and UK most notably – political differences over the role of the state and the governance of finance mostly turn on the particulars of policy implementation rather than on the issues fundamental to the organization of political community, such as ownership, equity, justice, and the accrual and expression of power and accountability. Neoliberalism has not only shed its once-radical profile; neoliberal arrangements are now unexceptional throughout much of the world, the default setting for a significant portion of the organization of political community, with the result that opposing views struggle to find purchase:

> Once upon a time, antineoliberal theory posited an opposition between the state and the free market, arguing that the antidote to the latter lay in the active intervention of the former. But the opposition is false, just another piece of the detritus of the modern history of capital. As states become mega-corporations ... they become inextricably part of the workings of the market and, hence, no longer 'outside', an antidote, or an antithesis from which to rethink or reconstruct the 'neoliberal paradigm'. This, in part, is why government is increasingly reduced to an exercise in the technical management of capital, why ideologically founded politics appear dead, replaced by the politics of interest and entitlement and identity – three counterpoints of a single triangle. And this is why the capillaries of neoliberal governance seem so firmly entrenched in the cartography of our everyday lives.
>
> *(Comaroff 2011, 146; Mudge 2011)*

But for all of the pervasiveness of neoliberalism, there is a certain sleight of hand at work in the contention that the state should be reduced to something akin to an 'emergency services' role, allowing dynamic entrepreneurship to flourish, since it does not stand up to the empirical evidence of high-risk state investments (especially in science and engineering) facilitating private gains (Mazzucato 2013). This socialization of risk/privatization of gains suddenly became highly visible and reached its apogee with the worldwide banking crisis. The subsequent financial turbulence brought with it predictions of the imminent death, demise or tempering of neoliberalism (Cahill 2011; Grugel and Riggirozzi 2012). Yet once the banking crisis had subsided (in large measure through public bail-outs), there was little corrective/preventive legislation to prevent a recurrence, nor a holding to account of the individuals and corporations responsible (Garrett 2014), nor, most remarkably, a serious and sustained challenge to the neoliberal paradigm (Mirowski 2013). This is despite the fact that the limitations of neoliberalism as a panacea have long been evident, recently to the point that a 2016 paper produced by the International Monetary Fund (IMF)'s own research department argued that 'no fixed agenda delivers good outcomes for all countries for all times. Policymakers, and institutions like the IMF that advise them, must be guided not by faith, but by evidence of what has worked' (Ostry *et al.* 2016, 41). However, the IMF's Chief Economist, Maurice Obstfeld, was quick to state that 'the article has been widely misinterpreted' – 'it [did] not signify a major change in the Fund's approach' and that the Fund had

> not fundamentally changed the core of our approach, which is based on open and competitive markets, robust macro policy frameworks, financial stability, and strong institutions. But it has added important insights about how best to achieve those results in a sustainable way.
>
> *(International Monetary Fund, 2016)*

More broadly, although neoliberal logic informed the regulatory arrangements which 'contributed to the financial crisis of 2008 by putting in place a set of opportunities and constraints that led to rapid growth in the market for asset-backed securities' (Major 2012, 536), neoliberalist principles remain the predominant ideological, institutional and technical governance instruments for configuring global, international and national socio-economic orders – and indeed, for addressing the financial turbulence for which they were partly responsible. The ongoing Greek debt crisis (Souliotis and Alexandri 2017; Konstantinidis 2016) is dramatic, but viewed against the history of neoliberal interventions, it is essentially an unexceptional case:

> [C]rises manifest themselves in specific 'domestic' contexts, each with their own history and internal logic, albeit the origins of such crises are rooted in the general dynamics of the global capitalist system and in the relations among its constituent national entities. [...] In cases where individual states, each with their own history, internal logic, needs, pressures and coercive powers,

have been unable or unwilling to refashion and sustain the requisite domestic social property relations, the ideological architecture of 'state failure' provides the latest imperial justification for interventionism and world-ordering.

(Ayers 2012, 581; 583–4)

The history of neoliberal outcomes, even on an abstracted view of them as technical fixes to macroeconomic frameworks, fiscal stability, soaring national debt or realignment of state–society institutional arrangements, is patchy at best; and in terms of human security and welfare, especially in the poorest states, often deleterious (Dell 1982). This is nowhere more evident than in the history of the Structural Adjustment Programme in southern Africa. The IMF's own commissioned study on its Enhanced Structural Adjustment Facility (ESAF) (IMF/Group of Independent Experts 1998, 9) had as part of its research remit the following, an implicit acknowledgment of scarcely avoidable 'collateral damage':

> To what extent and how has the social impact of ESAF-supported adjustment policies and reforms influenced the use and design of social safety nets, the level of public spending on social services like education, health, and rural development, and the design of the adjustment and reform measures themselves? How effective have the safety nets been in mitigating the effects of macroeconomic adjustment on the poorest members of society?

The findings were an astonishing catalogue of social deprivation and displacement, as the case of Zimbabwe illustrates (IMF/Independent Group of Experts 1998, 107):

> The deregulation of the labour market together with the reduced protection of manufacturing and the reduction in public expenditure produced a severe squeeze in the labour market. Both employment and real wages declined sharply. During 1991–96, formal sector employment in manufacturing fell by 9 per cent and real wages declined by 26 per cent. In public administration employment declined by 23 per cent and real wages fell by 40 per cent.

A summary and extended analysis of the study (Naiman and Watkins 1999) reveals that Zimbabwe was by no means the exception:

- Developing countries worldwide implementing ESAF programmes have experienced lower economic growth than those who have been outside of these programmes. African countries subject to ESAF programmes have fared even worse than other countries pursuing ESAF programmes; countries in Africa subject to ESAF programmes have actually seen their per capita incomes decline. It will be years before these populations recover the per capita incomes that they had prior to structural adjustment.

Africa under neoliberalism **5**

- While African countries urgently need to increase spending on health care, education and sanitation, IMF Structural Adjustment Programmes have forced these countries to reduce such spending. In African countries with ESAF programmes, the average amount of per capita government spending on education actually declined between 1986 and 1996.
- Neither IMF-mandated macroeconomic policies nor debt relief under the IMF-sponsored HIPC (Heavily Indebted Poor Countries) Initiative have sufficiently reduced these countries' debt burdens. Total external debt as a share of GNP for ESAF countries increased from 71.1 per cent to 87.8 per cent between 1985 and 1995. For southern Africa, debt rose as a share of GDP from 58 per cent in 1988 to 70 per cent in 1996. IMF debt relief has not sufficiently reduced the debt service burden of Uganda or Mozambique, the two African HIPC countries that have proceeded furthest under the HIPC initiative. Poor countries continue to divert resources from expenditures on health care and education in order to service external debt.

The important point about these and more recent neoliberal interventions and realignments is not that they inflict short-term damage on the livelihoods and social protections afforded to the poorest populations in order to secure the public good in the long term, but that they re-structure social relations in nearly every fundamental particular, constraining and shaping the opportunity of peoples to give communal and/or political expression to countervailing values. The extensive privatization and monetization of public goods and the shrinking of the compass of state authority (Mansfield 2008; Macdonald 2011) fracture important forms of public access, accountability, deliberation and an inclusive balancing of interests and costs – matters that are no less true in the developed world where the instruments of neoliberalism have also been applied (McGimpsey 2017). Even well-established welfare systems in the developed world are currently under pressure, at times driven by the professed need for 'austerity', but regardless, with the outcome that services are moving rapidly towards privatization. The costs of these many alterations to state–society relations, particularly in terms of social and political cohesion, are considerable – and many of them are as yet unmet:

> How we go about defining the 'public interest' or what constitutes a 'public good' is bound up with a shifting discourse focused on monetary rather than social objectives. Now that fiscal concerns have come to trump all others, it becomes harder to legitimate public goods driven by equity, environmental concerns and social justice criteria. In part this is because marketization processes often involve the 'unbundling' of socio-technical networks or systems, which can be seen as monopolies (e.g. transport system), in order to open up different parts of the network or system to competition and competitive forces. As a consequence, systemic planning is constrained, as are systemic solutions to critical problems that we face; for example, in order to mitigate climate change it will be necessary to systemically transform socio-technical

systems (e.g. housing, energy, transport), but this will be difficult if each part of the system is owned and controlled by different social actors. There is significant risk of lock-in to different market expectations, policies and structures, which means we will find it difficult to change course.

(Birch and Siemiatycki 2016, 194–5)

An additional element in the spread and consolidation of neoliberalism is that the means by which its principles can be enacted now extend beyond the International Financial Institutions (IFIs) and state regimes so disposed. Global capital – now vastly greater, more widely distributed and less restrained than at any time in history – effectively has no need for a clearly articulated ideological rationale: privatization, monetization and de-regulation suffice to ensure that market values and private profit will predominate, provided the way is cleared politically, legislatively or, in the poorest and least coherent states, by default (Raffer 2015). The conditions which facilitate the enactment of neoliberal principles and strictures are also wide-ranging, including 'weak' and/or 'failing' states in their many varieties and degrees (Taylor 2013); post-disaster recovery (Klein 2007); monetary and fiscal crises; the near-default of neoliberal reforms intended to promote 'free market democracy' (Holzner 2007; Centeno 1994); and the impetus to private gain by national regimes and private elites (Schwartz 2002). The scale on which developments can be conceived and the speed with which they can be designed, financed and initiated is breathtaking, because resources can be mobilized or purchased anywhere, whether for constructing shopping malls, golf clubs and gated communities which entail the shrinkage of public spaces (Voyce 2006), converting agriculture for global markets in place of local needs, establishing industrial enterprises for resource extraction and processing or constructing manufacturing and distribution hubs. To paraphrase Marx, all that is not profitable or which stands in the way of it, melts into air, people included – land-owning peasants and squatters on the margins of expanding cities; ways of life, their networks of social relations and physical supports destroyed or appropriated – now often propelled by remote or de-territorialized elites with no strong or enduring allegiance to any locale which would require them to secure themselves by way of sustainability.

So while not always expressed explicitly, the ideological components of neoliberalism are now concurrent with its programmatic and other forms of practical expression – and they have become mutually reinforcing (Morales *et al.* 2014). The acceleration of globalization in recent decades has proceeded similarly, the speed, scale and variety of its constituent developments often masking the larger, structural alterations that they bring about in aggregate. The emergence of the phrase 'governance without government', deployed to describe forms of non-authoritative but effective ordering and control (Rosenau and Czempiel 1992) carries with it meanings that are considerably more than socio-technical: it also describes the neoliberal diminution of options which privilege public goods; wide and inclusive democratic deliberation; solidarity with, and at least minimal support for, the least well-off; tax-generated programmes and/or subsidies for key social development projects and/or everyday sustenance; regulatory regimes to ensure the stability and sustainability of both human and natural systems; and whatever else might fall under the ethos 'government of, by and for the people' in any of the world's nation-states.

Africa and neoliberalism

Neoliberalism and the 'Arab Spring'

For reasons of political geography, culture and history, analyses focused on 'Africa' most often divide the continent between the North and sub-Saharan regions, diverse as these are in themselves. Yet for all the differences in their histories, polities, government structures and economies, the impacts of neoliberal structural adjustments on the poorest citizens of these nations and on their governments' subsequent ability to frame inclusive and beneficent public policy consistent with local conditions have a remarkable consistency. This is because the 'structures' subjected to adjustment have had profound impacts on the complex network of relationships between state, society and markets; and the instruments of structural adjustment – reduced government expenditure; privatization of state-controlled industries; currency devaluation; export promotion; raising interest rates; the removal of price controls – have had severe effects on the poor, including their access to education, health services through cost recovery and end-user fees, welfare entitlements and the rising cost of imports and small business loans. Quite aside from the internal difficulties that have long confronted majority populations in African countries, neoliberal regimes have also further exposed them to the harsh, competitive dynamics of globalization, thereby setting the stage for later cycles of crisis – including popular backlashes against austerity measures – and further rounds of restructuring. The experience of neoliberal reforms in Egypt over the course of four decades is a case in point.

Key to the austerity measures required for IMF and World Bank loans to Egypt in 1977 was the termination of subsidies of basic commodities and foodstuffs, including wheat, which sparked serious food riots. Even 30 years later, the majority of the population remained critically vulnerable to the familiar range of neoliberal instruments: 'It is estimated that in 2007, only eight million out of a population of 74 million had any disposable income at all, with the rest living at or below subsistence level' (Euromonitor International 2008), so then as before – and across the countries of the 'Arab Spring' (Bogaert 2013) – the imposition of neoliberal reforms required alternating cycles of political repression and stop-gap responses to popular dissent. By 2008 and the advent of the world food crisis, the Egyptian government was forced to use foreign reserves to buy wheat on the international market, while the army and Interior Ministry became involved in the manufacture and distribution of bread. Even so, the abiding slogan of the 2011 Egyptian uprising was 'bread, freedom, social justice' (Frerichs 2016).

While poverty is a pervasive feature of most societies, past and present, and can push some individuals towards desperate acts of violence in their struggle for survival, it is the realization of inequality that brings to the disadvantaged a sense of grievance. The advancement of the industrialized states' neoliberal agenda through globalization as an ideology for development has failed to deliver the promised macroeconomic stability and growth, with intended trickle-down benefits. Instead, globalization continues to increase the gap between rich and poor, within and between states, and the barren side of the fence becomes ever more crowded. Globalization thereby services the interests of its advocates, the elites of the core capitalist economies (and their counterparts in countries subjected to neoliberal reforms), at the expense and immiseration of the majority of people in developing economies – arguably a form of neo-colonialism. At the point where desperation meets grievance is where rebellion and radicalization are likely to ferment. The revolutionary uprisings in the Arab world and the Middle East, beginning in 2010 and ongoing, the continuing rumblings of radicalization in Greece in response to imposed austerity measures as conditions of bail-out loans and the wider turn to hard-right, populist and identity politics are worrying symptoms of these mounting pressures (Davidson and Saull 2016).

Importantly, despite the claims of democratic transition, the institutions of the Egyptian state have been consistently remodelled by neoliberalism as an enabling mechanism of the market. This is part of a change in the developmental strategy of the IFIs since the 1990s that emphasized the link between the functioning of the markets and their institutional governance. This strategy promotes the 'rule of law', 'decentralization', 'good governance' and other such measures with the supposed aim of reducing rent-seeking capabilities of the well-connected and in order to ensure greater transparency in economic affairs, but with the underlying aim of advancing the legitimacy for neoliberalism. The result is a tailoring of public institutions to the needs of the private sector while removing any ability of the state to intervene in the market.

While Tunisia and Egypt are already neoliberal, the Western neoliberal globalization ideology continues to strive for both economic and institutional restructuring towards still greater neoliberalism, as a 'solution' to the revolutionary discontent across North Africa from 2011 – an impetus extended to much of the world both before and since (Shefner 2011).

> At the core of this financial intervention in Egypt is an attempt to *accelerate* the neoliberal program that was pursued by the Mubarak regime. The IFI financial packages ostensibly promote measures such as 'employment creation', 'infrastructure expansion' and other seemingly laudable goals, but, in reality, these are premised upon the classic neoliberal policies of privatization, deregulation, and opening to foreign investment. Despite the claims of democratic transition, the institutions of the Egyptian state are being refashioned within this neoliberal drive as an enabling mechanism of the market. Egypt is, in many ways, shaping up as the perfect laboratory of the so-called post-Washington Consensus, in which a liberal-sounding 'pro poor' rhetoric – principally linked to the discourse of democratization – is used to deepen the

neoliberal trajectory of the Mubarak era. If successful, the likely outcome of this – particularly in the face of heightened political mobilization and the unfulfilled expectations of the Egyptian people – is a society that at a superficial level takes some limited appearances of the *form* of liberal democracy but, in actuality, remains a highly authoritarian neoliberal state dominated by an alliance of the military and business elites.

(Hanieh 2011)

Although the political outcomes of the revolts of 2011 resulted in two changes of regime (Egypt and Tunisia), in none of the affected states have the fundamental state and institutional arrangements or the domination of various elites undergone significant alteration; and ever-adaptable neoliberal values have not been displaced. As one study of the 'Arab Spring' aftermath noted,

Whatever the variations in political practices among [them], a deeper obstacle to democratic consolidation in all of them is that democratic procedures by themselves are unlikely to deliver solutions to problems rooted in a political economy where globalised neoliberalism dominates. This is particularly likely to disillusion those who backed political change in order to redress the wealth maldistribution under neoliberal crony capitalism. Revolution has so far remained purely political, with no attempts to attack unjust economic inequalities; at the same time, it actually worsened economic growth, and hence prospects for addressing unemployment, by deterring investors and tourism. What has changed for the unemployed is increased political freedom to express their frustrations.

(Hinnebusch 2015, 26–7)

Southern Africa

Perhaps in part because of the number and diversity of southern African states, the ways in which neoliberalist initiatives find purchase in the intersections of state formation, sociological makeup, political economy, governance structures, non-state institutions and other forms of socio-political and socio-economic organization find less extensive and comprehensive coverage than those of Latin America (Grugel and Riggirozzi 2009; Williams 2002). And although there are exceptions, even studies of development on a continental scale generally employ the North African/sub-Saharan divide (Villa-Vicencio *et al.* 2015). But for all the differences in their histories, endowments and political structures/orientations, southern African states are all subject to highly flexible neoliberalist rationales. Neoliberal logic is instrumental, its apparent ambivalence or inconsistency about the state and about state–society relations favouring opportunism over consistency or disinterested analysis. Nearly any condition, diagnosis of malaise or theoretical conception can be turned to its purposes, including models of state–society relations, both continentally and within individual states:

'State' and 'society' – the 'new paradigm' in the study of African politics that emerged at the end of the 1980s to rival the old nation-building approach – regards the state and its projects with new skepticism and rediscovers the local as the site of civil society, a vigorous, dynamic field of possibilities long suffocated by the state. In place of a modernizing national state bravely struggling against premodern ethnic fragmentation, the image now is of a despotic state and overbearing state that monopolizes political and economic space, stifling both democracy and economic growth. Instead of the main protagonist of development, the state (now conceived as flabby, bureaucratic and corrupt) begins to appear as the chief obstacle to it. What are called 'governance' reforms are needed to reduce the role of the state and bring it into 'balance' with civil society.

(Ferguson 2006, 95–6)

Given the social harms that neoliberal reforms routinely bring in their wake, it is hardly a surprise that they are so readily compatible with authoritarian regimes (Bruff 2014), but they have also been implemented by regimes that are ostensibly democratic, or which have broad appeal through inclusivist and pro-poor policies. Although no single factor is likely to have explanatory power, either fully or in all instances, one interesting pattern to have emerged in the scholarship on neoliberalism in Latin America is the role played by the level of institutionalization of the party system.

[R]egarding the factors that explain differences across leftist governments' economic policies [...] a key factor in these governments' ability to undertake drastic economic policy transformations is the degree of institutionalization of the party system. Countries with an institutionalized party system – those with a predictable, structured political process, a wide sense of legitimacy among the population, and a well-rooted tradition of playing by the rules of the game – are likely to preserve the pro-market status quo and conduct moderate economic transformations. Conversely, countries with a disjointed party system – those where party identities are weak among the population, party discipline is low, and the parties' internal life is loosely organized – tend to depart from the status quo and carry out drastic, unpredictable reforms.

(Flores-Macias 2012, 5; Roberts 2014)

Whether this applies to southern African states generally or in some instances awaits dedicated research. Regardless, the vulnerabilities of southern African states – including but extending beyond familiar weaknesses and crises – offer many channels and means by which neoliberal arrangements can be installed and entrenched. The larger point is that by narrowing and enforcing the basis on which interpersonal and institutional relations can be conducted, neoliberal arrangements become self-reinforcing. So for majority populations, securing adequate and affordable nutrition, paying for medical services, providing education for children and securing stable employment sufficient for these and other basic necessities are subject to market strictures determined not by wide deliberation and incremental adjustment, or for the purposes of social coherence and human welfare, but with a view to 'adjustments' that are removed from vital forms of individual and social security. Civil society and voluntary responses to the resultant provision shortfalls and hardships run the risk of complicity and normalization (Nihei 2010). Once established, neoliberal values find eventual expression in a very wide range of human systems and interactions, including, for example, urban environments and natural resource management – developments that are not particular to African states (Brenner and Theodore 2002; Heynen *et al.* 2007).

This is not to suggest that embedded neoliberalist arrangements are determinist, or that forms of resilience and resistance become wholly disempowered. After all, 'Neoliberalisation processes are ... polymorphic and produce place, scale and territory-specific forms of governance. [T]hey do not necessarily follow a linear "roll back–roll out" path. [T]hey generate their own forms and dynamics of incremental change' (Didier *et al.* 2013, 133). In the case of southern African states, the complex dynamics that continue to arise from post-colonial and post-apartheid transitions generate changes in social norms, expectations and forms of cultural and political organization that will not necessarily be compatible with the structuring of social relations according to neoliberal precepts, but which may instead heighten recent or pre-existing tensions and politicize the 'new normal' (Erasmus 2015).

But for many southern African states there are two more fundamental, underlying factors which precede and then interact with neoliberal arrangements. The first is that historically rooted and persistent problems prevent the establishment and succession of more than nominally democratic governments. So the inability to secure widespread allegiance to the state sufficient to overcome divisive and fractious identity politics makes them weak and/or corrupt in governance terms and vulnerable to loan conditions which ultimately make the socio-political and socio-economic conditions worse. Despite some significant advances and a now-secure core of democratic states in the region, the 'democratic turn' has lost momentum, with a firmly entrenched old guard holding out against popular expectation and international opprobrium (*The Economist* 2016). Even so, the history of both international loans and private investments to African governments demonstrate a remarkable normative flexibility, and an only intermittent concern for 'good governance':

> [A]n Organization for Economic Cooperation and Development (OECD) study of investment patterns in developing countries showed that all five top recipients of foreign investment in the period 1994–96 in Africa fell into the study's 'most risky' category; the list was headed by such unlikely paragons of 'good government' as Angola, Congo/Zaire, and Equatorial Guinea. Indeed, countries with raging civil wars and spectacularly illiberal governments have on a number of occasions proved to be surprisingly strong performers in the area of economic growth, as well. Angola, for instance, actually had one of

Africa's better rates of GDP growth during the war-torn (and, in human terms, quite horrific) 1980s, while Sudan's 8.1 percent annual GDP growth rate for the 1990s put it comfortably at the top of the continental pack, notwithstanding one of the most brutal and intractable wars in recent memory.

(Ferguson 2006, 95)

The second factor is the debilitating effects of widespread poverty. However, some caution is in order: aggregate figures for southern Africa as a whole can easily reinforce 'Africa the country' stereotypes, masking considerable differences between states, as well as the progress made in improving human security indices, however incrementally in some cases. According to the United Nations Development Programme (UNDP), eight southern African countries have between 55 and 73 per cent of their populations in 'severe multi dimensional poverty', but another four range between 1.3 per cent and 7.8 per cent; and '[e]ven though several African countries, including Ethiopia, Rwanda, Mozambique, Sierra Leone and Angola, fall into the Low Human Development group, they have made significant progress in increasing their HDI values' (UNDP 2016, 33). The same kinds of disparities are found across southern African states in respect of other fundamentals of human security and well-being: the burden of HIV and AIDS; infant mortality; education and sanitation to name but a few. Yet at the same time, measures of positive development are no less heterogeneous than those for underdevelopment. The latest United Nations Conference on Trade and Development (UNCTAD) statistics reveal an overall increase in foreign direct investment (FDI) inflows:

> driven by the Eastern and Southern African subregions, as others saw falling investments. In Southern Africa, flows almost doubled to $13 billion, mainly due to record-high flows to South Africa and Mozambique. In both countries, infrastructure was the main attraction, with investments in the gas sector in Mozambique also playing a role. In East Africa, FDI increased by 15 per cent to $6.2 billion as a result of rising flows to Ethiopia and Kenya. Kenya is becoming a favoured business hub, not only for oil and gas exploration but also for manufacturing and transport; Ethiopian industrial strategy may attract Asian capital to develop its manufacturing base. [...] Intra-African investments are [also] increasing, led by South African, Kenyan, and Nigerian TNCs.
>
> *(UNCTAD 2016, xix)*

The hopes invested in, and progress towards, an 'African Renaissance' (Asante 2007; Zeleza 2009) and the confident declarations of 'Africa rising' (Severino and Ray 2010; Rotberg 2013) appear to be bolstered by the more positive statistical indicators, however patchy. But the neoliberal grip on southern African states is both enabled and exacerbated by the political economy of underdevelopment. The recent surge of resource-secured loans, even with their attendant infrastructural supports – a key feature of Chinese loans directed towards natural resource extraction (Li *et al.* 2013) – does not necessarily weaken neoliberal arrangements, or socio-political and socio-economic configurations which are neoliberal in all but name:

> [Africa rising,] based on an intensification of resource extraction whilst dependency deepens, inequality increases and de-industrialisation continues apace, cannot be taken seriously. A model based on growth-for-growth's sake has replaced development and the agenda of industrialisation and moving Africa up the global production chain has been discarded. Instead, Africa's current 'comparative advantage' as a primary commodity exporter is celebrated and reinforced. History repeats itself.
>
> *(Taylor 2016, 8)*

On the view immediately above, the available alternatives to IFI conditionalities will entail similar risks and costs, even in the absence of determinedly neoliberal ends. The centres of gravity in both public and private finance are undergoing a re-configuration, most prominently by China eroding the predominance of largely Western-controlled IFIs and capital markets, in the form of commodity-secured loans and follow-on service contracts to African states. These are expected to reach US$1trillion by 2025 (Shih 2013); and China's nascent Asian Infrastructure Development Bank is likely to challenge the standing of the World Bank (Reuters 2015). But the sums involved are loans, not development assistance; and as the UNCTAD Investment Report pointed out, in Africa:

> Natural resources are mainly traded with extraregional countries, do not require much transformation (nor foreign inputs), and thus contribute little to African industrial development and its capacity to supply the growing internal demand. The high share of commodities in the region's exports together with inadequate transport, energy and telecommunications infrastructure is also a key factor hampering the development of regional value chains. Among the world's regions, Africa relies the least on regional interactions in the development of global value chains.
>
> *(UNCTAD 2016, 43)*

Because the Chinese government represents the collective interests of Chinese natural resource firms to negotiate with the host country, this powerful and coherent strategy has prompted one group of analysts to speculate 'whether Chinese firms will come to dominate the natural resources sector in Africa and other developing nations rich in natural resources' (Li *et al.* 2013, 319) – which has the potential to lock in underdevelopment and new or pre-existing modes of neoliberal organization.

Yet China's unique, 'one tier' government/corporate negotiating strategy highlights the importance of negotiating behaviours, especially now that public and private capital flows are more diffuse, with BRICS countries leveraging their economic weight not towards trying to reform multilateral institutions, but as part of generating a more heterogeneous order of global capital in which their policy preferences can at least sometimes find more purchase:

> With regard to global multilateral institutions, recent reform attempts have not significantly changed the clear mismatch between emerging powers' economic weight and their capacity to influence rule-setting within these governance structures. However, the BRIC countries have in recent years consolidated their autonomy and now significantly influence global capital flows, not only in the form of reserves but increasingly in terms of OFDI and development assistance. This catch-up process has already led to small but visible shifts in the global financial and monetary order. Assuming the absence of major crises, the economic weight of emerging powers is likely to further increase in the years ahead, which would sustain the momentum for the process of decentralization and reconfiguration of financial structures around new power centers.
>
> *(Huotari and Hanemann 2014, 307)*

Another analysis finds in the growing economic strength and the distinct social and political cultures of BRIC states an ability to mediate neoliberal demand:

> In all four [BRICS] countries, the role of the state as a critical actor in development was rediscovered and re-established in ways that go far beyond the modest institutionalist turn experienced by the Washington Consensus after the East Asian crisis. The endurance of heterodox economic traditions at a domestic level, the endogenous dynamics of the political system, and the extent to which corporate interests or mass publics mobilized against the pro-Washington Consensus technocratic elites have all contributed to bringing the state back in once again. The result of this was a proliferation of institutional and ideational hybrids that bore the imprint of distinctive 'edits' of the original Washington Consensus to make them compatible with the domestic context. These findings must, however, be interpreted with caution. These hybrids do not constitute a qualitatively different type or constitute a new and fundamental challenge to the current capitalist order. Nor do they serve as solid evidence for some counter-hegemonic 'state capitalist' economic model.
>
> *(Ban and Blyth 2013, 245–6)*

It would appear that one effective means of lessening the hold of externally generated neoliberal ends could turn on African states' ability to make effective use of their collective negotiating potential, particularly through sub-regional organizations such as the Southern African Development Community (SADC). However, the evidence to date is that no southern African state on its own has the economic or indeed political strength to mediate the neoliberal demands of multilateral institutions; and none of Africa's institutions yet have the political coherence or determination to act in concert at this level, or for these purposes (Hurt 2012). The already considerable and growing influence of Chinese investment, which is negotiated with individual states, might well serve as a disincentive to act collectively. However, BRICs countries and other 'rising powers' have developed powerful interests in Africa's natural resources, too – as well as in their growing markets, which opens up another line of possibilities for African states to more fully enter the world economy as a rule negotiator rather than as a rule-taker, in tandem or in partnership with states similarly disposed, if rather further along in the process (Vickers 2013). Because of the size of their economies, the BRICs states have some leeway in the negotiation and implementation of neoliberal conditionalities – a possibility not currently open to African states. And unlike the BRICs, they do not exert an aggregate effect on multilateral institutions or the dynamics of the global capital markets for self-determined policy purposes. Making Africa's regional and sub-regional organizations politically effective will require very considerable, coordinated leadership, in the absence of which, alternating cycles of resource-led underdevelopment and neoliberal 'adjustments' are likely to remain the order of the day.

Conclusion

Perhaps the most striking and enduring outcome of the global financial turbulence that erupted from 2008 is that neoliberalism, both as means and end, was not critically undermined and roundly discredited – still more, that it has been prescribed as a 'cure' for the woes of the global economy and for the conduct and performance of national economies (Aalbers 2013). Under any name, the impulse to extend and defend the interests of wealth accumulation is hardy perennial, but the international system, global capital and powerful globalizing dynamics are now configured in ways which give neoliberalism a multi-faceted and all but self-perpetuating character.

> It is sometimes argued that discussions of perceived neoliberalism are false, since there are no completely neoliberal systems. This is true, but at the same time an empty statement, as we should see neoliberalism – or, perhaps better, neoliberalization – as a process, not a condition. Moreover, neoliberal practice was never about total withdrawal of the state; it was about a qualitative restructuring of the state, involving not so much less state intervention as a different kind of state intervention, not aimed at the benefit of the population at large but at the benefit of a few. Neoliberal practice was all about redistribution, but not from the rich to the poor, but rather to the elites from everyone else.
>
> *(Aalbers 2013, 1084)*

Much hope is invested in the Sustainable Development Goals (SDGs) which could conceivably 'square the circle', enabling the poorest African states to secure decent and equitable levels of development for the poorest states and peoples, indirectly levelling the playing field of economics and trade so that they would be less subject to the externally generated neoliberal conditionalities which have been so injurious. The danger is that headline indicators such as GDP and low/middle income status will inhibit 'a shift from the conventional approach of pro-growth for poor people towards pro-poor growth; the need to take equity seriously and the need to address power relations while giving voice to the poor' (Kumi 2014, 547). And beneath the normative consensus of the SDGs, there is no shortage of business (and incentives) as usual. In a section devoted to private sector investment in the SDGs, the *World Investment Report 2014* noted that: 'Increasing private-sector involvement in SDG sectors can lead to policy dilemmas (e.g. public vs private responsibilities, liberalization vs regulation, investment returns vs accessibility and affordability of services); an agreed set of broad policy principles can help provide direction' (UNCTAD 2016, 151). Yet there is nothing in current patterns of investment that evinces dilemmas for either private or public investors in African states – nor for African governments, understandably keen to secure the immediate financial and infrastructural benefits of such arrangements – for example, in the implementation of China's Africa strategy. Rather,

> the fundamental flaw in the SDGs is the implicit assumption that the same economic system, and its still-present neoliberal governing rules, that have created or accelerated our present era of rampaging inequality and environmental peril can somehow be harnessed to engineer the reverse.
>
> *(Labonté 2016, 275; Murray 2011)*

Currently, both northern and southern African states are ill-placed to contend against the array of forces and actors which are integral to the global economy and with which they need to engage in order to secure their development needs and aspirations. The question for each of them – and for their collectivities – is whether and to what degree neoliberal demands can be mediated, since there is no shelter from globalizing dynamics. A degree of balancing of costs and benefits has proven possible in BRICs countries and elsewhere, but:

> For many developing countries a return to the policies of the past, where the state owned vast swathes of the productive sector and intervened in most aspects of private sector activity, does not seem likely … even if it were to be possible to follow such an interventionist path in the current world trading regime. Many of the fastest growing countries have benefited from the market-oriented policies of the past two decades, and the economic growth that countries such as Brazil and India witnessed in recent years as a consequence of these policies allowed progressive governments in many of these countries to mount expensive social transfer programmes that have benefited the poor in their countries. What is perhaps more likely to occur as a result of the [financial turbulence from 2008] is a rebalancing of the role of the state

Africa under neoliberalism **17**

and that of the market in many developing countries, and the emergence of a more synergistic relationship between the state and the private sector in Latin America, Africa and South Asia along the lines witnessed in an earlier period in East Asia.

(Sen 2011, 412)

If it is true that there is no escape from markets, it is no less the case that there is no escape from politics – and resistance to neoliberal strictures cannot be confined to the necessary work to make African regional organizations more effective with respect to the IFIs and inward investors, but must also include efforts in synch with other nations which have had greater success in asserting and implementing their more inclusive policy imperatives. Pressure from below also matters, albeit with a recognition that the daily struggle to create and maintain ways of life at the margins leaves little room for political activity directed towards improving conditions that are unlikely to have quick returns; and that political activism directed against unfair elections, autocratic rule and corruption will only bring a citizenry to the starting line of contending with the structural inequities set in place by neoliberalism.

The feat of neoliberalism having first escaped and then consolidated its hold after 2008 might signal less the enduring strength of the states and institutions that have long been its standard-bearers and more the persistence of neoliberal values, which might in time attach to the newer agents of global capital and inward investment. The gradual re-shaping of the global economy led by newly developed nations is not without hope; and Africa's very considerable natural resource endowments and the size of its markets give the continent's states considerable leverage in furthering at least some diminution of neoliberalism. At the same time,

> it would be a mistake ... to assume that only the redistributive state could control the destructive tendencies in capitalism. In fragile states where social democracy is effectively ruled out, owing to fragmented, poor societies and ineffective governance, community-based development offers important benefits through immersing the economy in grassroots reciprocity norms. People in small-scale communities can thereby satisfy their basic needs in difficult times and build satisfying personal relationships.
>
> *(Sandbrook 2011, 438)*

However, there is a caveat to this, which applies particularly to many African states:

> There is a dark side of community-based reciprocity too that needs to be acknowledged. It is often associated with a narrow communal identity that divides regional or national populations and with such debilitating practices as 'tribalism', patriarchy, intolerant religions, factionalism and nepotism. We must be wary of idealising *gemeinschaft*. In addition, it is difficult, though not impossible, to extend solidarity from the community to the regional or national level.

> [R]eciprocity is a fragile principle in the modern world, subject as it is to erosion by the individualism of market relations and external manipulation.
>
> *(Ibid.)*

Is a neoliberalist Africa sustainable? The sustainability of neoliberalism in any country has two fundamental aspects: the stability of its sources – that is, a coherent, stable and predictable international system and international political economy; and the limits of peoples and governments to absorb the relational and practical outcomes of neoliberal arrangements. The relational qualities of neoliberalism are deep and extensive, since they

> transmogrify every human domain and endeavor, along with humans themselves, according to a specific image of the economic [in which] all conduct is economic conduct; all spheres of existence are framed and measured by economic metrics, even when those spheres are not directly monetized.
>
> *(Brown 2015, 10)*

While it is obvious that there are *logical* limits to such things as resource depletion and environmental degradation, it is worth pondering whether a 'fully' globalized world (and concomitantly, a 'fully' neoliberalized world) is possible – whether human capacities and governance structures can continue a furtherance of neoliberal reconfigurations without undermining the interests that drive them? This applies particularly to the kinds of highly constrained room for manoeuvre left to majority populations and the forms of coercion required to commence and maintain neoliberal regimes – much as with any other form of governance that runs counter to prevailing norms, forcing the nature and pace of change (Taleb and Blyth 2011). Difficult as conditions are, there is no substitute for carefully determined, gradual and persistent political change. Neither attempts to engineer rapid socio-economic transformations nor catastrophic change are likely to include the poorest and weakest as beneficiaries. Strengthening African state and community agency to exploit the gradually shifting patterns of global capital remains the best hope for more inclusive and beneficent human development.

Note

1 Notable exceptions include the special 2015 issue of *Globalizations*, Markets and Development: Civil Society, Citizens and the Politics of Neoliberalism (3): 277–419; Mirowski (2013).

References

Aalbers, Manuel B. 2013. Neoliberalism is Dead … Long Live Neoliberalism! *International Journal of Urban and Regional Research* 37(3): 1083–90.

Asante, Molefi Kete. 2007. *An Afrocentric Manifesto: Toward an African Renaissance*. Cambridge: Polity Press.

Ayers, Alison J. 2012. An Illusion of the Epoch: Critiquing the Ideology of 'Failed States'. *International Politics* 49(5): 568–90.

Ban, Cornel and Blyth, Mark. 2013. The BRICs and the Washington Consensus: An Introduction. *Review of International Political Economy* 20(2): 241–55.

Birch, Kean and Siemiatycki, Matti. 2016. Neoliberalism and the Geographies of Marketization: The Entangling of State and Markets. *Progress in Human Geography* 40(2): 177–98.

Boas, Taylor C. and Gans-Morse, Jordan. 2009. Neoliberalism: From Liberal Philosophy to Anti-Liberal Slogan. *Studies in Comparative International Development* 44: 137–61.

Bogaert, Koenraad. 2013. Contextualizing the Arab Revolts: The Politics Behind Three Decades of Neoliberalism in the Arab World. *Middle East Critique* 22(3): 213–34.

Brenner, Neil and Theodore, Nikolas (eds). 2002. *Spaces of Neoliberalism: Urban Restructuring in North America and Western Europe*. Oxford: Blackwell.

Brown, Wendy. 2015. *Undoing the Demos: Neoliberalism's Stealth Revolution*. Cambridge, MA: Zone Books.

Bruff, Ian. 2014. The Rise of Authoritarian Neoliberalism. *Rethinking Marxism* 26(1): 113–17.

Burgin, Angus. 2012. *The Great Persuasion: Reinventing Free Markets Since the Depression*. Cambridge, MA: Harvard University Press.

Cahill, Damien. 2011. Beyond Neoliberalism? Crisis and the Prospects for Progressive Alternatives. *New Political Science* 33(4): 479–92.

Centeno, Miguel Angel. 1994. Between Rocky Democracies and Hard Markets: Dilemmas of the Double Transition. *Annual Review of Sociology* 20: 125–47.

Comaroff, John. 2011. The End of Neoliberalism? What Is Left of the Left. *Annals of the American Academy of Political and Social Science* 637: 141–7.

Davidson, Neil and Saull, Richard. 2016. Neoliberalism and the Far-Right: A Contradictory Embrace. *Critical Sociology*. DOI: 10.1177/0896920516671180.

Dell, Sidney. 1982. Stabilization: The Political Economy of Overkill. *World Development* 10(8): 597–612.

Didier, Sophie, Morange, Marioanne and Peyroux, Elisabeth. 2013. The Adaptative Nature of Neoliberalism at the Local Scale: Fifteen Years of City Improvement Districts in Cape Town and Johannesburg. *Antipode: A Radical Journal of Geography* 45(1): 121–39.

The Economist. 2016. The March of Democracy Slows, 20 August. www.economist.com/news/middle-east-and-africa/21705355-threats-democratic-rule-africa-are-growing-time-and-demography-are.

Erasmus, Zimitri. 2015. The Nation, its Populations and their Re-Calibration: South African Affirmative Action in a Neoliberal Age. *Cultural Dynamics* 27(1): 99–115.

Euromonitor International. 2008. *Consumer Lifestyles in Egypt*. London: Euromonitor International

Ferguson, James. 2006. *Global Shadows: Africa in the Neoliberal World Order*. Durham: University of North Carolina Press.

Flores-Macias, Gustavo A. 2012. *After Neoliberalism: The Left and Economic Reforms in Latin America*. Oxford: Oxford University Press.

Frerichs, Sabine. 2016. Egypt's Neoliberal Reforms and the Moral Economy of Bread: Sadat, Mubarak, Morsi. *Review of Radical Political Economics* 48(4): 610–32.

Garrett, Brandon L. 2014. *Too Big to Jail: How Prosecutors Compromise with Corporations*. Cambridge, Massachusetts: Belknap Press.

Grugel, Jean and Riggirozzi, Pía (eds). 2009. *Governance After Neoliberalism in Latin America*. Basingstoke: Palgrave.

Grugel, Jean and Riggirozzi, Pía. 2012. Post-Neoliberalism in Latin America: Rebuilding and Reclaiming the State after Crisis. *Development and Change*. 43(1): 1–21.

Hanieh, Adam. 2011. Egypt's 'Orderly Transition'? International Aid and the Rush to Structural Adjustment. *International Socialist Review* 78 (July). http://isreview.org/issue/78.

Heynen, Nik, McCarthy, James, Prudham, Scott and Robbins, Paul (eds). 2007. *Neoliberal Environments: False Promises and Unnatural Consequences*. London: Routledge.

Hinnebusch, Raymond. 2015. Change and Continuity after the Arab Uprising: The Consequences of State Formation in Arab North African States. *British Journal of Middle Eastern Studies* 42(1): 12–19.

Holzner, Claudio A. 2007. The Poverty of Democracy: Neoliberal Reforms and Political Participation of the Poor in Mexico. *Latin American Politics and Society* 49(2): 87–122.

Huotari, Mikko and Hanemann, Thilo. 2014. Emerging Powers and Change in the Global Financial Order. *Global Policy* 5(3): 298–310.

Hurt, Stephen R. 2012. The EU–SADC Economic Partnership Agreement Negotiations: 'Locking in' the Neoliberal Development Model in Southern Africa? *Third World Quarterly* 33(3): 495–510.

International Monetary Fund. 2016. IMF Survey: Evolution Not Revolution: Rethinking Policy at the IMF. www.imf.org/external/pubs/ft/survey/so/2016/POL060216A.htm.

International Monetary Fund/Group of Independent Experts. 1998. External Evaluation of the ESAF. www.imf.org/external/pubs/ft/extev/index.HTM.

Jones, Daniel Stedman. 2012. *Masters of the Universe: Hayek, Friedman, and the Birth of Neoliberal Politics*. Princeton: Princeton University Press.

Klein, Naomi, 2007. *The Shock Doctrine: The Rise of Disaster Capitalism*. London: Allen Lane.

Konstantinidis, Charalampos. 2016. The Neoliberal Restructuring of Agriculture and Food in Greece. *The Review of Radical Political Economics* 48(4): 544–52.

Kumi, Emmanuel. 2014. Can Post-2015 Sustainable Development Goals Survive Neoliberalism? A Critical Examination of the Sustainable Development–Neoliberalism Nexus in Developing Countries. *Environment, Development and Sustainability* 16(3): 539–54.

Labonté, Ronald. 2016. Health Promotion in an Age of Normative Equity and Rampant Inequality (Editorial). *International Journal of Health Policy and Management* 5(12): 675–82.

Li, Jing, Newenham-Kahindi, Aloysius, Shapiro, Daniel M. and Chen, Victor Z. 2013. The Two-Tier Bargaining Model Revisited: Theory and Evidence from China's Natural Resource Investments in China. *Global Strategy Journal* 3: 300–21.

Macdonald, Fiona. 2011. Indigenous Peoples and Neoliberal 'Privatization' in Canada: Opportunities, Cautions and Constraints. *Canadian Journal of Political Science* 44(2): 257–73.

Major, Aaron. 2012. Neoliberalism and the New International Financial Architecture. *Review of International Political Economy* 19(4): 536–61.

Mansfield, Becky (ed.). 2008. *Privatization: Property and the Remaking of Nature-Society Relations*. Oxford: Blackwell.

Mazzucato, Mariana. 2013. *The Entrepreneurial State: Debunking Public vs. Private Sector Myths*. London: Anthem Press.

McGimpsey, Ian. 2017. Late Neoliberalism: Delineating a Policy Regime. *Critical Social Policy* 37(1): 64–84.

Mirowski, Philip. 2013. *Never Let a Serious Crisis Go to Waste*. London: Verso.

Morales, Jérémy, Gendron, Yves and Guénin-Paracini, Henri. 2014. State Privatization and the Unrelenting Expansion of Neoliberalism: The Case of the Greek Financial Crisis. *Critical Perspectives on Accounting* 25: 423–45.

Mudge, Stephanie Lee. 2011. What's Left of Leftism? Neoliberal Politics in Western Party Systems, 1945–2004. *Social Science History* 35(3): 336–80.

Murray, Warwick E. 2011. Neoliberalism is Dead, Long Live Neoliberalism? Neostructuralism and the International Aid Regime of the 2000s. *Progress in Development Studies* 11(4): 307–19.

Naiman, Robert and Watkins, Neil. 1999. *A Survey of the Impacts of IMF Structural Adjustment in Africa: Growth, Social Spending, and Debt Relief.* Washington, DC: Center for Economic and Policy Research. http://cepr.net/documents/publications/debt_1999_04.htm.

Nihei, Norihiro. 2010. Reconsideration of the Problem of Complicity between Volunteering Activities and Neo-Liberalism. *International Journal of Japanese Sociology* 9(1): 112–24.

Ostry, Jonathan D., Loungani, Prakash and Furceri, Davide. 2016. Neoliberalism: Oversold? *Finance and Development.* 53(2). www.imf.org/external/pubs/ft/fandd/2016/06/ostry.htm.

Raffer, Kunibert. 2015. Neoliberalism and Global Capital Mobility: A Necessary Reconsideration of Textbook Trade Theory. *Brazilian Journal of Political Economy* 35(2): 267–84.

Reuters. 2015. China's AIIB to Offer Loans with Fewer Strings Attached-Sources, 1 September. http://af.reuters.com/article/commoditiesNews/idAFL4N1123AZ20150901.

Roberts, Kenneth M. 2014. *Changing Course in Latin America: Party Systems in the Neoliberal Era.* Cambridge: Cambridge University Press.

Rosenau, James and Czempiel, Ernst-Otto. 1992. *Governance Without Government: Order and Change in World Politics.* Cambridge: Cambridge University Press.

Rotberg, R. 2013. *Africa Emerges.* Cambridge: Polity Press.

Sandbrook, Richard. 2011. Polanyi and Post-Neoliberalism in the Global South: Dilemmas of Re-embedding the Economy. *New Political Economy* 16(4): 415–43.

Schwartz, Joseph M. 2002. Democracy Against the Free Market: The Enron Crisis and the Politics of Global Deregulation. *Connecticut Law Review* 35: 1092–124.

Sen, Kunal. 2011. 'A Hard Rain's a-Gonna Fall': The Global Financial Crisis and Developing Countries. *New Political Economy* 16(3): 399–413.

Severino, Jean-Michel and Ray, Olivier. 2010. *Africa's Moment.* Cambridge: Polity Press.

Shefner, Jon. 2011. Neoliberalism, Grievances, and Democratization: An Exploration of the Role of Material Hardships in Shaping Mexico s Democratic Transition. *Journal of World-Systems Research* 17(2): 353–78.

Shih, Toh Han. 2013. China to Provide Africa with US$1 Trillion Financing. *South China Morning Post*, 18 November. www.scmp.com/business/banking-finance/article/1358902/china-provide-africa-us1tr-financing.

Souliotis, Nicos and Alexandri, Georgia. 2017. From Embedded to Uncompromising Neoliberalism: Competitiveness Policies and European Union Interscalar Relations in the Case of Greece. *European Urban and Regional Studies* 24(3): 227–40.

Taleb, Nassim Nicholas and Blyth, Mark. 2011. The Black Swan of Cairo: How Suppressing Volatility Makes the World Less Predictable and More Dangerous. *Foreign Affairs* 90(3): 33–9.

Taylor, Andrew. 2013. *State Failure.* Basingstoke: Palgrave.

Taylor, Ian. 2016. Dependency Redux: Why Africa Is Not Rising. *Review of African Political Economy* 43(147): 8–25.

UNCTAD. 2016. *World Investment Report 2014.* http://unctad.org/en/PublicationsLibrary/wir2014_en.pdf.

UNDP. 2016. *Africa Human Development Report 2016: Accelerating Gender Equality and Women's Empowerment in Africa.* www.za.undp.org/content/dam/south_africa/docs/sa_AfHDR_2016_lowres_EN.pdf.

Vickers, Brendan. 2013. Africa and the Rising Powers: Bargaining for the 'Marginalized Many'. *International Affairs* 89(3): 673–93.

Villa-Vicencio, Charles, Doxtader, Erik and Moosa, Ebrahim Mbek (eds). 2015. *The African Renaissance and the Afro-Arab Spring.* Washington, DC: Georgetown University Press.

Voyce, Malcolm. 2006. Shopping Malls in Australia: The End of Public Space and the Rise of 'Consumerist Citizenship'? *Journal of Sociology* 42(3): 269–86.

Williams, Gareth. 2002. *The Other Side of the Popular: Neoliberalism and Subalternity in Latin America*. Durham: Duke University Press.

Zeleza, Paul Tiyambe. 2009. What Happened to the African Renaissance? The Challenges of Development in the Twenty First Century. *Comparative Studies of South Asia, Africa and the Middle East* 29(2): 155–70.

2

NEOLIBERALISM AND ECONOMIC GROWTH IN CONTEMPORARY AFRICA

Augustin Kwasi Fosu and Eric Kehinde Ogunleye

Introduction

Neoliberalism advocates the reliance on markets, rather than on government, to allocate resources. In the African development-economy context, this economic philosophy has promoted the private sector as the main engine of growth and development, especially in the wake of unfavourable economic outcomes after many years of reliance on government as the main agent of development in many African countries. Interestingly, and in contradiction to popular belief, heavy reliance on government in the immediate post-independence period was not necessarily the norm in Africa. There appeared to be roughly an equal share among African countries in terms of those following liberal versus market policies.[1]

Under neoliberalism, it is anticipated that growth and development will naturally follow a policy of liberalization, stabilization and privatization, *provided* that the government does its part by providing effective public goods. The adoption of this economic thought in the 1980s and thereafter was necessitated by the adverse economic, social and political crises experienced generally by African countries during the late 1970s. External debts were mounting due to high interest rates and economic mismanagement by governments, commodity prices were plummeting, fiscal deficits were worsening and terms of trade were deteriorating, with negative implications for economic growth and development. The poor state of African economies gave rise to the policy of neoliberalism initiated by the Bretton Woods Institutions (BWIs) as a potential solution to addressing the challenges faced by many African countries at the time.

The neoliberalism philosophy is contained in the 1981 BWI report entitled 'Accelerated Development in Sub-Saharan Africa: An Agenda for Action', the 'Berg Report'. The purpose of the report was to diagnose the challenges facing

Africa and to recommend solutions. One key conclusion of the report was that bad governance and internal policies initiated and implemented by African countries were responsible for the poor state of the economic health of the continent. Generally, the proposed solutions included liberalizing markets, anti-inflationary macroeconomic stabilization and other market-based and private sector-driven policies. The report also proposed strict debt management, control of budget deficits, massive privatization of state-owned enterprises and reduced fiscal spending, including attenuating government subsidies for consumption goods and social services. Prominent among these policies were currency devaluation and trade liberalization aimed at achieving an economically healthy and stable external balance.

Neither of the two main regional bodies in Africa – the Economic Commission for Africa (ECA) and Organization of African Unity (OAU), now African Union (AU) – agreed with or accepted the conclusions and recommendations of the report. Prior to the report, the ECA and OAU had developed policy prescriptions for tackling the observed challenges facing the region. These included the Monrovia Declaration of Commitments, Lagos Plan of Action and Final Act of Lagos.

There has been a serious debate on the effects of neoliberalism on economic growth in African countries. These views range from those of the BWI, African institutions and African and other intellectuals. While certain parties have argued that the effects were positive (World Bank 1994; Christiaensen *et al.* 2001), others have posited that they were negative, going further to argue that they were responsible for the reversal of the progress made in the 1960s and early 1970s (Mkandawire and Soludo 1999; UNECA 1989). Impatience in getting results from its implementation, lack of wide consultation, its one-size-fits-all approach, insufficient attention to social sector development and institutional weakness have been cited as reasons behind the failure. Yet others have opined that the effects were mixed (Easterly 2000, 2005; Klasen 2003).

This chapter chronicles neoliberalism and economic growth in Africa. Following this introduction, the second section assesses pre-neoliberalism growth initiatives championed by Africans and African institutions. The third section reviews the thrust of neoliberalism in Africa, focusing on its tenets and history. The fourth section examines recent African economic growth performance. The fifth section focuses on the effects of neoliberalism on economic growth in Africa, while the sixth section concludes the chapter.

Pre-neoliberalism growth initiatives in Africa

Several growth initiatives were initiated by Africans and African institutions, especially the ECA, prior to the emergence of neoliberalism. There has been active debate about these initiatives before, during and immediately after decolonization, ranging from the Bandung Conference of 1955 to the Final Act of Lagos. A brief highlight of these initiatives is presented below with a view to highlighting their strengths and weaknesses.[2]

The Bandung Conference

Apart from the struggle for political independence, the 1955 African–Asian Conference,[3] otherwise known as the Bandung Conference, was one of the earliest self-determination efforts by African countries on political, economic and social governance. It was the first large-scale meeting between the newly independent Asian and African countries purposely to promote Afro-Asian economic, political and cultural cooperation. It was also meant to serve as a forum for opposing colonialism, neo-colonialism and any form of recolonization by the United States, the Soviet Union, France and any other 'imperialistic' nation for that matter (Kanza 1975). African countries used the opportunity to forge alliances with fellow developing countries from other regions, with a view to pressing for political self-determination, mutual respect for sovereignty, non-interference in internal political and economic affairs, and non-aggression.

The Communiqué from the conference placed emphasis on the need for developing African and Asian countries to reduce their economic dependence on the developed nations, through improved provision and exchange of technical assistance and expertise on developmental issues amongst themselves. Specifically, it was agreed that the countries would maintain a middle ground on the Cold War raging at the time between Western democracies and Communist nations. They also agreed to wean themselves off Western aid and to rely instead on each other for mutual economic development. Also emphasized was the urgent need to establish regional training and research institutes that would help build the capacity of African and Asian countries on political and economic governance and management of science, technology and innovation.

The Bandung Conference was, indeed, the first conscious effort among African and Asian countries aimed at forming alliance among themselves as developing countries, with a view towards self-reliance for initiating and implementing development policies. Participating countries adopted five principles based on 'Peaceful Coexistence': (1) Mutual respect for sovereignty and territorial integrity; (2) Mutual non-aggression; (3) Non-interference in each other's internal affairs; (4) Equality and mutual benefit; and (5) Peaceful coexistence (Larkin 1975). With this, African countries engaged in a political, economic and social South–South alliance.

To a large extent, this conference achieved its objectives. First, the creation of the Non-Aligned Movement in 1961 was a by-product of the Communiqué signed at the end of the conference. This allowed most African countries to maintain a neutral stand throughout the Cold War period. Second, the conference pushed the African decolonization and self-determination agendas, making the United States and other Western countries quicken the pace of decolonization as several African countries were granted political independence shortly thereafter. Ultimately, the conference provided a voice for African countries and amply demonstrated that they could be a positive force in global political, economic and social development.

However, the alliance forged through this conference was unsustainable. Attempts to follow up with a Second Asian-African Conference ten years later in

Algeria in 1965 was unsuccessful, given the Sino-Soviet split and removal of the Algerian government led by Ben Bella. Ever since, no further attempt has been made to reconvene the conference, thus making it impossible to assess and monitor progress on the original agreements. The only attempt was made on the fiftieth anniversary of the conference in 2005 to launch the New Asian-African Strategic Partnership (NAASP). However, divergent views, loyalties and ideologies were obvious during the conference, thus weakening the synergy among the countries. Within Asia were countries exhibiting alliances with the United States, while China showed covert sympathy for the Communist system. Furthermore, besides the declarations made at the conference, there was no specific implementation strategy developed to ensure success of the initiatives.

The Monrovia Declaration of Commitments

Recognizing that African countries that had recently secured political independence were facing an immense development crisis, certain African intellectuals were determined to ensure that the countries and the continent as a whole did not become marginalized in the emerging New International Economic Order. Thus they led political leaders in a search for a development paradigm that might be distinct from those advocated by the Western world, recognizing the peculiarities and intricacies of African countries (Adedeji 2002).

This search culminated in the publication in 1976 of the *Revised Framework of Principles for the Implementation of the New International Order in Africa* by the ECA. The main thesis of this publication was that any successful and enduring development policy for Africa must be based on four fundamental principles: self-reliance, self-sustainment, democratization and equitable distribution of the dividends of development through the eradication of unemployment and mass poverty. The report reviewed the trends in economic, political and social policy programmes in Africa over 1950–74, and recommended specific actions, with stated implications of each for accelerated development in Africa.

The basic premise underlying the above thesis was that the negative effects of global economic shocks and the inability of developed countries to address them resulted in the apparent weak structure of the African economies. The objective, therefore, was to proffer measures that would help restructure the economic base of African countries with a view to reversing the trend. Driven by this goal, African leaders adopted in July 1979 a far-reaching regional approach based on collective self-reliance, the *Monrovia Declaration of Commitments of the Heads of State and Government of the OAU on the guidelines and measures for national and collective self-reliance in economic and social development for the establishment of a new international economic order*: the *Monrovia Declaration*.

The motivation for the Monrovia Declaration was the shared thoughts of African political leaders that the continent had been a victim of the negative effects of global development strategies by developed nations,[4] resulting in stagnation through exposure of the continent to the social and economic vagaries of the industrial countries. Another factor giving rise to the Monrovia Declaration was that the adoption of development policies based on the modernization thesis had not yielded the expected results; hence, there was now the need to adopt home-grown growth strategies (Ankie 1982). Strong emphasis was placed on regional integration through creation of an African Common Market that would drive economic integration.

An important weakness of this initiative, however, was that it was a declaration of several commitments devoid of specific strategies for achieving the stated commitments of promoting growth within the defined context. Adopting concrete measures for implementing the declarations was postponed until the Extraordinary Session of the Heads of State and Government in Lagos that gave birth to the Lagos Plan of Action.

Lagos Plan of Action

To correct the visible anomaly of structural problems in African countries through concretization of a specific strategy for implementing the Monrovia Declaration of Commitments, the Second Extraordinary Session of the Heads of States and Governments of the OAU was convened in July 1980 in Lagos, Nigeria. One key submission was that the long years of colonial exploitation was a major factor responsible for economic backwardness of the region. Emerging from the session were the Lagos Plan of Action (LPA) and the Final Act of Lagos (FAL), both of which also had as their intellectual and theoretical base the ECA's *Revised Framework of Principles for the Implementation of the New International Order in Africa*.

The LPA articulated specific strategies for achieving the objectives set out in the Monrovia Declaration. One important feature of the LPA is its comprehensiveness. The Plan covers almost all spheres and sectors of African economies. Specifically, the following areas were covered: food and agriculture; natural resources; industry; science and technology; energy; transport and communication; trade and finance; human resource development and utilization; economic and technical cooperation; environment and development; least-developed African countries; women and development; development planning; statistics; and population.

The LPA first provided a comprehensive review of the status quo, identified the challenges constraining key sectors and finally provided action plan(s) for dealing with the identified challenges. Another interesting feature of the Plan is that the proposed action plans were categorized into what needed to be done at regional, sub-regional and local levels, thus identifying the role of each stakeholder in the value chain.

One important weakness of the Plan, however, was its apparent one-sidedness. Foreign colonial powers were blamed for all the economic woes facing the continent while exonerating African leaders. This bias has been considered a faulty foundation for the LPA, thus undermining the genuineness of its policy prescriptions. For this reason, the Plan has been dubbed 'economically illiterate' (Clapham 1996, 176). Indeed, many African leaders lacked accountability and transparency in their style of leadership. A number of them had become autocratic. And several were so corrupt that rather than focusing on the business of governing the people and promoting their welfare, their focus was rather on self-enrichment through mismanagement, misallocation and misappropriation of public funds. They were busy building empires in foreign countries rather than basic infrastructures for their people. Furthermore, the LPA advocated a continuation of the import substitution industrialization strategy, despite the mounting evidence that such a strategy had failed miserably (Ergas 1987).

Final Act of Lagos

The Final Act of Lagos was a resolution among African heads of state and government on the required action for achieving successful implementation of the Monrovia Declaration and Lagos Plan of Action (OAU 1980). Integration at both sub-regional and sectoral levels was to be inaugurated as soon as possible. Both the Secretary-General of OAU and the Executive Secretary of ECA were assigned the task of working out the appropriate modalities for achieving the integration.

The state was also ratified as the engine of growth, and thus required strengthening, notwithstanding the fact that in many cases it was a culprit in the dismal economic state of affairs during the post-independence era.

Neoliberalism in Africa

In the early 1980s, the World Bank conducted an independent assessment of African countries and arrived at the conclusion that these countries faced structural challenges – the Berg Report (World Bank 1981). According to a World Bank source, the study was motivated by a memorandum from the African Governors of the World Bank to the Bank's President in 1979, 'expressing their alarm at the dim economic prospects for the nations of Sub-Saharan Africa and asking that the Bank prepare "a special paper on the economic development problems of these countries" and an appropriate program for helping them' (World Bank 1981, 1).

Several policy prescriptions based on the neoliberal philosophy were recommended for implementation across all African countries. This became the basis for the World Bank/IMF intervention popularly known as Structural Adjustment Programmes (SAPs). There are differing opinions on the impact of this policy on economic performance of African countries. While there are beliefs that the programme was successful, others believe that it was a failure.

The Berg Report provided an intellectual basis for the subsequent World Bank economic and social policy interventions in Africa. It underscored the depth of African economic crisis; discussed the factors underlying the slow economic growth; provided an analysis of the required policy changes, new priorities and programme orientations needed to promote and sustain faster growth; and concluded with a set of recommendations. While the focus of the report on African economies was almost as comprehensive as the LPA, its policy prescriptions have been described as an antithesis of the LPA in every respect (Soludo 2003).

Neoliberalism and economic growth   **29**

In assessing the root and nature of the economic crisis that faced Africa, the study identified 'internal constraints based on "structural" factors that evolved from historical circumstances or from the physical environment' (World Bank 1981, 4). Specifically, the constraints identified included underdeveloped human resources, the economic disruption that accompanied decolonization and post-colonial consolidation, climatic and geographic factors hostile to development, and rapidly growing populations.

The Berg Report identified a broad range of factors militating against African development: internal, external and domestic policy inadequacies. The internal constraints were believed to be structural in nature and 'evolved from historical circumstances or from the physical environment' (World Bank 1981, 4). On the other hand, external factors were thought to be alien to the continent, emanating from economic situations in foreign countries and international economic transactions. Factors identified in this category included stagflation in industrial countries, relatively slow growth of trade in the primary products characteristic of Africa's production, adverse terms of trade in copper and iron ore and higher energy prices.

The most critical problems of policy inadequacies in African countries were identified. These included: inappropriate exchange rate and trade policies that overprotected industry, held back agriculture and absorbed much administrative capacity; little attention accorded to administrative constraints in mobilizing and managing resources for development; overextension of the public sector due to weaknesses of planning, decision-making and management capacities; and tax, exchange rate and pricing policies that were biased against agriculture.[5] Most of the blame on slow growth in Africa was assigned to low agricultural growth. In turn, getting the prices wrong and excessive government interference in the markets and private enterprises were faulted. Thus the background was set for the ensuing neo-liberal policies.

To improve production, three policy prescriptions were proposed: (1) suitable trade and exchange rate policies; (2) increased efficiency of resource use in the public sector; and (3) improvement in agricultural policies. Agriculture was projected not as a backward sector, but as an engine of growth for African countries as opposed to the LPA that arrogated this role to the state. The key role for agriculture was to be achieved through improved incentives and infrastructure services to farmers.

As part of SAPs, shifts in fiscal and macroeconomic policies were proposed. Of particular importance was the need to achieve macroeconomic stability involving low inflation, and also to create the macroeconomic environment for private sector operations. Furthermore, the proposed fiscal policies involved downsizing government for purposes of budget deficit reductions and for improvements in the efficiency of both private and public sector activities. The public sector retrenchment was also intended to relieve pressure on available financial resources in order to prevent crowding out of the private sector, through higher interest rates or via higher taxes. In addition, direct production of goods or services by government – as

30 A. K. Fosu and E. K. Ogunleye

in manufacturing, mining, marketing and transportation – was often fraught with inefficiencies. Thus, government was required to limit engagements in these activities and to rationalize its expenditures for basic 'non-essential' public services such as in defence, education and health.

The set of neoliberal policies advocated by the Bank, popularly referred to as the 'Washington Consensus' (WC),[6] has certainly received its share of criticisms. One such criticism is that there was neglect of the initial conducive environment and conditions required to render its policy prescriptions more effective. This is the sequencing issue. For instance, while improved productivity and openness were prescribed, it would have been more appropriate to ensure that the supply constraints, particularly those in agriculture, were first given greater attention. Furthermore, institutions that were underdeveloped should have been accorded priority. With such proper sequencing, the affected economies and particularly their agricultural sectors could have better withstood the competitive and supply pressures resulting from foreign exposure. Indeed, the appropriateness of this sequencing criticism was acknowledged in World Bank (1994) as one of the major factors constraining the success of neoliberalism in Africa's financial sector.

In response to the above criticisms, the WC as initially proposed was adjusted over time (World Bank 1989). Although the macroeconomic stabilization and liberalization goals remained intact, the policy was gradually refocused from the short-term to the medium-term, and finally to the long-term. The timeframe for achieving the macroeconomic goals was extended from three to five years, and then later to 15 years. Further changes entailed mitigating the adverse social impacts, as in the case of Ghana's Programme of Action to Mitigate the Social Cost of Adjustment (PAMSCAD) (Fosu 2013a). Greater focus was also placed on poverty reduction, with absolute poverty reduction as a major objective for both macro and sectoral policies.

Thus the strategy proceeded from the 'stabilization' phase of the early 1980s to the mid-1980s, to the 'adjustment with growth' phase that lasted throughout the rest of the 1980s. The strategy was advanced further to the 'adjustment with poverty alleviation' phase that started in the early 1990s. Moreover, the country-specific World Bank-assisted Poverty Reduction Strategy Papers (PRSPs) were initiated in 1999, with poverty reduction as a key objective of the growth strategy. Championed by the BWIs, the core pillars of the PRSPs are macroeconomic and structural policies, improved governance, prioritization of appropriate sectoral policies and programmes and realistic costing of proposed projects. The PRSPs were designed to ensure a comprehensive process that is country-driven, participatory, broad-based, result-oriented, multidimensional and development partner-coordinated (Fosu and Ogunleye 2015).

Most African governments generally accepted the neoliberal economic policies that were introduced in the 1980s, mainly because their economies were in tatters. Regarding Ghana, one of the first early reformers, Fosu (2013a, 271) writes:

> The rationale for adopting the above strategy was simply the critical condition of Ghana's economy. The government had nowhere to turn but to the

World Bank and IMF for financial support in return for economic reform. For example, appeals to the socialist countries, particularly the Soviet Union, during the drought of the early 1980s resulted in little support, thus virtually foreclosing alternatives to accepting the capitalist-based reform.

Post-independence growth performance: pre-reform versus reform

As Figure 2.1 shows, per capita GDP growth was generally strong over 1961–75, a period that is often referred to as 'Africa's golden era' (Adedeji 2002). During this period, exports, agricultural production and manufacturing grew at substantial rates (Adedeji 2002). About 70 per cent of the countries could be classified as strong or good performers. Agriculture was the dominant driver of the economies during this period, employing a greater percentage of the population and generating substantial foreign exchange. Towards the end of the 1970s, however, the picture changed and per capita growth turned negative, with the downward trend actually beginning in the mid-1970s.

Nonetheless, as Figure 2.1 further shows, per capita GDP growth has resurged with a positive trend since the mid-1990s. Beginning in the early 2000s, moreover, Sub-Saharan Africa (SSA)'s rate of growth has actually outstripped that of the world, suggesting per-capita-income convergence. Indeed, employing data on real consumption rather than national income or GDP, Young (2012) finds that SSA's growth has been even faster.

As expected, economic growth has been transformed to substantial increases in income, as measured by per capita GDP, and also to development in terms of human development or poverty reduction. For example, per capita GDP rose from $1,163 (2005 constant US dollars) in 1990 to $1,779 in 2010. And the human

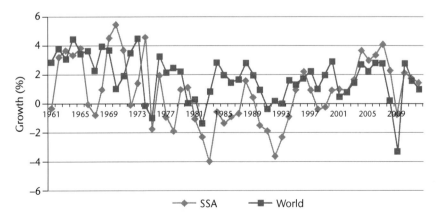

FIGURE 2.1 Real per capita GDP annual growth, Africa vs. world (1961–2012)

Source: World Development Indicators Online, World Bank (2015a).

development index increased from 0.387 to 0.468 over the same period, while the poverty rate at $1.25 declined to 48.5 per cent in 2010 from its zenith of nearly 60 per cent in 1993 (Fosu 2015b). Growth has arguably contributed to this improvement in human development. It is estimated, for instance, that income growth, relative to changes in income distribution, was the main factor explaining the progress on poverty in the region (Fosu 2015a), consistent with the global evidence (Dollar and Kraay 2002).

Neoliberalism – a boon or a bane?

Much of the evidence on neoliberalism's impact is based on African growth and development performance in the 1980s and early 1990s. However, in our view, that would be premature. Many of these countries were either still undergoing adjustment or had not even started the process. According to data presented by Salinas *et al.* (2015), only Botswana and Mauritius attained 'stability/liberalization' prior to the mid-1980s, joined by Ghana, Mali and Uganda in the mid-to-late 1980s, and then by many more countries in the 1990s. Thus, while the various criticisms levelled against neoliberalism on theoretical grounds might be correct, the empirical evidence of poor or good performance in the 1980s and early 1990s should not necessarily be attributed to economic liberalization. It seems appropriate, therefore, to exclude from the present chapter all such empirical studies. Instead, we rely on relatively recent evidence for the post-mid-1990s period that is more likely to reflect the era of stabilized structural adjustment for most African countries.

Deteriorating terms of trade (TOT) constituted a considerable part of the explanation for SSA's poor economic performance during the late-1970-to-early-1980 period, with the TOT index decreasing by at least 20 per cent between its high level in the early 1960s and the low in the early 1980s (Figure 2.2). In order to better understand what other factors might have also contributed to the dismal growth record, we need to further examine economic growth.

Table 2.1 presents the decomposition of SSA per-worker real GDP growth by half-decade periods over 1960–2000. First, consistent with the data in Figure 2.1,

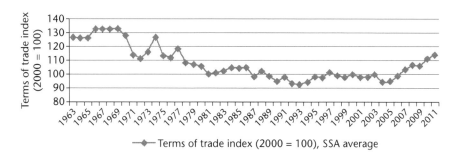

FIGURE 2.2 Terms of trade index (1963–2011), sub-Saharan Africa

Source: African Development Indicators Online, World Bank (2015b).

Neoliberalism and economic growth **33**

TABLE 2.1 Growth decomposition for sub-Saharan Africa

Year	Growth of real GDP per worker	Contribution of physical capital per worker	Growth in estimated per worker	Education residual*
1960–64	1.33	0.53	0.12	0.68
1965–69	1.74	0.80	0.20	0.75
1970–74	2.33	1.05	0.22	1.06
1975–79	0.19	0.74	0.24	−0.79
1980–84	−1.70	0.16	0.29	−2.16
1985–89	0.45	−0.22	0.34	0.33
1990–94	−1.74	−0.08	0.30	−1.95
1995–2000	1.51	−0.12	0.26–1.37	
Total	0.51	0.36	0.25–0.09	

Source: Fosu (2013b) [original *source*: Ndulu and O'Connell (2003)].

Notes
* Measure of growth of total factor productivity (TFP).

The data are based on 19 SSA countries with comparable data over time. Despite the rather small sample size, note that these countries represent all sub-regions of SSA, as well as 72 per cent of SSA's population and the bulk of the region's GDP.

the table shows that the first decade and a half registered the largest growth, and that the rate increased steadily, reaching as high as 2.3 per cent annual rate in 1970–74, before falling precipitously to only 0.2 per cent in 1975–79. Then it became substantially negative during both 1980–84 and 1990–95, before turning significantly positive in 1995–2000.

Second, the substantially positive growth during 1960–1974 was attributable equally to growth in per capita physical capital and total factor productivity (TFP), while the anaemic growth in 1975–79 was explained by mainly negative TFP growth. Third, the substantially negative growth rates during 1980–84 and 1990–94 were attributable primarily to declining TFP, while the resurgence in growth in 1995–2000 was due mainly to improvements in TFP. Thus productivity appears to have been a major factor in the African growth record, consistent with previous findings that productivity has been a more important factor than the level of (physical) investment in explaining Africa's generally dismal historical growth record (Devarajan *et al.* 2001, 2003).

Country growth evolution

While the SSA-wide evidence seems considerable, as the aforementioned account demonstrates, we further present in this section some data on post-independence country growth evolution that might further bolster the above aggregate evidence. Table 2.2 reports per-capita country GDP growth by half-decades for 1961–2014. In the earlier 1961–75 period when SSA as a whole experienced relatively high growth, most of the SSA countries also performed well. And when growth was considerably negative during the 'lost decade' of the mid-1970s to early 1990s,

TABLE 2.2 Per capita GDP growth (annual percentage) for SSA countries between 1961 and 2014, five-year averages (per cent)

Country	61–65	66–70	71–75	76–80	81–85	86–90	91–95	96–00	01–05	06–10	11–14	Average
Angola						0.58	−6.78	3.42				−0.93
Bénin	1.65	0.67	−0.89	1.40	1.72	−1.06	0.54	1.95	0.57	0.78	2.44	0.89
Botswana	3.62	7.70	14.19	7.99	6.30	8.48	1.84	3.23	2.18	2.81	4.04	5.67
Burkina Faso	1.58	1.21	1.25	1.48	1.62	0.35	1.18	3.82	3.34	2.94	2.10	1.90
Burundi	−0.08	5.15	−0.59	1.86	2.32	0.42	−4.45	−2.93	−1.00	0.88	0.93	0.23
Cape Verde					4.64	2.20	8.01	9.44	4.13	5.29	1.03	4.96
Cameroon	0.46	−0.86	3.88	3.85	6.16	−5.13	−4.50	1.90	1.06	0.32	2.44	0.87
Central African Rep.	−1.13	1.11	−0.03	−1.68	−0.62	−2.17	−1.44	−0.80	0.20	1.14	−8.70	−1.28
Chad	−1.30	−0.48	−1.39	−6.41	6.56	−1.21	−0.81	−0.88	12.85	1.50	2.04	0.95
Comoros					1.25	−1.36	−1.97	0.65	−0.16	−0.84	0.32	−0.30
Congo, Dem. Rep.	0.18	0.94	−0.24	−4.18	−0.73	−3.01	−10.53	−6.36	0.69	2.19	4.52	−1.50
Congo, Rep.	0.69	2.05	4.78	2.12	7.40	−2.93	−2.10	−0.21	1.63	2.20	1.72	1.58
Côte d'Ivoire	3.92	5.07	1.63	−0.07	−3.73	−2.41	−1.86	0.40	−1.84	0.10	3.51	0.43
Equatorial Guinea					−1.80	−3.24	11.86	51.62	26.09	1.17	−2.72	11.85
Eritrea								0.93	−0.81	−2.86	2.46	−0.07
Ethiopia						1.88	−2.15	1.59	3.62	7.96	7.40	3.38
Gabon	6.85	3.43	15.84	−1.88	−0.07	−1.03	0.45	−2.08	−0.51	−0.71	3.22	2.14
Gambia			2.36	1.36	−0.65	−0.48	−0.92	1.57	−0.12	1.37		0.56
Ghana	0.10	0.77	−2.65	−0.84	−3.46	1.91	1.48	1.92	2.39	3.83	6.06	1.05
Guinea						−0.35	0.26	0.73	0.82	−0.81	−2.27	−0.27
Guinea-Bissau			1.37	−2.34	4.22	1.50	0.90	−2.83	−0.38	1.03	−0.03	0.38
Kenya	0.24	2.36	6.11	2.43	−1.28	1.98	−1.49	−0.39	1.01	2.32	2.65	1.45
Lesotho	5.69	0.72	3.52	7.45	0.27	3.27	2.44	2.15	2.13	4.30	3.04	3.18
Liberia	0.92	4.00	−1.14	−0.84	−4.76	−15.85	−21.63	30.74	−5.51	3.21	3.59	−0.66
Madagascar	−1.09	1.98	−2.15	−1.41	−4.11	−0.20	−3.28	0.62	−0.43	0.05	−0.31	−0.94

Malawi	2.26	2.38	4.64	1.74	−0.98	−2.98	2.61	1.25	−0.63	3.98	1.14	1.40
Mali			1.65	3.05	1.17	0.71	0.67	1.57	3.22	1.59	−0.11	1.50
Mauritania	8.42	2.40	−2.18	−0.05	−1.89	−0.28	0.35	−0.66	1.56	2.60	3.00	1.21
Mauritius					3.54	6.63	3.67	4.62	2.36	4.13	3.25	4.03
Mozambique					−6.38	5.21	−0.17	8.76	5.79	4.45	4.20	3.12
Namibia					−2.70	−1.57	0.69	0.71	3.63	2.90	3.17	0.98
Niger	3.24	−3.15	−4.81	2.40	−4.96	−0.35	−2.53	−0.74	0.25	1.33	2.24	−0.64
Nigeria	2.36	3.27	3.19	1.02	−5.08	−1.16	−1.99	0.71	8.34	4.41	2.43	1.59
Rwanda	−3.55	4.42	−2.13	6.72	−0.83	−1.93	−0.22	3.78	5.02	5.47	4.51	1.93
Sao Tome and Principe									2.33	3.52	2.28	2.71
Senegal	−0.80	−0.92	−0.55	−1.36	−0.02	−0.73	−0.88	1.57	1.92	0.69	0.44	−0.06
Seychelles	1.04	3.63	4.88	6.88	0.01	4.77	1.41	4.17	−0.61	2.86	5.50	3.14
Sierra Leone	2.99	2.63	0.42	0.05	−1.44	−1.41	−4.59	−0.68	3.14	2.79	8.88	1.16
Somalia	−3.19	1.61	1.93	−5.17	2.59	0.43						−0.30
South Africa	4.09	2.91	1.35	0.89	−1.14	−0.68	−1.23	0.41	2.33	1.69	0.74	1.03
South Sudan											−12.32	−12.32
Sudan	−0.77	−1.48	1.80	−0.66	−2.44	1.79	1.89	3.06	3.42	4.23	4.68	1.41
Swaziland			6.37	0.02	2.15	9.01	0.82	0.83	1.34	0.86	0.87	2.47
Tanzania							−1.42	1.68	4.27	2.84	3.49	2.17
Togo	8.41	2.20	1.08	2.55	−3.74	−0.56	−1.84	1.86	−1.55	0.45	2.61	1.04
Uganda						1.53	3.66	2.88	3.23	4.51	2.15	2.99
Zambia	2.96	−1.65	−1.05	−2.99	−2.80	−1.35	−2.66	0.89	3.50	5.61	3.25	0.34
Zimbabwe	0.21	5.86	1.40	−1.62	0.36	1.15	−0.78	1.03	−7.90	−2.93	5.38	0.20
SSA simple average	1.67	2.00	1.88	0.70	−0.08	0.01	−0.87	3.03	2.13	2.12	1.98	1.16
World Bank SSA weighted average	2.70	2.05	1.57	0.17	−1.78	−0.94	−1.78	0.56	2.47	1.97	1.41	1.20

Source: World Development Indicators, World Bank (2015a).

most of the countries similarly experienced near-zero or negative growth. Furthermore, the growth resurgence since the mid-1990s has involved a clear majority of African countries.

Explaining the growth record

The source of the contraction by the end of the 1980s, according to Fosu (2010a) was mainly the deterioration in TFP, the result of idle capacity, which presented a primary impediment to industrialization in Africa (Mytelka 1989). The supply shocks of the 1970s and early 1980s, both negative and positive, arguably contributed to the creation of the policy syndromes that resulted in poor growth (Fosu 2008a). Furthermore, of countries bucking the trend (at least 1.0 per cent per-capita growth), TOT appreciation was a common feature. However:

> Negative terms of trade provide only a partial explanation for the dismal performance. For example, among the countries registering negative growths in GDP, while Ghana, Mozambique, Niger, Namibia and Nigeria experienced substantial losses in terms of trade in the early 1980s, Togo, Mali and Madagascar did not. What appears to be a relatively common feature is that most of these poor-performing economies were saddled with control regimes inherent in the socialistic strategy of development: e.g. Ethiopia, Ghana, Madagascar, Mali, Mozambique, Niger, Nigeria and Togo.
>
> *(Fosu 2010a, 65)*

Moreover, although much of the poor growth in the early 1990s could be attributable primarily to severe political instability and deterioration in TOT, there were a number of countries registering decent growth:

> The following countries registered decent growth (at least 1.0 percent per capita GDP growth): Botswana, Burkina Faso, Cape Verde, Equatorial Guinea, Eritrea, Ghana, Lesotho, Malawi, Mauritius, Namibia, Seychelles, Sudan, and Uganda (Table 2.1). What is interesting about this list of countries is that only a small number of them experienced appreciable terms of trade (TOT) improvements during the late 1980s or early 1990s. Instead, most of these countries were 'syndrome-free' and many had adopted structural adjustment programs (SAPs), such as Burkina Faso, Ghana, Namibia and Uganda, suggesting that for such countries reforms may have aided growth.
>
> *(Fosu 2010a, 66)*

The policy-syndrome explanation

'Policy syndromes'[7] have been a main culprit explaining Africa's poor post-independence history of economic growth. Recent studies find that the prevalence of a syndrome-free (SF) regime – a peaceful regime with reasonable market-friendly policies (Fosu and O'Connell 2006) – is positively correlated with SSA growth. For example, as Figure 2.3 shows, the frequency of SF was high in the 1960s and early 1970s when growth was also high; low in the late 1970s and 1980s, a period of dismal growth; and high in the 1990s when growth was decent. Indeed, Fosu and O'Connell (2006) find that over the 1960–2000 sample period, attaining SF was a necessary condition for sustaining growth and a near-sufficient condition for preventing a growth collapse. They find further that the presence of SF tended to add as much as 2 percentage points, on average, to annual per capita GDP growth. More recently, Fosu (2013b) provides an even larger estimate for the impact of SF when it is endogenized. Similarly, Salinas *et al.* (2015, 101) find that those SSA countries 'that maintained political stability and significantly liberalized their economies experienced high and relatively stable growth in income per capita, even as high generally as the growth seen in ASEAN-5 countries'. Thus attaining SF appears to be a powerful instrument for achieving growth in SSA.

An important question, then, is how is the prevalence of SF correlated with neoliberalism? There is currently no precise answer to this question. However, what is apparent is that the resurgence of SF appears to have occurred under neoliberalism. Despite the usual risk of *post-hoc ergo propter hoc*, it seems reasonable to assume that SF was the result of neoliberalism. Theoretically, if neoliberalism attenuated rent-seeking opportunities and rents associated with control regimes, then it should raise SF. If so, then we could attribute the growth-enhancing role of SF, at least in great part, to neoliberalism.

An illustrative case – Ghana

Ghana is often cited as a 'success' case under neoliberalism (see, for example, Fosu 2013a). We provide here additional evidence in support of this view, and on two

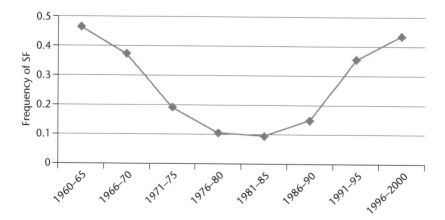

FIGURE 2.3 Evolution of a syndrome-free (SF) regime, SSA (1960–2000)
Source: Figure based on data from Fosu (2013b, Table 2, 529).

specific dominant criticisms against neoliberalism: (1) reductions in social spending, and (2) deindustrialization.

As Figure 2.4 shows, Ghana's per capita growth shows a definite downward trend shortly after independence when control policies were in place, but then an upward trend following the liberalization that actually began in April 1983 under the Economic Recovery Programme (ERP) (see Fosu 2012a for details). Furthermore, not only has the post-ERP remained positive but it has been relatively stable. The growth has also led to steady increases in per capita income as well as to increases in the human development index and substantial reductions in poverty (Fosu, 2013a).

Following years under a control regime, Ghana's per capita GDP had declined from nearly $500 (2000 constant US dollars) in the early 1960s to just a little over $300 by 1983 (Figure 2.5). Under neoliberalism, however, it more than doubled to $765 by 2014 from this pre-liberalization value. Interestingly, SSA's median per capita GDP rose only modestly even during the 'golden era' but fell in the 1980s, consistent with the above growth evidence (Figure 2.5). However, it exhibited a positive trend from the early 1990s, a period that was coincidental with neoliberalism.

In both cases of reductions in social expenditure and deindustrialization, the basic argument is that government financial support for the respective programmes had to be curtailed under pressure from the BWIs as a budget-balancing mechanism, and as a way to attenuate relative participation of government in the economy. Considering the former charge first, this view might hold in certain countries; however, there is little evidence that spending on the social sector (education and health) was *on average* lower during the structural adjustment period compared with other periods (Fosu 2007, 2008a, 2010b). Instead, spending in these

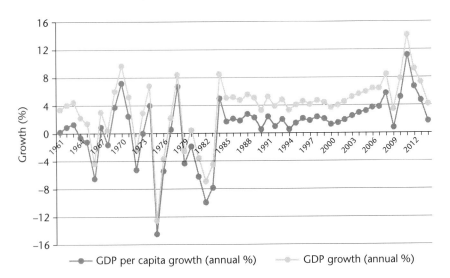

FIGURE 2.4 Ghana's real GDP and real per capita GDP growth (per cent) (1961–2014)

Source: World Development Indicators Online, World Bank (2015a).

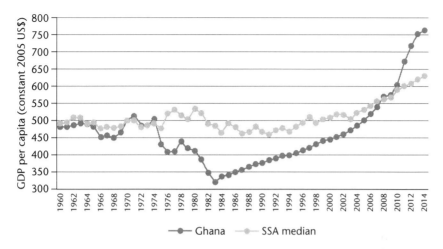

FIGURE 2.5 Ghana's GDP per capita vs. SSA median (constant 2005 US$) (1960–2014)

Source: World Development Indicators, World Bank (2015a).

social sectors had actually fallen already before the neoliberalization policy of the SAPs, likely as a result of binding budget constraints in many African countries.

Similarly, deindustrialization had also begun in many African countries prior to the SAPs. The case of Ghana, one of the early showcases of structural adjustment in Africa, is particularly instructive. By the time of the economic reforms implementation in 1983, the share of industry in GDP was as low as 7 per cent; however, this share rose to at least 25 per cent by 1993 following SAP (Fosu 2013a). Similarly, the manufacturing share of exports that was as high as 14 per cent in 1975 fell to 4 per cent in 1982 (just before the reforms), but rose to about 9 per cent by 1995. At the same time, the manufacturing share of exports increased from less than 1 per cent in 1982 to 15 per cent by 2000. Besides, the share of exports in GDP had also increased from less than 5 per cent in 1982 to over 30 per cent by 2000 (Fosu 2013a, Table 13.2). That exports and their manufacturing share had substantially increased following structural adjustment is especially significant, given the favourable implications of these variables for sustained growth (Fosu 1990a, 1990b).

Sustainability of growth under neoliberalism

As argued above, economic growth in Africa has improved under neoliberalism. But how sustainable is it? To properly answer this question, it is important that we understand the underlying determinants of economic growth in Africa, to begin with. These include: initial conditions; governance/institutions; the external sector; and policy choices.

Initial conditions are a major determinant of economic growth. Colonial legacy (Acemoglou *et al.* 2001), slavery (Nunn 2008), geography (Bloom and Sachs 1998) and ethnic division (Easterly and Levine 1997) have been cited among the initial conditions not favouring African economic growth. Acemoglou *et al.* (2001) argue that the hostile environment of much of the African sub-continent compelled European colonizers to engage in exploitative activities that led to unfavourable institutions hostile to economic growth. Previously African intellectuals, under the Lagos Plan of Action, for instance, had argued that European colonizers destroyed traditional institutions and had carved out the region in such a manner that growth was inhibited. Both arguments, therefore, point in the same direction in terms of the negative implications for growth, though they emphasize different tenets. Indeed, the apparently poor policy choices made by the post-independence policymakers (Sachs and Warner 1997) could be attributable to such legacies (Ndulu *et al.* 2008a).

In Nigeria, for example, while indirect rule was instituted in the northern part of the country, direct rule was adopted for the southern part of the country. The colonial authorities had surreptitiously elevated certain ethnic groups above the others, thus creating a polarized society with negative implications for growth, including under-provision of essential public goods (Kimenyi 2006). Nor was infrastructure well-developed, as the primary objective was to extract mineral resources. Ultimately, areas with marked differences were nonetheless thrown together as countries, which could hardly constitute nation-states. In contrast, Botswana was never colonized, thus allowing the country to use its own traditional systems to develop good institutions that have served the country well in terms of promoting relatively high growth performance (Robinson 2013; Fosu and Ogunleye 2015).

Nunn (2008) found that the slave trade depleted the sub-continent of human capital, with adverse implications for growth, while Bloom and Sachs (1998) emphasize the role of geography. The latter points to the harsh ecological conditions at work in the tropics, including the prevalence of malaria, and argues that geography does not favour relatively high growth in much of the region. Others have also found ethnic division as a deterrent to growth in Africa, mainly because it tends to lead to the choice of bad policies (Easterly and Levine 1997).

Quality of governance and institutions is critical for growth. The main issues about governance and institutions hinge on quality, capability, commitment and credibility of governance and institutions. Indeed, there are claims that the failure of African countries to significantly drive sustained economic growth and development is almost synonymous with governance failure (Levine and Renelt 1992; Sachs and Warner 1997). Macroeconomic stability has been found to be critical to development 'success' (Fosu 2013c, 2013d), while political stability positively influences macroeconomic stability, and conversely (Barro and Lee 1993). Illustrating with the case of Ghana, Aryeetey and Tarp (2000) demonstrate that political instability contributes significantly to macroeconomic instability. Furthermore, elite instability, which reflects poor governance, has exacted a toll on African development, either by depressing growth (Fosu 1992, 2001b, 2002a, 2003) or by reducing the rate at which growth is transformed to human development (Fosu 2002b, 2004).

Indeed, Rodrik *et al.* (2004) have demonstrated that institutions are so crucial that they can overcome adverse initial conditions. And Fosu (2013e) assigns to

Neoliberalism and economic growth **41**

improved institutions a major role for the greater resilience of African economies to the recent economic crisis. However, achieving quality institutions requires much time and effort.

A related issue is if democratic institutions are best for growth in Africa. Fosu (2008c), for instance, finds that 'advanced-level' democracies are growth-enhancing in Africa, while 'intermediate-level' democracies tend to retard growth.[8] Thus, the role of democracy in creating growth-promoting institutions is not straightforward.

African growth responds to the external environment. Even though 'openness' can exert a powerful positive effect on the growth of African economies it can also subject these economies to certain risks, such as shocks from financial and currency crises (Fosu 2001c, 287):

> The 'contagion' effect can be substantial, and the 'speculative attacks' may lead to overshooting of the long-run equilibrium exchange rates. Such short-run equilibria can be destabilizing and highly deleterious to both economic and political institutions. It is thus conceivable that these 'short-run' disturbances would have medium- or even long-term adverse impacts on affected economies.

Gyimah-Brempong (1991) found a statistically significant negative impact of export instability on economic growth for 1960–86. However, Fosu (1991) found for 1970–86 that the effect of export instability is consequential only when it is transmitted into capital (investment) instability. Nonetheless, there appears to be an unambiguous negative effect of import instability on growth (see Helleiner 1986 and Fosu 2001a).

External aid and debt are additional external factors that might help shape economic growth in Africa. That aid may have assisted post-conflict economies get back on their feet and prevent recurrence of conflict appears incontrovertible (Collier 2005). The directional impact of aid, however, has been quite ambiguous. Despite the seemingly robust finding that policies served an intermediating role in the transmission of eternal aid to growth (Burnside and Dollar 2000), subsequent evidence has been rather murky. A most recent review of the evidence suggests, however, that the long-run causal growth impact of aid on growth is small, though positive (Arndt and Jones 2015).

Relatedly, the effect of external debt on economic growth in Africa has been estimated to be negative (Ojo and Oshikoya 1995; Elbadawi *et al.* 1996; Fosu 1996, 1999; Iyoha 1999). Nonetheless, Fosu (1996) found the debt effect to be not only nonlinear but also non-monotonic: positive initially but negative at a sufficiently high level of debt.

The policy choice of political leaders is crucial. The anti-growth policy syndromes pursued by many African governments have been found to be responsible for the dismal performance of their respective economies in the late 1970s and the 1980s. In the absence of such policies, African countries could have improved their per capita GDP growth by an average of *at least* 2 percentage points (Fosu and O'Connell

2006). This potential growth loss is huge, given that per capita growth has averaged less than 1.0 per cent over the entire post-independence period. The good news, though, is that as the prevalence of syndrome-free regimes has resurged since the 1990s so has growth. To sustain the recent growth, therefore, African leaders must ensure that policy syndromes are avoided.

Conclusion

Growth was robust for Africa until about the mid-1970s. Then it declined substantially in the late 1970s through the early 1990s. It is important to emphasize, though, that the record differed significantly across countries. The positive growth record of the 'golden era' was not necessarily exhibited by those countries with government as the leader of the development process. Indeed, countries like Botswana, Côte d'Ivoire, Kenya, Lesotho, Malawi, Nigeria, Seychelles, Sierra Leone and Togo, which pursued more economically liberal policies, grew faster during this period than their counterparts. The difference in performance could be explained by the relatively inefficient growth process led by governments, as in the case of Ghana and Zambia at the time.

There is little doubt that the supply shocks of the late 1970s and 1980s negatively influenced African countries generally, but especially those countries that employed overvaluation of domestic currencies as part of dealing with such TOT shocks. Indeed, policy syndromes proliferated during this period as part of governments' efforts to adjust to these shocks, in turn causing or exacerbating the growth decline (Fosu 2008b). The economic reforms – neoliberalism – engendered by the Bretton Woods Institutions were not effectively implemented in most of these countries until the 1990s. Although these reforms may have worsened the economic and social situations in certain countries, as governments were required to limit their role in the economy in exchange for financial support, the evidence does not, on average, support the view that it was these reforms that led to the growth declines of the 1980s and early 1990s. Instead, TOT shocks were considerably responsible. And, in the early 1990s when Africa experienced substantial growth declines, countries escaping these declines were mostly those that had actually undergone reforms.

Syndrome-free regimes have now resurged in African countries since the 1990s, and so has growth. Such resurgence has occurred under neoliberalism. Despite the usual challenge of attribution, it seems likely that greater institutional democracy that has accompanied neoliberalism in the region has helped to reduce the capricious nature of the executive branch of government that may have spawned the policy syndromes to begin with. As Fosu (2013b), for instance, finds, raising the level of executive constraint in Africa could actually increase the prevalence of syndrome-free regimes, and hence growth, independently or via reducing the potentially adverse effects of ethnic division.

In retrospect, it is unclear if the aforementioned strategies proposed by African institutions and intellectuals would have accorded African countries a better development trajectory. Constructing accurate counterfactuals is, of course, a very difficult task. Nevertheless, to the extent that such strategies might have led to greater participation by government in the development process, it is doubtful that a better outcome would have emerged. After all, without the appropriate checks and balances, many of the African governments might have resorted to business-as-usual, which previously generated the policy syndromes in the first place.

The key policy strategy should now be to ensure that capabilities – physical, institutional and human capital – are strengthened. Indeed, development 'success' strategies in more advanced countries and across the developing world have been those where capabilities were created, via orthodox or heterodox policies, and markets have been mainly relied on to allocate resources (Fosu 2013c, 2013d). Capability creation, including fortifying markets by government, would, therefore, appear to constitute a critical role for governments. And, in this regard, development partners also have an important role to play, especially in supporting institutional building.

Having quality institutions is particularly crucial for sustaining growth. As the African Economic Research Consortium (AERC) Growth Project has amply demonstrated, it was the existence of weak institutions that seemed to have fostered the policy syndromes, especially in the presence of shocks from the external environment. Hopefully, as African countries increasingly attain 'advanced-level' democracy, growth sustainability will endure.

Notes

1 Approximating a government-dominated development process as one with 'state controls', roughly 33 per cent of country years during 1960–65 would be attributed to the government-led paradigm and 67 per cent market-led (Fosu 2013b, Table 2, 529). Alternatively, one could adopt the terminology of a 'syndrome-free' regime as a peaceful regime with reasonably market-friendly policies (Fosu and O'Connell 2006; Collier and O'Connell 2007). Then the division between government-led and market-led during the same period is approximately 50:50. This empirical evidence is derived from the 'Explaining African Economic Growth' Collaborative Research Project of the African Economic Research Consortium (AERC) – The Growth Project (see Ndulu et al. 2008a, 2008b).
2 For further details, see Fosu and Ogunleye (2015).
3 African countries in attendance were Egypt, Ethiopia, Gold Coast (now Ghana), Liberia, Libya and Sudan.
4 These include First Yaoundé Convention (1964–69) between the European Community and the 18 African ex-colonies gaining political independence. The Convention was signed on 20 July 1963 and entered into force on 1 June 1964. At the expiration of the First Convention, the Second Yaoundé Convention (1971–75) was signed on 29 July 1969 and entered into force on 1 January 1971. Another similar unfulfilled strategy was the Lomé Convention, a trade and aid agreement between the European Union (EU) and 71 African, Caribbean and Pacific (ACP) countries, first signed in February 1975 in Lomé, Togo.
5 For a detailed analysis of such policies, see Bates (1981).
6 The 'Washington Consensus' is characterized by fiscal discipline; trade liberalization; liberalization of (inward) foreign direct investment; privatization; strong protection of property rights; reordering of public expenditure priorities towards public goods (e.g.

health and education); liberalized interest rates; tax reform involving broad tax base and moderate marginal rates; and deregulation to ease barriers for firms' entry and exit of sectors (Williamson 1990). There have been subsequent revisions, but this definition constitutes Williamson's original characterization (Fosu 2013a).

7 'Policy syndromes' is used here to mean 'state controls', 'adverse redistribution', 'suboptimal intertemporal resource allocation' and 'state breakdown/failure'; the presence of none of these syndromes is the 'syndrome-free' (SF) regime which is found to be growth-enhancing (see Fosu and O'Connell 2006; Ndulu et al. 2008a, 2008b).

8 'Advanced-level' democracies in the African sample are estimated as those countries with the level of the index of electoral competitiveness in excess of 4.4 (0.0–7.0 range); below that threshold are 'intermediate-level' democracies.

References

Acemoglou, D., Johnson, S. and Robinson, J. 2001. The Colonial Origins of Comparative Development: An Empirical Investigation. *American Economic Review* 91(5): 1369–401.

Adedeji, A. 2002. From the Lagos Plan of Action to NEPAD and from the Final Act of Lagos to the Constitutive Act: Whither Africa. Keynote address presented at the African Forum for Envisioning Africa, Nairobi, Kenya, 26–29 April.

Ankie, M. M. H. 1982. *The World in Global Development*. London: Macmillan.

Arndt, C. and Jones, S. 2015. Assessing Foreign Aid's Long-Run Contribution to Growth and Development. *World Development* 69: 6–18.

Aryeetey, E and Tarp, F. 2000. Structural Adjustment and After: Which Way Forward? In Aryeetey, E., Harrigan, J. and Nisanke, M. (eds) *Economic Reforms in Ghana: The Miracle and the Mirage*. Oxford: James Currey and Woeli Publishers.

Barro, R. and Lee, J-W. 1993. International Comparisons of Educational Attainment. *Journal of Monetary Economics* 32(3): 363–94.

Bates, R. 1981. *Markets and States in Tropical Africa: The Political Bias of Agricultural Policies*. Berkeley: University of California Press.

Bloom, D. E. and Sachs, J. D. 1998. Geography, Demography, and Economic Growth in Africa. *Brookings Papers on Economic Activity* 2: 207–95.

Burnside, C. and Dollar, D. 2000. Aid, Policies, and Growth. *American Economic Review* 90(4): 847–68.

Christiaensen, L. J., Demery, L. and Paternostro, S. 2001. *Growth, Distribution and Poverty in Africa: Messages from the 1990s*. Washington, DC: The World Bank.

Clapham, C. 1996. *Africa and the International System*. Cambridge: Cambridge University Press.

Collier, P. 2005. Economic Policy in Post-Conflict Societies. In Fosu, A. K. and Collier, P. (eds) *Post Conflict Economies in Africa*. New York: Palgrave/Macmillan.

Collier, P. and O'Connell, S. 2007. Opportunities and Choices. In Ndulu, B., O'Connell, S., Bates, R., Collie, P. and Soludo, C. (eds) *The Political Economy of Economic Growth in Africa 1960–2000*. Cambridge: Cambridge University Press.

Devarajan, S., Easterly, W. and Pack, H. 2001. Is Investment in Africa Too High or Too Low? Macro and Micro-Evidence. *Journal of African Economies* 10: 81–108.

Devarajan, S., Easterly, W. and Pack, H. 2003. Low Investment Is Not the Constraint on African Development. *Economic Development and Cultural Change* 51(3): 547–71.

Dollar, D. and Kraay, A. 2002. Growth is Good for the Poor. *Journal of Economic Growth* 7(3): 195–225.

Easterly, W. 2000. *The Effect of IMF and World Bank Programs on Poverty*. Mimeo. Washington, DC: The World Bank.

Easterly, W. 2005. What Did Structural Adjustment Adjust? The Association of Policies and Growth with Repeated IMF and World Bank Adjustment Loans. *Journal of Development Economics* 76(1): 1–22.

Easterly, W. and Levine, R. 1997. Africa's Growth Tragedy: Policies and Ethnic Divisions. *Quarterly Journal of Economics* 112(4): 1203–50.

Elbadawi, I. A., Ndulu, B. N. and Ndung'u, N. (1996). Debt Overhang and Economic Growth in Sub-Saharan Africa. In Iqbal, Z. and Kanbur, R. (eds) *External Finance for Low Income Countries*. Washington DC: IMF.

Ergas, Z. (ed.). 1987. *The African State in Transition*. London: Macmillan.

Fosu, A. K. 1990a. Exports and Economic Growth: The African Case. *World Development* 18(6): 831–5.

Fosu, A. K. 1990b. Export Composition and the Impact of Exports on Economic Growth of Developing Economies. *Economics Letters* 34(1): 67–71.

Fosu, A. K. 1991. Capital Instability and Economic Growth in Sub-Saharan Africa. *Journal of Development Studies* 28(1): 74–85.

Fosu, A. K. 1992. Political Instability and Economic Growth: Evidence from Sub-Saharan Africa. *Economic Development and Cultural Change* 40: 829–41.

Fosu, A. K. 1996. The Impact of External Debt on Economic Growth in Sub-Saharan Africa. *Journal of Economic Development* 21(1): 93–118.

Fosu, A. K. 1999. The External Debt Burden and Economic Growth in the 1980s: Evidence from Sub-Saharan Africa. *Canadian Journal of Development Studies* 20(2): 307–18.

Fosu, A. K. 2001a. Economic Fluctuations and Growth in Sub-Saharan Africa: The Importance of Import Instability. *Journal of Development Studies* 37(3): 71–84.

Fosu, A. K. 2001b. Political Instability and Economic Growth in Developing Economies: Some Specification Empirics. *Economics Letters* 70(2): 289–94.

Fosu, A. K. 2001c. The Global Setting and African Economic Growth. *Journal of African Economies* 10(3): 282–310.

Fosu, A. K. 2002a. Political Instability and Economic Growth: Implications of Coup Events in Sub-Saharan Africa. *American Journal of Economics and Sociology* 61(1): 329–48.

Fosu, A. K. 2002b. Transforming Growth to Human Development in Sub-Saharan Africa: The Role of Elite Political Instability. *Oxford Development Studies* 30(1): 9–19.

Fosu, A. K. 2003. Political Instability and Export Performance in Sub-Saharan Africa. *Journal of Development Studies* 39(4): 68–82.

Fosu, A. K. 2004. Mapping Growth into Economic Development: Has Elite Political Instability Mattered in Sub-Saharan Africa? *American Journal of Economics and Sociology* 63(5): 37–156.

Fosu, A. K. 2007. Fiscal Allocation for Education in Sub-Saharan Africa: Implications of the External Debt Service Constraint. *World Development* 35(4): 702–13.

Fosu, A. K. 2008a. Implications of External Debt-Servicing Constraint for Public Health Expenditure in Sub-Saharan Africa. *Oxford Development Studies* 36(4): 363–77.

Fosu, A. K. 2008b. Anti-Growth Syndromes in Africa: A Synthesis of the Case Studies. In Ndulu, B. O'Connell, S., Bates, R., Collier, P. and Soludo, C. (eds) *The Political Economy of Economic Growth in Africa, 1960–2000*. Cambridge: Cambridge University Press.

Fosu, A. K. 2008c. Democracy and Growth in Africa: Implications of Increasing Electoral Competitiveness. *Economics Letters* 100: 442–4.

Fosu, A. K. 2010a Africa's Economic Future: Learning from the Past. *CESifo Forum* 11(1): 62–71.

Fosu, A. K. 2010b. The External Debt-Servicing Constraint and Public-Expenditure Composition in Sub-Saharan Africa. *African Development Review* 22(3): 378–93.

Fosu, A. K. 2012a. The African Economic Growth Record, and the Roles of Policy Syndromes and Governance. In Noman, A., Botchwey, K., Stein, H. and Stiglitz, J. (eds)

Good Growth and Governance in Africa: Rethinking Development Strategies. Oxford: Oxford University Press.

Fosu, A. K. 2013a. Country Role Models for Development Success: The Ghana Case. In Fosu, A. K. (ed.) *Achieving Development Success: Strategies and Lessons from the Developing World*. Oxford: Oxford University Press.

Fosu, A. K. 2013b. African Economic Growth: Productivity, Policy Syndromes and the Importance of Institutions. *Journal of African Economies* 22(4): 523–51.

Fosu, A. K. 2013c. Development Success: Historical Accounts from the More Advanced Countries. In Fosu, A. K. (ed.) *Development Success: Historical Accounts from More Advanced Countries*. Oxford: Oxford University Press.

Fosu, A. K. 2013d. Achieving Development Success: Synthesis of Strategies and Lessons from the Developing World. In Fosu, A. K. (ed.) *Achieving Development Success: Strategies and Lessons from the Developing World*. Oxford: Oxford University Press.

Fosu, A. K. 2013e. Impact of the Global Financial and Economic Crisis on Development: Whither Africa? *Journal of International Development* 25(8): 1085–104.

Fosu, A. K. 2015a. Growth, Inequality, and Poverty in Sub-Saharan Africa: Recent Progress in a Global Context. *Oxford Development Studies* 43(1): 44–59.

Fosu, A. K. 2015b. Growth and Institutions in African Development. In Fosu, A. K. (ed.) *Growth and Institutions in African Development*. Abingdon: Routledge.

Fosu, A. K. and O'Connell, S. A. 2006. Explaining African Economic Growth: The Role of Anti-Growth Syndromes. In Bourguignon, F. and Pleskovic, B. (eds) *Annual Bank Conference on Development* Economics. Washington, DC: World Bank.

Fosu, A. K. and Ogunleye, E. K. 2015. African Growth Strategies: The Past, Present and Future. In Lin, J. and Monga, C. (eds) *Handbook of Africa and Economics: Policies and Practices*. Oxford: Oxford University Press.

Gyimah-Brempong, K. 1991. Export Instability and Economic Growth in Sub-Saharan Africa. *Economic Development and Cultural Change* 39(4): 815–28.

Helleiner, G. K. 1986. Outward Orientation, Import Instability and African Economic Growth: An Empirical Investigation. In Lall, S. and Stewart, F. (eds) *Theory and Reality in Economic Development*. London: Macmillan.

Iyoha, Milton A. 1999. External Debt and Economic Growth in Sub-Saharan African Countries: An Econometric Study. AERC Research Paper No. 90. Nairobi: African Economic Research Consortium.

Kanza, T.M. 1975. Chinese and Soviet Aid to Africa; An African View. In Weinstein, W. (ed.) *Chinese and Soviet Aid to Africa*. New York: Praeger Publishers.

Kimenyi, M.S. 2006. Ethnicity, Governance and the Provision of Public Goods. *Journal of African Economies, Supplement* 1(15): 62–99.

Klasen, S. 2003. What Can Africa Learn from Asian Development Successes and Failures? *Review of Income and Wealth* 49(3): 441–51.

Larkin, B. D. 1975. *Chinese Aid in Political Context 1971–1975*. In Weinstein, W. (ed.) *Chinese and Soviet Aid to Africa*. New York: Praeger Publishers.

Levine, R. and Renelt, D. 1992. A Sensitivity Analysis of Cross-Country Growth Regressions. *American Economic Review* 82(4): 942–63.

Mkandawire, T. and Soludo, C. C. 1999. *Our Continent, Our Future: African Perspectives on Structural Adjustment*. CODESRIA (Council for the Development of Social Science Research In Africa), Dakar: Africa World Press.

Mytelka, L. K. 1989. The Unfulfilled Promise of African Industrialization. *African Studies Review* 32(3): 77–138.

Ndulu, B. and O'Connell, S. 2003. *Revised Collins/Bosworth Growth Accounting Decompositions*, AERC Explaining African Economic Growth Project. www.swarthmore.edu/SocSci/soconne1/documents/Revised%20colbos%20tables.pdf.

Ndulu, B. O'Connell, S., Bates, R., Collier, P. and Soludo, C. (eds) 2008a. *The Political Economy of Economic Growth in Africa 1960–2000, Vol. 1*. Cambridge: Cambridge University Press.

Ndulu, B., O'Connell, S., Azam, J-P., Bates, R.H., A. K. Fosu, A.K., J. W. Gunning, J.W. and Njinkeu, D. (eds) 2008b. *The Political Economy of Economic Growth in Africa 1960–2000, Vol. 2, Country Case Studies*. Cambridge: Cambridge University Press.

Nunn N. (2008). The Long Term Effects of Africa's Slave Trades. *Quarterly Journal of Economics* 123(1): 139–76.

OAU. 1980. *The Lagos Plan of Action for the Economic Development of Africa, 1980–2000*. Addis Ababa: Organization of African Unity.

Ojo, O. and Oshikoya, T. 1995. Determinants of Long-Term Growth: Some African Results. *Journal of African Economies* 4(2): 163–91.

Robinson, J. 2013. Botswana as a Role Model for Country Success. In Fosu, A. K. (ed.) *Achieving Development Success: Strategies and Lessons from the Developing World*. Oxford: Oxford University Press.

Rodrik, D., Subramanian, A. and Trebbi, A. 2004. Institutions Rule: The Primacy of Institutions Over Geography and Integration in Economic Development. *Journal of Economic Growth* 9(2): 131–65.

Sachs, J. D. and Warner, A. M. 1997. Sources of Slow Growth in African Economies. *Journal of African Economies* 6(3): 335–76.

Salinas, G., Gueye, C. and Korbut, O. 2015. Impressive Growth in Africa under Peace and Market Reforms. *Journal of African Economies* 24(1): 101–27.

Soludo, C. C. 2003. In Search of Alternative Analytical and Methodological Frameworks for an African Economic Development Model. In Mkandawire, T. and Soludo, C. C. (eds) *African Voices on Structural Adjustment*. CODESRIA/IDRC, Dakar: Africa World Press.

UNECA. 1989. *African Alternative Framework to Structural Adjustment Programmes for Socio-Economic Recovery and Transformation*. UNECA: Addis Ababa.

Williamson, J. 1990. What Washington Means by Policy Reform. In Williamson, J. (ed.) *Latin American Adjustment: How Much Has Happened?* Washington, DC: Institute for International Economics.

World Bank. 1981. *Accelerated Development in Sub-Saharan Africa: An Agenda for Action*. Washington, DC: World Bank.

World Bank. 1989. *Sub-Saharan Africa from Crisis to Sustainable Growth: A Long-Term Perspective Study*. Washington DC: World Bank.

World Bank. 1994. *Adjustment in Africa: Reforms, Results, and the Road Ahead*. Washington, DC: The World Bank.

World Bank. 2015a. *World Development Indicators Online*, Washington DC: World Bank.

World Bank. 2015b. *African Development Indicators Online*, Washington DC: World Bank.

Young, A. 2012. The African Growth Miracle. *Journal of Political Economy* 20: 696–739.

3

AS THE GLOBAL COMMODITY SUPER-CYCLE ENDS, AFRICANS CONTINUE UPRISING AGAINST 'AFRICA RISING'

Patrick Bond

Introduction: Africans uprising

The conditions for reproduction of daily life in Africa have not improved as a result of the frenetic expansion of global capitalism in the age of neoliberalism, given that this process has for the past third of a century entailed structural adjustment austerity imposed by the Bretton Woods Institutions, has been carried out by dictatorships or at best semi-democratic regimes, has had the effect of deepening Resource Curses due to extractive industry exploitation and has amplified other political, economic and ecological injustices. The 'Great Recession' the world entered from 2007 exacerbated these problems. As a result, contrary to 'Africa rising' rhetoric, a new wave of protests has arisen across the continent since 2010. The African Development Bank (AfDB) commissions annual measurements based upon journalistic data, which suggest that major public protests rose from an index level of 100 in 2000 to nearly 450 in 2011. Instead of falling back after the Arab Spring – especially acute in Tunisia, Egypt and Morocco – the index of protests rose higher, to 520 in 2012, as Algeria, Angola, Burkina Faso, Chad, Gabon, Morocco, Nigeria, South Africa and Uganda maintained the momentum of 2011 (AfDB *et al.* 2013). In 2013, the index rose still higher, to 550 (AfDB *et al.* 2014). In 2014, it fell back just slightly, but as in the earlier years, the main causes of protest were socio-economic injustices (AfDB *et al.* 2015). There are all manner of reasons for dissent, but according to Agence France Press and Reuters reports, the vast majority since 2011 were over inadequate wages and working conditions, low quality of public service delivery, social divides, state repression and lack of political reform. A good share of the turmoil in Africa prior to the 2011 upsurge took place in the vicinity of mines and mineral wealth, as reflected in mappings of the Armed Conflict Location Event Data (PRIO).

Ironically, as the uprisings gathered steam, this was an era advertised in the mainstream press as 'Africa rising' (e.g. Perry 2012 Robertson 2013). Per capita gross domestic product (GDP) levels rose rapidly, with most of the gains occurring from 1999–2008. There was even a momentary hoax-type claim from the African Development Bank's economist Mthuli Ncube in April 2011, endorsed by the *Wall Street Journal*, that 'one in three Africans is middle class' with the absolute number varying from 313 to 350 million (Ncube 2013). Ncube defines 'middle class' as those who spend between $2 [*sic*] and $20 per day, with 20 per cent in the $2–4/day range and 13 per cent from $4-$20. Both ranges are poverty-level in most African cities, whose price levels leave them amongst the world's most expensive. The share of Africans living above $20/day ('rich' according to Ncube – but middle class in any reasonable narrative) has been steadily decreasing since 2000, from 8 per cent to 5 per cent, Ncube's own data indicate.

As the commodities super-cycle is now definitively over and as corporate investment more frantically loots the continent (as argued below), the contradictions may well lead to more socio-political explosions. The idea of a 'double movement' – that is, social resistance against marketization, as suggested by Karl Polanyi (1944) in *The Great Transformation* – applies to Africa in part because of the 'IMF Riots' that spread across the continent during the 1980s and democratization movements in the 1990s, but also because of the intense protest wave beginning in 2011. As

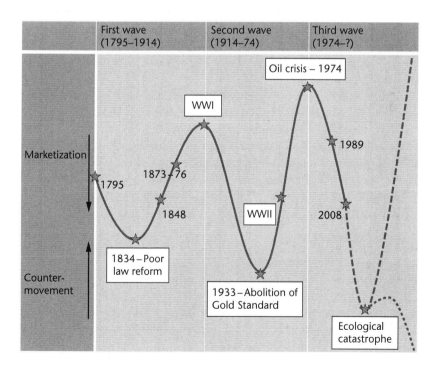

FIGURE 3.1 Polanyi's 'double movement' in the West, with socio-ecological uprisings anticipated

Source: Burawoy (2013).

reinterpreted by Michael Burawoy (2013), the double movement will necessarily tackle climate change and related problems such as the food shortages that are causing such intense battles in drought-stricken sites, including Darfur, the Horn of Africa and so many others on the horizon.

As the AfDB conceded in its 2015 list of 'top drivers' of protests, per capita GDP growth did not prevent mass protests for 'wage increases and better working conditions followed by demands for better public services ... [because] lived poverty at the grassroots remains little changed despite the recent growth episode'. One of the central reasons for the disconnect between 'Africa rising' and the poverty of the continent's majority is illicit financial flow as well as *legal* financial outflows – in the form of profits and dividends sent to transnational corporate (TNC) headquarters, profits drawn from minerals and oil ripped from the African soil.

Africa looted – but less so in future?

A general case must be made, repeatedly, against TNCs based on their excessive profiteering and distortion of African economies. The worst form of foreign direct investment (FDI) tends to come solely in search of raw materials, without reinvestment in either beneficiation systems or other fixed capital. But from 2011–15, FDI began to stall, because commodity prices crashed, especially in 2015. If 2002 is set at an index level of 100, the overall global price index of all commodities rose to 390 by 2008, crashed back to 190 in 2009, and again rose to nearly 400 in 2011. The fall from 2011–14 was to 350 but then in 2015 there was a crash to 160, before a subsequent 2016–17 rise to 230.

The slowing of FDI inflows is promising in part because the 2002–11 commodity super-cycle is now decisively over, so the extractive industries' extreme pressures on people and environments will probably slow dramatically. Although traumatic job losses are on the cards (Anglo American announced in mid-2015 that a third of its South African mining jobs will be shed, with probable asset sales to India's quite predatory lead mining house, Vedanta), it could also mean less financial looting of Africa. The argument along these lines proceeds through six points.

Illicit financial flows

First, the category of so-called 'illicit financial flows' (IFFs) reflects many of the corrupt ways that wealth is withdrawn from Africa, mostly in the extractives sector. TNC tactics include mis-invoicing inputs, transfer pricing and other trading scams, tax avoidance and evasion of royalties, bribery, 'round-tripping' investment through tax havens and simple theft of profits via myriad gimmicks aimed at removing resources from Africa. Examples abound:

- In South Africa, Sarah Bracking and Khadija Sharife conducted a study for Oxfam (2014) showing De Beers mis-invoiced $2.83 billion of diamonds over six years.

- The Alternative Information and Development Centre (Forslund 2014) found that Lonmin's platinum operations – notorious at its Marikana mine for the massacre of 34 of its wildcat-striking mineworkers in 2012 – has also spirited hundreds of millions of dollars offshore to Bermuda since 2000.
- The Indian mining house Vedanta's chief executive arrogantly bragged at a Bangalore meeting how in 2006 he spent $25 million to buy Zambia's Konkola Copper Mines (KCM), which is Africa's largest, and then reaped at least $500 million profits from it annually, apparently through an accounting scam (Lusakatimes.com 2014). In August 2015, Zambian communities appeared in the London courts trying to halt Vedanta's KCM toxic pollution (Vidal 2015); and at seven protest sites across the world the vibrant *Foil Vedanta* movement showed how inspiring the networked transnational activists can be. The firm's share price fell 61 per cent in 2015 and its critics can claim at least some credit.

The most profound analysis of IFFs on a continental scale has been conducted by Burundian political economist Leonce Ndikumana, a professor at the University of Massachusetts-Amherst, who argues that:

> Globalisation and unregulated finance have also facilitated the expansion of capital flight and illicit financial flows from African countries. In the four decades to 2010, Africa lost about US$1.3 trillion through capital flight, or US$1.7 trillion including interest earnings. This vastly exceeds the continent's liabilities to the rest of the world. Ironically, this has made the most capital-starved continent a net creditor to the rest of the world.
>
> *(Ndikumana 2015)*

In addition to tireless researchers and activists, there are also policy-oriented NGOs working against IFF across Africa and the south, including several with northern roots like Trust Africa, Global Financial Integrity, Tax Justice Network, Publish What You Pay and Eurodad. Battling IFFs – for example, in the Trust Africa 'Stop the Bleeding' campaign – is one means of giving hope to so many who want Africa's scarce revenues to be recirculated inside poor countries, not siphoned away to offshore financial centres. However, the implicit theory of change adopted by the head offices of many such NGOs (e.g. in the Soros circuits) is dubious, if they argue that because *transparency* is like a harsh light that can disinfect corruption, their task is mainly a matter of making capitalism cleaner by bringing problems like IFFs to light. To their credit, many NGOs and allied funders (e.g. Trust Africa) and grassroots activists generated sufficient advocacy pressure to compel the African Union and UN to commission an IFF study led by former South African President Thabo Mbeki. Reporting in mid-2015 and using a conservative methodology, his estimate is that IFFs from Africa exceed $50 billion a year (Report of the High Level Panel 2015), which he subsequently revised to $80 billion.

The IFF looting is mostly, but not entirely, related to the extractive industries. On an even more narrow accounting than Mbeki's, according to the United

Nations Economic Commission on Africa (UNECA 2015), $319 billion was robbed from 2001–10, with the most theft in metals, $84 billion; oil, $79 billion; natural gas, $34 billion; minerals, $33 billion; petroleum and coal products, $20 billion; crops, $17 billion; food products, $17 billion; machinery, $17 billion; clothing, $14 billion; and iron and steel, $13 billion. The charge that Africa is 'Resource Cursed' fits the data well.

From IFFs to LFFs

But even if IFFs were reduced, there is another reason that FDI leaves Africa much poorer: what can be termed *licit* financial flows (LFFs). These are legal profits and dividends sent home to TNC headquarters after the FDI begins to pay off. They are hard to pin down but can be found within what is called the 'current account', along with trade. According to the International Monetary Fund's database, the last 15 years or so witnessed mostly evenly balanced trade between sub-Saharan African countries and the rest of the world, with a slight surplus (more exports than imports) from 2000–08, and then a slight deficit, growing in 2014.

The current account measures not only whether imports are greater than exports, but also the flows of profits, dividends and interest, known as the balance of payments (this category does not include longer investment covered by the 'capital accounts'). Africa had a fair balance (and even in 2005–08 a surplus) but since 2011 has rapidly fallen into the danger zone, with a current account deficit at 3.3 per cent of GDP in 2015. Some of the continent's largest economies – Nigeria, Egypt, South Africa, Algeria and Angola – are in especially bad shape due partly to crashing mineral and oil prices in a context where TNCs repatriate an exorbitant share of the profits.

FDI in retreat

Third, the legal LFFs are volatile, no more so than in Africa where FDI has fallen from its $66 billion peak annual inflow in 2008 to a recent level around $50 billion. That fall cannot entirely be accounted for by the shrunken global commodities markets and the end of the Chinese growth miracle. The UN Conference on Trade and Development (UNCTAD) has also recorded a sharp rise since 2001 of 'new national investment policies that are restrictive', although Africa has been slow to keep up with that trend. South Africa's policy of Black Economic Empowerment (which compels around a quarter of local corporate ownership to be held by black South Africans) is one example of contested sovereignty, in which international pressure has come to bear against those desiring a different African power structure. (That incident led to the SA Trade Minister, Rob Davies, abrogating various bilateral investment treaties.)

There is also the overall problem of the capitalist crisis as it appears in 2017: what political economists term capital's worsening 'overaccumulation', or glutting of markets. As a result, nearly everywhere, FDI is in retreat, with 16 per cent less flowing globally in 2014 than in 2013, followed by a 7 per cent decline in 2015, according to UNCTAD's 2015 and 2016 *World Investment Reports*. In 2008, 2009 and 2012, there were also impressive double-digit declines in the rate of FDI growth from the prior year. This is potentially very good news for those concerned that TNCs exploit through LFFs, in Africa and elsewhere.

Foreign debt explodes

However (and fourth), getting the aforementioned current account deficit under control in turn requires either that exchange controls be applied and foreign debt be questioned (e.g. on grounds of the international Odious Debt doctrine), or that state elites attract yet more new FDI, so as to have hard currency on hand to pay back old FDI, or to take on new foreign borrowings so as to make payments on home-bound TNC profits and dividends. In order to make those payments, foreign debt is soaring. For sub-Saharan Africa, what was $200 billion in foreign debt from 1995–2005 (when G7 debt relief shrunk it 10 per cent), is now nearly $400 billion. In South Africa's case alone, the debt soared from the $25–35 billion range then to nearly $150 billion in 2017 – that is, from 20 per cent of GDP in 2005 to more than 50 per cent now. The last time even a 40 per cent foreign-debt/GDP ratio was reached was in 1985, and the result – thanks also to anti-apartheid activist sanctions pressure against bankers – was that apartheid President PW Botha defaulted.

Exploitation also comes from within Africa

Fifth, more nuance is important in terms of *which* firms are expropriating vast sums by a variety of means. It is not only Western TNCs which looted this continent for centuries. The single biggest country-based source of FDI in Africa is internal, from South Africa. A dozen companies with Johannesburg Stock Exchange listings draw out excessive FDI profits: British American Tobacco, SAB Miller breweries (which in 2016 was acquired by US-based Anheuser Busch), the MTN and Vodacom cellphone networks, Naspers newspapers, four banks (Standard, Barclays, Nedbank and FirstRand), the Sasol oil company and the local residues of the Anglo American Corporation empire. The result is the systematic internal looting of Africa by South Africa, especially as the main retail chains – for example, Walmart-owned Massmart and its affiliates – use the larger market in the south to achieve economies of scale in production that then swamp and wipe out Africa's basic-needs manufacturing sector.

At the same time, since the late 1990s, South Africa's current account deficit has soared because the country's biggest companies nearly without exception relocated to London or New York, and took LFFs with them: Anglo American (the gigantic mother firm) and its historic partner De Beers, plus SAB Miller, Investec bank, Old Mutual insurance, Didata, Mondi Paper, Liberty Life insurance, Gencor (BHP Billiton) and a few others. Exchange controls are desperately needed before, as some local commentators predict, capital flight lands South Africa in a foreign debt crisis like that of 1985, which brought the dreaded emergency IMF loan (Bond 2015).

54   P. Bond

In mid-2015, the South African Reserve Bank revealed that in the two previous years, Johannesburg firms had drawn in only half as much in profits ('dividend receipts') from their overseas operations as TNCs were taking out of South Africa. But that was a step up from the 2009–11 period when local TNCs pulled in only a third of what foreigners took out. It appears that Johannesburg companies have been busier securing profits from the rest of Africa in the past few years, as mining, cellphones, banking, brewing, construction, tobacco, tourism and other services from South Africa became more available throughout the rest of the continent.

Yet more public subsidization of FDI?

Sixth, a threat arising from the trend of declining FDI is renewed and yet more frenetic mining and petroleum extraction. To this end, vast public subsidies may become available through a new 'Programme for Infrastructure Development for Africa'. The donor-supported, trillion dollar project is mainly aimed at extraction, and its transport along new roads, railroads, pipelines and bridges to new ports, along with electricity generation overwhelmingly biased towards mining and smelting. If they materialize, subsidies of this sort will bring back the worst of the FDI, especially from Brazil-Russia-India-China-South Africa (BRICS) companies like Brazil's Vale mining (in Mozambique), Russia's Rosatom nuclear (with its proposed $100 billion South African deal), India's Vedanta and various Chinese parastatal firms – and Johannesburg corporations. Many of the BRICS firms appear oriented mostly to depleting Africa's 'natural capital', a term used by economists to describe natural resource endowments.

Although the end of the commodity super-cycle will mean a lower rate of extraction, this should not blind patriotic Africans to the continent's residual colonial-era bias towards depletion of non-renewable minerals, oil and gas (the exploitation of which leaves Africa far poorer in net terms than anywhere else). That bias left the continent's net wealth to shrink rapidly over the last few years, as even the World Bank (2011) details in its *Wealth of Nations* series, that 88 per cent of sub-Saharan African countries suffered net negative wealth accumulation in 2010. The contrast with Latin America and East Asia is striking.

In addition, a Group of 20 (G20) Compact with Africa was launched in 2017 by Wolfgang Schäuble, the German finance minister who in 2000 was forced to resign his post as conservative party leader due to corruption. The Compact stresses public subsidies to reduce risk and increase profits from TNC investment in Africa. A 'C20' (2017) group of civil society critics expressed concern not only about Schäuble's top-down process (unlike Tony Blair's 2005 Commission for Africa, no Africans were involved in drawing up the G20-IMF-World Bank Compact), but also:

> higher costs for the citizens, worse service, secrecy, loss of democratic influence and financial risks for the public ... and the multinational corporations involved demand that their profits be repatriated in hard currency – even

though the typical services contract entails local-currency expenditures and revenues – and that often raises African foreign debt levels, which are now at all-time highs again in many countries.

The crisis continues through land grabs, climate change and militarization

Another devastating feature of African political economy and political ecology is the certain demise of the peasantry once climate change hits. Already, farming is threatened in states like Ethiopia and Mozambique as a result of land grabs by Middle Eastern countries and India, South Africa and China (Ferrando 2013). Climate change will affect the most vulnerable Africans in the poorest countries, who are already subject to extreme stress as a result of war-torn socio-economic fabrics in West Africa, the Great Lakes, North Africa and the Horn of Africa. The Pentagon-funded University of Texas's Robert S. Strauss Center (2016) is acutely concerned about the extent to which social unrest will emerge as a result. The growing role of the US military's Africa Command in dozens of African countries bears testimony to the overlapping desire to maintain control amidst rising Islamic fundamentalism from the Sahel to Kenya, sites also in the vicinity of large petroleum reserves (Turse 2017).

Ending the looting and roasting of Africa

To halt uncompensated depletion, to address climate change properly (for example, with systematic demands for 'climate debt' reparations to be paid to African climate victims) and to prevent the BRICS from adopting explicitly sub-imperial accumulation strategies will require more coherence from those engaged in the African uprisings noted above. One process along these lines is the traditional class struggle and, as noted earlier, the demand for higher wages and better working conditions consistently ranked as the main reason for protests in recent years. Much labour movement activism is, however, rooted in micro-shopfloor and industry-level sectoral demands. Shifting to a broader ideological terrain, to national policy contestation and to Africa-wide solidarity is much harder, as the South African xenophobic upsurges of 2008, 2010 and 2015 (and in between) show. Nevertheless, Africa is ripe for a renewed focus on class struggle. The World Economic Forum's (WEF's) regular *Global Competitiveness Reports* rank African workers as extremely militant. The WEF asks representative samples of corporate managers to rate 'cooperation in labour–employer relations' in each country, measured on a scale of 1 to 7, from 'generally confrontational' to 'generally cooperative'. Table 3.1 reveals the 2013 results from 148 countries. Of the 39 African countries surveyed, 30 were higher than (or at) the world mean level of militancy (4.3). From 2012–14, South Africa ranked as the most militant.

Once this vital component of 'Africans uprising', labour, rises in unison with community, environmental, women's and other groups against the 'Africa rising'

56 P. Bond

TABLE 3.1 Africa's relative labour militancy according to World Economic Forum Competitiveness rankings for 140 countries (7 = most cooperative, 1 = most confrontational); world's ten most placid working classes, plus those African working classes above the world mean

#	Economy	
1	Switzerland	6.1
2	Denmark	6.1
3	Singapore	6.0
4	Norway	6.0
5	Japan	5.7
6	Austria	5.7
7	Sweden	5.7
8	Netherlands	5.6
9	Qatar	5.6
10	Luxembourg	5.6
77	Mali	4.3
79	Botswana	4.3
80	Uganda	4.2
85	Malawi	4.2
88	Madagascar	4.2
91	Ghana	4.1
92	Egypt	4.1
94	Namibia	4.1
96	Gabon	4.1
99	Cameroon	4.1
101	Kenya	4.0
103	Ethiopia	4.0
104	Seychelles	4.0
108	Sierra Leone	4.0
109	Tanzania	4.0
110	Zimbabwe	3.9
111	Cape Verde	3.9
114	Morocco	3.9
115	Lesotho	3.8
117	Mauritania	3.8
118	Liberia	3.8
119	Chad	3.7
120	Guinea	3.7
123	Mozambique	3.7
125	Tunisia	3.6
128	Algeria	3.6
135	Burundi	3.4
140	South Africa	2.5

Source: World Economic Forum (2015).

constituency of extractive industries and neoliberal policy managers, a different set of policies will be advocated. An egalitarian economic argument will be increasingly easier to make now that global capitalism is itself forcing Africa towards rebalancing. This will ultimately compel a much more courageous economic policy, potentially including:

- in the short term, a reimposition of exchange controls to better control both IFFs and LFFs, then a lowering interest rates to boost growth, with an audit of 'Odious Debt' before further repayment, and better control of imports and exports;
- adoption of an ecologically sensitive industrial policy aimed at import substitution, sectoral re-balancing, social needs and true sustainability;
- an increase in state social spending, paid for by higher corporate taxes, cross-subsidization and more domestic borrowing (and loose-money 'Quantitative Easing', too, if necessary);
- a reorientation of infrastructure to meet unmet basic needs, and expansion/maintenance/improvement of the energy grid, sanitation, public transport, clinics, schools, recreational facilities and internet; and
- in places like South Africa and Nigeria replete with fossil fuels, adopt 'Million Climate Jobs' strategies to generate employment for a genuinely green 'Just Transition'.

These are radical-sounding policies. But assuming state power can be won in a democratic election (far-fetched everywhere in the short term, to be sure), they are attractive to those Africans with even a 'Keynesian' worldview – and nearly all NGOs and funders are operating on this turf. Indeed, John Maynard Keynes was the most brilliant economist of the last century, when it came to saving capitalism from its worst excesses. As he put it in his 1933 *Yale Review* essay, 'National Self-Sufficiency':

> I sympathise with those who would minimise, rather than with those who would maximise, economic entanglement among nations. Ideas, knowledge, science, hospitality, travel – these are the things which should of their nature be international. But let goods be homespun whenever it is reasonably and conveniently possible and, above all, let finance be primarily national.
>
> *(Keynes 1933)*

Today we might term this the 'globalization of people and de-globalization of capital' and it is a perfect way to sloganize a sound, short-term economic strategy – 'transitional demands', if you like – appropriate for what we might hope will be a post-FDI world. In Africa, Samir Amin (2011) – the continent's greatest political economist, and in his 80s and still active – has argued this sort of delinking strategy since the 1960s. It is time those arguments were dusted off and put to work, to help Africans continue to rise (Ekine 2011; Biney 2013; Mampilly 2013) against the 'Africa rising' meme and all that it represents. Those who would dispute this line of argument must confront evidence of the futility of Africa's export-led economic fantasies, in view of the continuing Great Recession: the dramatic downturn in world trade over the past few years, the decline in rich country GDP to a 2 per cent annual level and recessionary conditions in emerging markets.

And as a final clarion call for radical re-envisaging of African political economy, there is also a political-ecological imperative to reboot the fossil fuel-addicted sectors of the economy, as the world necessarily moves to post-carbon economies. Naomi Klein's (2014) book *This Changes Everything* bears witness to the need to restructure a great many areas of life:

- energy (oil/coal to renewables);
- transport (private to public, shipping to local production);
- urban form (from sprawling suburbs to compact cities);
- housing/services (from hedonism to socio-ecological);
- agriculture/food (from semi-feudal, sugar-saturated, carbon-intensive plantation-grown to organic, cooperative and vegetarian-centric);
- production (from multinational-corporate capitalist logic to 'Just Transition' localization, eco-social planning and cooperation);
- consumption (from advertisement-driven, high-carbon, import-intensive and materialistic to de-commodified basic-needs guarantees and eco-socially sound consumption norms);
- disposal (from planned obsolescence to 'zero-waste');
- health, education, arts and social policy (from capitalist-determined to post-carbon, post-capitalist);
- social/private space (from durable race/class/gender segregation to public space, recreation, desegregation and human liberation).

This, then, is the major challenge for Africans who rise up against injustice, especially in forms which can generate solidarity with the rest of the world's progressive people. It is only in sketching out contradictions and opportunities that we can project forward several decades. But at this critical juncture as the commodity super-cycle's denouement now makes obvious the need for change, at least it is evident that Africans are not lying down.

References

African Development Bank, OECD Development Centre, UN Development Programme and Economic Commission for Africa. 2013. *African Economic Outlook*. www.africaneconomicoutlook.org.

African Development Bank, OECD Development Centre, UN Development Programme and Economic Commission for Africa. 2014. *African Economic Outlook*. www.africaneconomicoutlook.org.

African Development Bank, OECD Development Centre, UN Development Programme and Economic Commission for Africa. 2015. *African Economic Outlook*. www.africaneconomicoutlook.org.

Amin, Samir. 2011. An Arab Springtime? *Monthly Review*, 2 June. http://monthlyreview.org/commentary/2011-an-arab-springtime.

Biney, Ama. 2013. Is Africa Really Rising? *Pambazuka News*, 31 July and 4 September. http://pambazuka.org/en/category/features/88748.

Bond, Patrick. 2015. SA Bonded to a Stupid Economy. *Mail & Guardian*, 24 July. http://mg.co.za/article/2015-07-24-bonded-to-a-stupid-economy/.

Bracking, Sarah and Sharife, Khadija. 2014. Rough and Polished: A Case Study of the Diamond Pricing and Valuation System. LCSV Working Papers Series, No. 4. www.escholar.manchester.ac.uk/api/datastream?publicationPid=uk-ac-man-scw:226968&datastreamId=FULL-TEXT.PDF.

Burawoy, Michael. 2013. Marxism After Polanyi. In Williams, Michelle and Satgar, Vishwas (eds) *Marxisms in the 21st Century: Crisis, Critique and Struggle*. Johannesburg: Wits Press.

C20. 2017. The G20's Compact With Africa. *Pambazuka News*, 4 May. www.pambazuka.org/economics/g20%E2%80%99s-compact-africa.

Ekine S. 2011. Defiant in the Face of Brutality: Uprisings in East and Southern Africa. *Pambazuka News*, 2 June. http://pambazuka.org/en/category/features/73738.

Ferrando, Tomaso. 2013. Global Land Grabbing: A European Self-Critique. Unpublished manuscript. https://papers.ssrn.com/sol3/papers.cfm?abstract_id=2290352.

Forslund, Dick. 2014. Press Release: Lonmin, the Marikana Massacre and the Bermuda Connection. Alternative Information Resource Centre, 3 December. http://aidc.org.za/press-release-lonmin-the-marikana-massacre-and-the-bermuda-connection/.

Keynes, John Maynard. 1933. National Self-Sufficiency. www.panarchy.org/keynes/national.1933.html.

Klein, Naomi. 2014. *This Changes Everything: Capitalism vs The Climate*. New York: Simon & Schuster.

Lusakatimes.com. 2014. Video of Vedanta Boss Saying KCM Makes $500 Million Profit Per Year, 13 May. www.lusakatimes.com/2014/05/13/video-vedanta-boss-saying-kcm-makes-500-million-profit-per-year/.

Mampilly, R. 2013. Urban Protests and Rural Violence in Africa: A Call for an Integrated Approach. African Futures Forum, Social Science Research Council, New York, 4 February. http://forums.ssrc.org/african-futures/2013/02/04/urban-protests-and-rural-violence-in-africa-a-call-for-an-integrated-approach/#sthash.4KB0d0vO.dpuf.

Ncube, M. 2013. The Middle of the Pyramid: Dynamics of the African Middle Class. Tunis: African Development Bank. www.afdb.org/fileadmin/uploads/afdb/Documents/Publications/The%20Middle%20of%20the%20Pyramid_The%20Middle%20of%20the%20Pyramid.pdf.

Ndikumana, Leonce. 2015. How Africa Can Overcome Being Marginalised in the Global Economy. *The Conversation*, 2 July. http://theconversation.com/how-africa-can-overcome-being-marginalised-in-the-global-economy-43873.

Perry A. 2012. Africa Rising. *Time*, 3 December.

Polanyi, K. 1944. *The Great Transformation: The Political and Economic Origins of Our Time*. Boston: Beacon Press.

PRIO. *Armed Conflict Location Event Data*. www.prio.org/Data/Armed-Conflict/Armed-Conflict-Location-and-Event-Data/.

Report of the High Level Panel on Illicit Financial Flows from Africa. 2015. *Illicit Financial Flow*. www.uneca.org/sites/default/files/PublicationFiles/iff_main_report_26feb_en.pdf.

Robert S. Strauss Center for International Security and Law, Program on Climate Change and African Political Stability. 2016. *Final Program Report: 2009–2016*. Austin: University of Texas.

Robertson, C. 2013. Why Africa Will Rule the 21st Century. *African Business*, 7 January. http://africanbusinessmagazine.com/features/profile/why-africa-will-rule-the-21st-century.

South African Reserve Bank. 2015. *Full Quarterly Bulletin*, No. 276.

Turse, N. 2017. America's War-Fighting Footprint in Africa. *Pambazuka News*, 4 May. www.pambazuka.org/human-security/america%E2%80%99s-war-fighting-footprint-africa.

UNCTAD. 2015. *2015 World Investment Report*. http://unctad.org/en/PublicationsLibrary/wir2015_en.pdf.

United Nations Economic Commission for Africa (UNECA), High Level Panel on Illicit Financial Flows from Africa. 2015. *Illicit Financial Flows: Why Africa Needs to Track It, Stop It and Get It*. www.uneca.org/sites/default/files/PublicationFiles/illicit_financial_flows_why_africa_needs.pdf.

Vidal, John. 2015. Zambian Villagers Take Mining Giant Vedanta to Court in UK Over Toxic Leaks. *Guardian*, 1 August. www.theguardian.com/global-development/2015/aug/01/vedanta-zambia-copper-mining-toxic-leaks.

World Bank. 2011. *The Changing Wealth of Nations*, Washington, DC: World Bank.

World Economic Forum 2015. *Global Competitiveness Report, 2015–2016*. www3.weforum.org/docs/gcr/2015-2016/Global_Competitiveness_Report_2015-2016.pdf.

4

NEOLIBERALISM, URBANIZATION AND CHANGE IN AFRICA

Pádraig Carmody and Francis Owusu

Introduction

One of the defining features of the neoliberal regime of accumulation is inequality. This presents challenges for political regime maintenance in Africa and elsewhere, which increasingly find expression in cities. Cities are centres of capital accumulation globally, but they also are places where the majority of humanity lives. As such, they are the primary crucibles or arenas where the contradictions between use and exchange value play out. Cities are also increasingly interlinked, globally, allowing for greater flows of value and the spatial displacement of contradictions through the urban grid or network, in particular through the rapid growth of the informal sector. Thus inter- and intra-urban relations, and those between cities and their hinterlands, largely determine the evolution of these spaces.

To date, the 'urban crisis' has been manifest primarily in the cities of the Global South. While neoliberalism was posited as the solution to global development problems, the neoliberalization of urban spaces in Africa does not seem to be capable of meeting the challenges of poverty, security and climate change; in fact, it is contributory to them. However, there has recently been a new approach to mitigating the urban contradictions generated by neoliberalization – the creation of 'world city' developments in Africa or heterotopias (attempts to enact utopias). This chapter explores how these neoliberal urban developments in Africa are attempting to incorporate global urban forms and the role this is playing in the continent's (under)development. We argue that addressing urban challenges requires more creative solutions than those offered by the ideationally, if not practically, defunct ideology of neoliberalism and call for restructuring the accumulation processes in ways that can unleash the growth potential of African cities to benefit the mass of residents who reside in them, rather than just their elites.

Urbanization and development – is Africa different?

According to the *2014 World Urbanization Prospects* (UN Department of Economic and Social Affairs 2014), 54 per cent of the world's population now resides in urban areas and this number is projected to increase to 66 per cent by 2050. The urban population of the world has grown rapidly from 746 million in 1950 to 3.9 billion in 2014. Continuing population growth and urbanization are projected to add 2.5 billion people to the world's urban population by 2050. Africa and Asia, which currently contain nearly 90 per cent of the world's rural population, are expected to contribute massively to this global urban population growth by 2050. Indeed, Africa is experiencing phenomenal urban growth and urbanization. Over the past three decades, the region's urbanization rate has steadily increased faster than any other region in the world. According to the UN-HABITAT (2010), in 2009, Africa's total population for the first time exceeded one billion, of which 395 million (or almost 40 per cent) lived in urban areas. The percentage of the population which is urban in Africa is projected to increase to 56 per cent by 2050. Consequently, Africa is currently urbanizing faster than it did in the late 1990s and is expected to become the fastest urbanizing region from 2020 to 2050 (UN Department of Economic and Social Affairs 2014).

Although urbanization is often presented as a challenge to the development aspirations of African countries, the process itself is not necessarily a bad thing for a country or continent. Indeed, most analysts agree that urbanization can – and often does – contribute to or precipitate economic and social development. For example, urbanization leads to economies of scale in the provision of water, health, education, electricity and other services. Industries benefit from concentration of suppliers and consumers and they allow for savings in communications and transport costs. Cities serve as commercial, administrative and growth centres and are generally places for production and consumption of goods and services. Cities also provide big, differentiated labour markets and often help to generate new ideas and accelerate the pace of development of technological innovation and dissemination. Indeed, the countries with the fastest rate of urbanization are those with the best economic performance and shared prosperity (Henderson 2003, 2010).

The connection between urbanization and growth has been challenged in the African context in several studies (Freire *et al.* 2014; Ravallion *et al.* 2007). The argument is that urban economies in sub-Saharan Africa have not historically been well integrated into the global economy, and they depend on the export of natural resources and agricultural products in order to import manufactured goods. Poor public services, infrastructure and city management all obstruct economic growth in sub-Saharan Africa's cities. In addition, Africa's rapid urbanization is occurring in a context of slums and poverty. For instance, according to the UN-HABITAT (2008), over 43 per cent of Africa's urban populations live below the poverty line, with many countries recording over 50 per cent poverty rates. Africa's urban slum populations also continue to grow – slum and informal settlements proliferation account for almost all of the current urban spatial growth in some of the fast-growing

African cities. For instance, Nairobi's slums account for about a quarter of the total population of the metro area, estimated to be around 4.3 million (UN-HABITAT 2013). Poverty, deprivation, crime, violence and general human insecurity have become more widespread in many African cities, especially in the slums. In sum, one of the greatest challenges facing Africa today relates to how to unleash the potential benefits of the region's rapid urbanization, especially in the context of the dominance of neoliberal policies and the spread of globalization.

Neoliberalism and globalization in African cities

Globalization and the spread of neoliberalism have drastically shaped the way cities are developing across the globe. Neoliberalism in the African context was initiated through the imposition of Structural Adjustment Programmes (SAPs) from the early 1980s. These essentially transformed the state's role into a gatekeeper of the neoliberal project and market; attempting to ensure a stable investment climate and keeping in check those marginalized by neoliberalism (Peck and Tickell 2002; Afenah 2009). Globalization also refers to worldwide processes of interaction and integration among the people, companies and governments of different nations that have intensified since the late 1980s, driven in part by international trade and investment and aided by information technology that make the world more integrated and therefore interdependent (Murphy and Carmody 2015). Globalization is a much broader and multidimensional process than the transnational economic transactions that undergird neoliberalism; the connections between globalization and neoliberalism are not straightforward (Litonjua 2008; Heron 2008).

The world economy is largely organized around and through cities and so-called 'world cities' are playing increasingly important roles in the globalization process. Indeed, cities are no longer mere points of production and exchange of goods and services; they have become places where people and products are linked to the wider world (Robinson 2006). As a result, today's global urban system is dominated by a small number of centres that are the command and control points for global capitalism. Such world cities are distinguished not by their size or their status as capital cities of large countries but by the range and extent of their economic power. They are locations for the key individual institutions and organizations which manage, manipulate, dictate and determine the formation and distribution of capitalism across the world, and therefore occupy dominant positions in the global urban hierarchy.

Although most world cities are located in the developed countries (Robinson 2006), other cities are increasingly playing significant roles in the globalization process. Some geographers have taken this argument further by showing that even poorer cities also serve productive functions (Grant and Nijman 2002). For instance, cities of the Global South are increasingly becoming central to capital accumulation globally, both as centres of production (Shanghai), ownership (in the platinum industry, for example, in the case of Johannesburg) and as new markets for Northern and other transnationals through so-called 'bottom of the pyramid' strategies, which seek to consumerize the poor through selling small packets of washing powder, for example, as the poor cannot afford the outlay for larger boxes of it. Some African cities consequently serve ownership functions, as centres for the receipt of surplus capital from Northern and Eastern countries and as new markets for transnationals, such as beverage or mobile phone companies. Indicative of this imaginative and empirical shift, Coca-Cola recently relocated its African headquarters from England to Johannesburg in South Africa.

According to some urban theorists, cities in the Global South also serve as 'holding centres' for populations that are surplus to the requirements of global capital accumulation. The point is germane in the African context where a large percentage of the urban population continues to derive its livelihood from the informal sector, which is related to the broader structure of political economy. Much has been written about the so-called resource curse in Africa, which often manifests itself in the form of corruption, slow economic growth, Dutch disease, economic narrowing and conflicts (Owusu *et al.* 2014). While we do not have the space in this chapter to engage extensively with this concept, we do note that the resource dependence of many African economies creates problems, not only at the level of the polity or macro-economy, but at the urban scale, where formal sector livelihoods are often in short supply. This has resulted in the majority of urban populations working in the informal economy.

Writing in the 1970s, Milton Santos (1979) argued that rather than being a temporary aberration, the informal sector was functionally articulated and reproduced through its interaction with the formal economy – for example, through the provision of cheap wage goods. Thus rather than the informal economy being reflective of exclusion, the so-called dual economy was functional to the broader demands and structural nature of (underdeveloped) capitalist accumulation (Portes and Walton 1981; Castells and Portes 1989). Most of the population of African cities are then both included and excluded along different dimensions. They may be simultaneously excluded from public services and included in the consumption and production dynamics of the informal economy and global capitalism. This urban structure of inclusionary exclusion is itself then reflective of the broader politico-economic dynamics of resource dependence, which in turn is a reflection of the way in which Africa has historically been subordinately incorporated into the global economy.

Recently, within geography, there has been a debate about the ontological status of cities. Neil Brenner (2014, 15) has questioned 'established understandings of the urban as a bounded, nodal and relatively self-enclosed sociospatial condition in favour of more territorially differentiated, morphologically variable, multiscalar and processual conceptualizations'. Malaquais (2007, 32) argues that 'it would be significantly more productive to discuss cities more generally, with given African cities as starting points, as prototypes for an emerging, global form of urbanity', whereas Simone (2004) writes of the 'transterritorial city'. We accept the unbounded view of urban areas in Africa and seek to build on these insights through an examination of the role that utopian urban developments play – and as seems likely, will increasingly play – in the continent.

Neoliberal planning: contradiction in terms?

Since planning as a profession derives its relevance from the state, neoliberalism with its focus on reducing the role of the state has had significant implications for urban planning. From a neoliberal perspective, much urban planning is seen as distorting land markets and increasing transaction costs through bureaucratization of the urban economy (Wright 2013), although others with critical perspectives see planning as largely serving the needs of capital (Rankin 2009). According to Gleeson and Low (2000, 135), neoliberalism undercuts the very basis of planning as a tool for correcting and avoiding market failure and privileges a 'minimalist form of spatial regulation whose chief purpose is to facilitate development'. As Tasan-Kok and Baeten (2012) argue, planning is a prerequisite for neoliberal urban development precisely because a system based on market-oriented dynamics can only function if land-use decisions are regulated by planning institutions. Neoliberalism, however, presents many challenges to planners, including the effects of 'downsizing of local government, a simplification of public planning processes, and an emphasis on production and economic efficiency rather than redistribution and fairness' (Sager 2011, 180).

According to Afenah (2009, 3), the practical effects of neoliberalism on urban policy can be seen at various scales: in the neighbourhood, city and metropolitan region; and 'through the reorientation from redistribution to competition, institutional rescaling (giving greater powers to sub- and supranational levels) and through the revitalisation of the urban economy through privatisation, liberalisation, decentralisation, de-regulation and increased fiscal discipline'. These neoliberal challenges to core planning ideas have led some to question the concept of 'neoliberal planning', stressing the contradictory relationship between neoliberalism and planning. For instance, Tasan-Kok and Baeten (2012) argue that as urban planning becomes increasingly neoliberal and 'entrepreneurial', serious contradictions arise in the governance of cities. Baeten (2012) also discusses the planner's impossible task of serving private profit-seeking interests while actually seeking the public betterment of cities. He argues that neoliberalism seems to have reduced urban planning 'to a mere facilitator of "market forces" in the city'; that urban dwellers cannot simply 'lay claims on the city government to guarantee their well-being' and, as a result, '[t]he city as right, as entitlement, is slowly being replaced with the city as possibility and opportunity' (Baeten 2012, 206–7).

Neoliberalism has significantly curtailed the role of the state in Africa, and along some dimensions, incapacitated and weakened the planner's toolkit for dealing with the problems of African cities. In addition, the focus of urban planners across Africa seems to have shifted from making the city a decent place to live for its residents to a place of elite consumption and production, the benefits of which are meant to trickle down. As a result of resource constraints, Africa planners have only tinkered at the margins of the enormous urban problems in the region. As will be shown in the next two sections, the result has been the inability to respond to unprecedented urban growth, with 6,000 people migrating to Lagos a day (Grant 2015), the pervasive lack of urban amenities, widespread poverty and the resultant slumification of African cities. The limited success of the neoliberal-inspired narrow economic focus of much of the planning efforts in the region is a testimony to the bankruptcy of this mode of planning.

Neoliberal planning, globalization and African cities

'Good urban governance' has been presented as the key to the resolution of the challenges of poverty, poor and patchy service delivery and other urban ailments. The relationship between urban governance and neoliberalism has been explored elsewhere (see Obeng-Odoom 2013). Here, we explore whether or not the new worlding practices associated with the current round of urban globalization have the capacity or potential to substantively alter the dynamic of the political economy of urbanism in Africa. As a strategy for overcoming the current ailments and contradictions of the dominant, informal urban mode of capital accumulation (at least in terms of employment), many cities are seeking to become 'world cities'. They are doing this in order to ground mobile, transnational capital and other flows deemed as developmentally positive. However, these plans confront the reality of large-scale informality in African cities, with which these developments are articulated.

One of the ways in which African political and planning elites are seeking to overcome this legacy of urban underdevelopment, reflected in the prevalence of informality in Africa cities, is through the creation of new types of urban development. These efforts have taken a variety of forms ranging from special economic zones (SEZs) to financial services centres. SEZs, for instance, are essentially hybrids that bring the conditions of labour of the informal sector into the formal sector through often largely deregulated labour markets, for example (Cross 2010). The other new types of developments, such as Eko Atlantic in Nigeria, discussed in more detail below, add spatial and functional dimensions to this inclusionary exclusion process. In other words, while such developments are exclusionary in terms of their spatiality, they are also inclusionary in the ways that they serve to globalize functional dualism. This new type of functional dualism requires that African cities not only serve labour reserve functions, but through the provision of wage goods and services, the informal sector also services globalized financial and other activities. Furthermore, the informal sector is itself subject to worlding practices, through slum tourism, for example. Mega urban developments and attempts to formalize the informal sector, then, represent two neoliberal approaches to the urban crisis in Africa.

Globalization and the heterotopian imperative in Africa

The new international division of labour characterized by export processing manufacturing has bypassed most of Africa because the region is perceived as lacking infrastructure, a sufficiently skilled human resource base and capacity for effective state intervention. In contrast, state-led development in China has dramatically reduced the costs of manufactured exports, with which Africa cannot compete

(Lee 2014). As a result of these and other issues, there are often higher real product wages in Africa than in other competitor regions. Indicators of Africa's economic marginalization until the recent growth turnaround included a decline in Africa's share of foreign direct investment (FDI) from 1.8 per cent of global FDI inflows in 1986–90 to 0.8 per cent in 1999–2000, with about half of all FDI in the extractive sectors (e.g. oil and gas, mining, timber, etc.) that have little value added (Dupasquier and Osakwe 2005); a decrease in manufacturing value added; and stock markets that often attract only local stocks. While the continent has more recently seen a substantial increase in foreign investment, this is heavily concentrated in the resource sector. This generates imperatives to look for new sources of connection to the global economy.

Air transportation is a major driver of globalization and can therefore indicate the status of African cities in globalization (Bassens *et al.* 2012). Here too, a study by Otiso *et al.* (2011) concluded that, although some African cities, notably Johannesburg, Cairo, Cape Town, Nairobi, Casablanca, Durban and Tunis, have become important hubs in Africa's air transport network, the continent is still not as well integrated into the global economy from an airline connectivity standpoint. Moreover, the continent's cities do not rank high on the global urban network despite significant increases in their globality in the current round of restructuring associated with financialization and informationalization. In fact, most of the cities identified above largely handle non-African passenger flows, with about 80 per cent of passengers also carried by non-African carriers. The context described above has provided an imperative for African planners to look for new sources of connection to the global economy.

Given the limitations on planning practice posed by the operation of a 'free' market economy, cities around the world, including major African cities, are adopting other strategies to enhance their competitive advantages in attracting capital, tourists, knowledge workers and other flows judged beneficial to economic development. In Cape Town and Johannesburg, for example, there is a heavy emphasis on making them 'world cities' (Beavon 2004). Richard Florida's (2002) work on the importance of the creative class and fostering urban amenities, services and environments conducive to attracting them has been particularly important. Some cities in both the Global North and South now market themselves as homonormative, although this has its own exclusions and contradictions. Examples of worlding practices being adopted in Africa include the development of new financial services/utopian centres and new technology cities and hubs. These new developments seek to overcome previous problems or urbanization through the development of new forms of connection to the global economy, as will be detailed below.

Neoliberal heterotopias: case study examples

The most high-profile urban developments of recent years have not been about restructuring the accumulation processes within extant cities but centre on new types of additive urban development which ostensibly attempt to: (1) work from a tabula rasa; and (2) on that basis, forge new connections with the international economy. According to Foucault (1984, 3), heterotopias are 'a kind of effectively enacted utopia'. There are a variety of examples of heterotopic developments under construction across the continent, including Modderfontein (South Africa), Eko Atlantic (Nigeria) and Konza Techno City (Kenya).

Modderfontein (Johannesburg), South Africa

The 'Heartland' development at Modderfontein near Johannesburg in South Africa is being built by the Hong Kong-listed property developer Zendai. The Modderfontein development markets itself as becoming the 'New York of Africa' or 'the future capital for the whole of Africa' (Dai Zhikang quoted in Sowetan Live 2015) when it is completed. Its development is facilitated by the existence of a large parcel of undeveloped land between Johannesburg's international airport and the city. Some have questioned whether other property development capital from overseas will follow in substantial amounts, given Modderfontein's exceptional geography.

This new 'mega-city' is meant to serve as a financial services hub and capitalize on South Africa's role as a gateway to the rest of the continent for other investors. Johannesburg still dominates South Africa's urban hierarchy, with 74 per cent of the country's corporate headquarters located there (Rogerson and Rogerson 2014). In terms of its micro-spatiality, the city has experienced substantial restructuring since the end of apartheid, as corporate offices have left the downtown in favour of suburban and securitized locations such as Sandton, in the north of the city (Beavon 2004). However, in the case of the Modderfontein development, it represents not just suburbanization, but ex-urbanization, where a new city is meant to be created *de novo*, without the extant problems of congestion and crime, which have bedevilled Johannesburg. It therefore represents an attempted erasure of the socio-historical conditions which have produced Johannesburg as a particular type of space.

Modelled on urban developments in China, Modderfontein represents a 'dream world' of neoliberalism (Davis and Monk 2007), where socio-economic contradictions and tensions are spatially excluded from the purview of the city. According to the promotional literature for the development, 'Zendai's plan is to create a city which provides the ultimate solution in terms of convenience, sustainability, integrated development and prosperity. Live, work, play and learn are key focus areas of the development.' Through this erasure then, the groundwork is laid for a new, more productive engagement with the global economy. As such this represents a particular type of 'space of exception'; not just in the sense that it will apply for special economic status from the South African government, but also, according to Zendai, for the Chinese government's 'overseas economic trade and cooperative park' status.

While being in line with the neoliberal principles of attracting foreign investment, the Modderfontein development will be highly planned and designed to attract and cater to very particular types of people. There is to be a 'silver industry and retirement community' and an 'international residential community' who will be able to avail themselves of the 'themed entertainment centre, international conference and exhibition centre'. There will also be education and sports centres and a light industry and business, trade and logistics park. The development is meant to be self-contained for its residents, while reaching outwards into the global economy in a classic enclave form. Whether there is a need for this new office development can be questioned given an inner city vacancy rate of 16.6 per cent in Johannesburg and almost 10 per cent in 'decentralized office nodes'.

Eko Atlantic (Lagos), Nigeria

Eko Atlantic, currently under construction on reclaimed land off the coast of Lagos and inaugurated by former US President Bill Clinton, has a similar utopian/dystopian or heterotopian vision. Lagos, a mega-city with an estimated population of over 15 million, has experienced spectacular population growth and spatial expansion in the past four decades. Even though growth rates have slowed down since the late 1980s, the city is facing many severe urban problems. Its burgeoning population is marked by high rates of poverty and income inequality (UN-HABITAT 2010). The city is also known for urban decay as reflected in overcrowded housing, congested traffic, inadequate sanitation and social services, and a high unemployment rate. In addition, many residents are crowded into limited space threatened by sea-level rise, ocean surges and extreme weather events. Despite these problems, this city remains the economic pulse of the largest economy in Africa, with the economy of Lagos, by itself, now bigger than the economy of Kenya, East Africa's largest economy. This has put pressure on urban infrastructure, in addition to resulting in substantial rises in property prices in Lagos Island in particular, where many of the urban elite live (Global Property Guide 2014).

Eko Atlantic is an attempt to rearticulate this mega-city's relations with the global political economy so that it becomes a world, or perhaps even, in time, a global city (Sassen 1991). Funded jointly by the Lagos state government, South EnergyX Nigeria Limited (a subsidiary of the Chagoury Group) and other African and international banks, Eko Atlantic is being promoted nationally and internationally as a model of private–public partnership. The project, which is being implemented by experienced international architectural design and engineering firms, is the highest profile example of the so-called eco-cities that are currently in vogue across Africa. Drawing from the language of eco-cities, this ambitious project is presented as a green development which will protect Lagos from storm flooding and rising sea levels, even though some critics have pointed out the many ways in which the project has failed to follow the eco-cities principles (Grant 2015). Eko Atlantic and the Great Wall of Lagos sea revetment are expected to help to reverse coastal erosion and relieve some of the pressure on land and resources in Lagos. Like Modderfontein, Eko Atlantic is marketed with a pro-business message: a world class-city that will 'become the new financial epicentre of West Africa by the year 2020' (www.ekoatlantic.com). This model city will be privately administered and supplied with electricity, water, mass transit, sewage and security and will help 'update and transform Lagos' notoriously bad international reputation as a poster-child of crime and urban dysfunction' (Grant 2015, 321). When completed, Eko Atlantic will include 3,000 new buildings zoned in ten separate districts over 10 square kilometres of reclaimed land, complete with waterfront areas, tree-lined streets, efficient transport systems and mixed-use plots that combine residential areas with leisure facilities, offices and shops. It is projected to house many businesses, 250,000 residents, serve as the workplace for 150,000 people and support an additional 190,000 commuters.

That the project is targeting the international market can be seen from such comparisons as 'This will support a new urban development the size of the Manhattan district of New York City' (www.ekoatlantic.com). However, as Grant (2015) notes, the risk of abandoning traditional African cities, such as Lagos, through the promotion of such detached new cities explicitly geared towards serving elites and international capital is very real. More importantly, Eko Atlantic does not address the multifold problems of Lagos discussed above, and may indeed exacerbate them. For instance, it is doubtful that many jobs would be created beyond those that will be available during the construction. Other critics, such as Martin Lukacs (2014), argue that Nigeria's super-rich are using projects such as Eko Atlantic to exploit the crisis of climate change to increase inequality and seal themselves off from its impacts.

Konza Techno City (Nairobi), Kenya

In Kenya, there is also an initiative to build a new high-tech city/centre outside of Nairobi called Konza Techno City, which is being promoted by the Kenya Information, Communications and Technology Board. In the media and academic literature there has been substantial interest and, some might argue, these have hyped the creation of a 'silicon savannah'. In part, this enthusiasm is built on initiatives such as the i-Hub, which has attracted much media attention. While the i-Hub has several thousand members, its primary function is the creation of mobile phone applications, which are notoriously difficult to make profitable, even though some are spectacularly successful. Mobile phones and laptops are distributed or inverse infrastructures, with low sunk costs. Laptops can also serve as means of production for symbolic analysts (Reich 1991) to develop applications and other computer programs. This tendency towards the democratization of the ownership of some limited means of production is, however, offset by the imperative to be able to computer programme in order to take advantage of it. In addition, the distributed nature of the infrastructure associated with these new technologies undermines the generation of rents, vital for economic development. Therefore, the potential for tech-driven economic transformation should not be over-sold or over-estimated in Eastern Africa, even as there are some important new developments such as IBM establishing its first African lab in Nairobi. Nairobi or Konza are nowhere near establishing the conditions to become a technopolis.

Conclusion: beyond neoliberal planning: the search for creative solutions

In sum, these planned urban developments can be characterized as utopias, dystopias or heterotopias not because they will, if completed, generate substantial economic benefits in the form of job creation, linkage, multiplier and accelerator effects. However, through their representations, micro-spatialities and external foci, they discursively erase the deepening contradictions of the urban agglomerations with which they are associated. As such they can be seen as yet other examples of the unequalization of space and class associated with global neoliberalism, even as they attempt to reverse marginalization through greater integration into the global economy. The new exclusions that they generate may further deepen the structural violence experienced by the majority of the population. So while the gaze of their planners/developers is utopian, the impacts may be partially dystopian.

Africa is undergoing a profound urban transformation and is charting its own distinctive path to modernity (Chabal 2009). Current trends indicate deepening income inequality, with profound social, economic and political ramifications. Johannesburg is the city in Africa with the highest Gini coefficient at 0.7, and consequently it is not coincidental that it also has an extremely high crime rate. While the extent of crime should not be sensationalized or over-played, structural violence begets direct economic violence, which is resulting in securitization and deeper entrenchment of anomie and exclusion reflected in the urban morphology of the city – urban splintering. This urban splintering does not any longer, it appears, just take the form of gated communities, but of whole new cities being planned to discursively and spatially erase, bypass or circumvent the often predominantly informal mode of reproduction and capital accumulation of the cities to which they are to be attached or articulated. They are to be 'spaces of exception' linked to the global economy in ways distinctive from their 'host' cities. As these new spaces develop, the mode of urban governance which they deploy will be interesting and vitally important. Will these new spaces be securitized, like other urban enclaves such as Sandton in Johannesburg, to try to enable the partial detachment from host society dynamics in order to better and deeper integrate into transnationalized circuits of capital accumulation? Will urban splintering (spatial disarticulation) result in new transnational linkages between urban enclaves and result in the global splintering of space? Will the Southization of the Global North (Comaroff and Comaroff 2012) articulate with its analogue in the South to deepen the neoliberal global social formation currently crystalizing?

Carmody and Owusu (2016, 70) write that 'similar to the way in which indigenous Kenyans were simultaneously needed and rejected by the colonial city council in Nairobi, refugees and other African migrants now fill this ambiguous position'. Utopias can never be achieved in practice and their attempted construction results in new exclusions, as evinced by current spatial forms under construction. However, exclusion or detachment from the reality of the host society can never be achieved, given heterotopic dependence on labour power for their construction and operation. Furthermore, in a dialectical interplay, revenge may be meted out to the neo-revanchist cities under construction through violent crime within and beyond their boundaries. The class war manifest in neoliberalism then experiences sociospatial contradictions and instability despite this attempted socio-spatial fix.

While some of the new heterotopias either in the process of planning or under construction in Africa have their inspiration and finance from the 'Global East', the question still remains whether they represent a form of neo-developmentalism or neoliberalism? Although Africa is often written about, mistakenly, as marginal to the dynamics of global capital accumulation, cities in Africa are set to become, even more than before, some of the primary centres where the social and economic contradictions of neoliberalizing capitalism play out. The urbanization of neo-liberalism in turn produces new opportunities for development, in addition to con-tradictions. As such, African cities, or many of them, represent the neoliberal frontier. Beall and Fox (2009) argue that development thinking is preoccupied with two themes: progress and differentiation. This neoliberal frontier may evince both, along different dimensions.

Rather than housing, poor sanitation, poverty, crime or other symptoms being the main problems in African cities, it is the urban and the global mode of accumulation and livelihoods which is the structural root of these symptoms. In the current round of urbanization in Africa, different forms compete, and to some extent, come into conflict. Under national developmentalism, the two circuits of the urban economy (formal and informal) were highly articulated and interdependent. Under the current round of neoliberal 'glurbanization' there is an attempt being made through worlding practices to restructure (some) space outwards, and, in the process, further disarticulate the urban economy. These patterns of spatial restructuring, however, will be incap-able of overcoming the urban crisis on the continent, manifest in high levels of unem-ployment, poor housing and poverty, because of their limited nature, lack of productive focus and the new exclusions which they produce.

An alternative strategy of urban governance must start from a focus on the underlying structural issues and the necessity and potential for their resolution. A productivist focus would strategically identify those economic sectors in which competitive advantage, internal market deepening and opportunities for import substitution could be developed. Thus, urban governance must be reconceptual-ized as being part of a broader programme of structural transformation. According to Turok (2013, 66), 'possible examples of technologically realistic products [that African cities could produce] include fertilizers, chemicals, plastics and other petro-leum products, construction materials, plant and equipment, pipes, electrical cables, pylons, buses and railway rolling stock'. New spatial instruments such as SEZs, eco-industrial parks and others may play a part in this but the strategic vision must be broader, involving the beneficiation of resources, for example, and the develop-ment of linkage and multiplier effects which may be achieved through these. Fundamentally then, this comes down to the nature of the state and whether it is developmental.

Much research on the development of African cities has adopted a scalar focus on the local state. Yet, actor-network theory has encouraged us to examine the imbrications and impacts of actors and artefacts into assemblages. However, while a useful heuristic device, the ontological boundaries of assemblages are open to debate, as local states are also imbricated with national ones, which in turn articulate with transnational actors such as corporations. The global neoliberalizing assemblage then consists of a multiplicity of actors whose interests overlap and conflict depending on the precise issue area. Whereas the strategic impetus of corporations is profit, states have a more complex mix of motives, including, often, the preservation and deepening of the conditions for capital accumulation, the desire to achieve legitimacy or hegemony and to perpetuate regime maintenance. This configuration creates both constraints and points of action for social movements, developmentally oriented bureaucrats and other potentially progressive social forces. The development of cities is therefore fundamentally a project imbued with class (Obeng-Odoom 2013). As the Chief Operating Officer of Zendai South Africa noted in relation to Modderfontein, 'the project will be market driven, and depending on what our clients or developers want, the sky is the limit' (for some) (quoted in Sowetan Live 2015). Grounding urban development so that it produces sustainable livelihoods for the majority of the city's inhabitants, rather than new forms of exclusion, must be the primary goal of those struggling for a different, better and more inclusive future.

Acknowledgments

Many thanks to Prof. Andrew McLaran for his comments. Pádraig Carmody also thanks Jayne and Chris Rogerson for their advice and guidance on sources, and their hospitality. Any errors of fact or omission are of course ours.

References

Afenah, A. 2009. Conceptualizing the Effects of Neoliberal Urban Policies on Housing Rights: An Analysis of the Attempted Unlawful Forced Eviction of an Informal Settlement in Accra, Ghana. Development Planning Unit, University College London. www.ucl.ac.uk/bartlett/development/sites/bartlett/files/migrated-files/WP139_Afia_Afenah_Internet_copy_0.pdf.

Baeten, G. 2012. Neoliberal Planning: Does It Really Exist? In Tasan-Kok, T. and Baeten, G. (eds). *Contradictions of Neoliberal Planning: Cities, Policies and Politics*. The GeoJournal Library, 102. Dordrecht: Springer.

Bassens, D., Derudder, B., Otiso, K. M., Storme, T. and Witlox, F. 2012. African Gateways: Measuring Airline Connectivity Change for Africa's Global Urban Networks in the 2003–2009 Period. *South African Geographical Journal* 94(2): 103–19.

Beall, J. and Fox, S. 2009. *Cities and Development*. London: Routledge.

Beavon, K. 2004. *Johannesburg: The Making and Shaping of the City*. Pretoria: University of South Africa Press.

Brenner, N. (ed.). 2014. *Implosions/Explosions: Towards a Study of Planetary Urbanization*. Berlin: Jovis.

Carmody, P. and Owusu, F. 2016. Neoliberalism, Urbanization and Change in Africa: the Political Economy of Heterotopias. *Journal of African Development* 18: 61–73.

Castells, M. and Portes, A. 1989. World Underneath: The Origins, Dynamics, and Effects of the Informal Economy. In Portes, A., Castells, M. and Menton, L. A. (eds) *The Informal Economy: Studies in Advanced and Less Developed Countries*. Baltimore: John Hopkins University Press.

Chabal, P. 2009. *Africa: The Politics of Suffering and Smiling*. London: Zed/Pietermaritzburg: University of KwaZulu-Natal Press.

Comaroff, Jean and Comaroff, John L. 2012. Theory from the South: Or, How Euro-America Is Evolving Toward Africa. *Anthropological Forum* 22(2), 113–31.

Cross, J. 2010. Neoliberalism as Unexceptional: Economic Zones and the Everyday Precariousness of Working Life in South India. *Critique of Anthropology* 30(4): 355–73.

Davis, M., and Monk, D. B. 2007. *Evil Paradises: Dreamworlds of Neoliberalism*. New York and London: New Press.

Dupasquier, C. and Osakwe, P. N. 2005. *Foreign Direct Investment in Africa: Performance, Challenges and Responsibilities*. African Trade Policy Centre (ATPC) Work in Progress No. 21, Economic Commission for Africa.

Florida, R. L. 2002. *The Rise of the Creative Class: and How It Is Transforming Work, Leisure, Community and Everyday Life*. New York: Basic Books.

Foucault, Michel. 1984. Of Other Spaces: Utopias and Heterotopias. http://web.mit.edu/allanmc/www/foucault1.pdf.

Freire, Maria E., Somik, Lall and Leipziger, Danny. 2014. Africa's Urbanization: Challenges and Opportunities. Washington DC: The Growth Dialogue, Working Paper No. 7. www.growthdialogue.org/sites/default/files/documents/GD_WP7_web_8.5x11%20(3).pdf.

Gleeson, B. and Low, N. 2000. Revaluing Planning: Rolling Back Neo-Liberalism in Australia. *Progress in Planning* 53(2): 83–164.

Global Property Guide. 2014. www.globalpropertyguide.com/Africa/Nigeria.

Grant, R. 2015. *Africa: Geographies of Change*. Oxford: Oxford University Press.

Grant, R. and Nijman, J. 2002. Globalization and the Corporate Geography of Cities in the Less-Developed World. *Annals of the Association of American Geographers* 92(2): 320–40.

Henderson, J. V. 2003. Urbanization and Economic Development. *Annals of Economics and Finance* 4: 275–341.

Henderson, J. V. 2010. Cities and Development. *Journal of Regional Science* 50(1): 515–40.

Heron, Taitu 2008. Globalization, Neoliberalism and the Exercise of Human Agency. *International Journal of Politics, Culture & Society* 20: 85–101.

Lee, M. 2014 *Africa's World Trade: Informal Economies and Globalization from Below*. London: Zed Books.

Litonjua, M. D. 2008. The Socio-Political Construction of Globalization. *International Review of Modern Sociology* 34(2): 253–78.

Lukacs, M. 2014. New, Privatized African City Heralds Climate Apartheid. *Guardian*, 21 January. www.theguardian.com/environment/true-north/2014/jan/21/new-privatized-african-city-heralds-climate-apartheid.

Malaquais, D. 2007. Douala/Johannesburg/New York: Cityscapes Imagined. In Murray, M. J. and Myers, G. A. (eds) *Cities in Contemporary Africa*. Basingstoke: Palgrave Macmillan.

Murphy, J. and Carmody, P. 2015. *Africa's Information Revolution: Technical Regimes and Production Networks in South Africa and Tanzania*. Oxford: Wiley-Blackwell.

Obeng-Odoom, F. 2013. *Governance for Pro-Poor Development: Lessons from Ghana*. London and New York: Routledge.

Otiso, K.M., Derudder, B., Bassens D., Devriendt L. and Witlox, F. 2011. Airline Connectivity as a Measure of the Globalization of African Cities. *Applied Geography* 31: 609–20.

Owusu, F., D'Alessandro, C. and Hanson, K. T. 2014. Moving Africa Beyond the Resource Curse: Defining the 'Good Fit' Approach Imperative in Natural Resource Management and Identifying the Capacity Needs. In Hanson, K. T., D'Alessandro, C. and Owusu, F. (eds) *Managing Africa's Natural Resources: Capacities for Development*. Basingstoke: Palgrave Macmillan.

Peck, J. and Tickell, A. 2002. Neoliberalizing Space. *Antipode* 34: 380–404.

Portes, A. and Walton, J. 1981. *Labor, Class and the International System*. New York: Academic Press.

Rankin, K. N. 2009. Critical Development Studies and the Praxis of Planning. *City* 13(2–3): 219–29.

Ravallion, M., Chen, S. and Sangraula, P. 2007. New Evidence on the Urbanization of Global Poverty. www.gtap.agecon.purdue.edu/resources/download/3430.pdf.

Reich, R. B. 1991. *The Work of Nations: Preparing Ourselves for 2lst-Century Capitalism*. London: Simon & Schuster.

Robinson, Jennifer 2006. *Ordinary Cities: Between Modernity and Development*. London: Routledge.

Rogerson, C. M. and Rogerson, J. M. 2014. Johannesburg 2030: The Economic Contours of a 'Linking Global City'. *American Behavioural Scientist* 59(3): 347–68.

Sager, T. 2011. Neo-Liberal Urban Planning Policies: A Literature Survey 1990–2010. *Progress in Planning* 76: 147–99.

Santos, Milton. 1979. *The Shared Space: the Two Circuits of the Urban Economy in Underdeveloped Countries*. London: Methuen.

Sassen, S. 1991. *The Global City*. Princeton: Princeton University Press.

Simone, A. M. 2004. *For the City Yet to Come: Changing African Life in Four Cities*. Durham, NC: Duke University Press.

Tasan-Kok, T. and Baeten, G. (eds). 2012. *Contradictions of Neoliberal Planning: Cities, Policies and Politics*. The GeoJournal Library, 102. Dordrecht: Springer..

Sowetan Live. 2015. Construction Starts on New Gauteng 'City', 8 January. www.sowetanlive. co.za/business/2015/01/08/construction-starts-on-new-gauteng-city--.

Turok, I. 2013. Linking Urbanisation and Development in Africa's Economic Revival. In Parnell, S. and Pieterse, E. A. (eds) *Africa's Urban Revolution*. London: Zed.

United Nations Department of Economic and Social Affairs, Population Division. 2014. *2014 World Urbanization Prospects* (ST/ESA/SER.A/352). https://esa.un.org/unpd/wup/publications/files/wup2014-highlights.Pdf.

UN-HABITAT. 2008. *The State of African Cities 2008: A Framework for Addressing Urban Challenges in Africa*. Nairobi: UN-HABITAT.

UN-HABITAT. 2010. *The State of African Cities 2010: Governance, Inequality and Urban Land Markets*. Nairobi: UN-HABITAT.

UN-HABITAT. 2013. *State of the World's Cities 2012–13: Prosperity of Cities*. Nairobi: UN-HABITAT.

Wright, I. 2013. Are We All Neoliberals Now? Urban Planning in a Neoliberal Era. Unpublished manuscript prepared for the 49th ISOCARP Congress. www.isocarp.net/Data/case_studies/2412.pdf.

5

FROM URBAN CRISIS TO POLITICAL OPPORTUNITY

African slums

Jeffrey W. Paller

Studies of urbanization in Africa emphasize the failure of neoliberal policies and structural inequalities brought about by globalization. Yet these studies overlook the underlying political dynamics that contribute to the rise of slums across the continent. This chapter demonstrates how the informal social and political networks that underlie state–society relations in Africa contribute to the growth of slums. Rather than taking the conventional top-down approach to the so-called urban crisis, evidence from Ghana demonstrates how slum dwellers are active participants, and sometimes beneficiaries, in the development of informal settlements. I show how politicians' political survival calculations; community leaders' attempts to build followings and amass wealth; and insecure land rights contribute to urban governance. For many Africans, slums provide independent space to accumulate political power. The chapter suggests rethinking the scholarly and policy debate from one of an 'urban crisis' to 'political opportunity'.

Africa is urbanizing at a rate of 3.5 per cent per year during the past two decades, the highest regional urbanization rate in the world (African Development Bank 2012). Leading scholars of African urban studies go as far as to call the situation a 'revolution' (Parnell and Pieterse 2014). A result of this rapid urbanization is the growth of slums across the continent, where an estimated 200 million people live (Vidal 2010), equalling 62 per cent of the urban population in sub-Saharan Africa (UN-HABITAT 2010; Arimah 2010).[1] The inability of African governments to provide public goods and services to their urban populations, the increase of urban poverty and the rising number of slums across the continent have led a number of experts to suggest that Africa is experiencing an urban crisis (Tibaijuka 2004; Bond 2000; Hove *et al.* 2013).

This chapter suggests shifting the scholarly and policy debate from an urban crisis to political opportunity. This is because the dual transition of rapid urbanization and political liberalization across the continent provides new spaces for the accumulation of political power. Slums are at the forefront of these political struggles, as previously marginalized communities demand citizenship rights and seek inclusion into democratic polities (Holston 2008).

I focus on three political opportunities that slums offer politicians, community leaders and urban residents. First, slums offer politicians large voting blocs and 'political muscle' to win election campaigns. Second, slums offer community leaders the chance to act as brokers between politicians and residents, allowing them to extend their personal rule and territorial authority at the grassroots. Third, slums offer urban residents opportunities to profit from the provision of public goods and services through the informal sector. I demonstrate how this focus on political opportunities is more in line with the empirical realities of urban Africa. It also provides a partial explanation for the continued growth of slums that extend beyond arguments about globalization, neoliberal restructuring and failures in urban planning.

Urban Ghana provides a useful case study to assess the effects of political liberalization and rapid urbanization on African polities. I specifically use references to the neighbourhoods of Old Fadama and Ga Mashie in Accra, as well as Tulako in Ashaiman. I conducted ethnographic research to uncover the informal networks, processes of politics and spontaneity of decision-making in slum environments. I add additional evidence from an original household survey in Ghanaian slums.[2] The chapter demonstrates how slum leaders and residents are active participants, and sometimes beneficiaries, in the growth of slums.

African slums in the age of neoliberalism

Conventional wisdom attributes the rise of slums in the developing world, particularly in Africa, to an outgrowth of broader processes of globalization. Rising globalization has contributed to the growth of mega-cities, which has left huge portions of these populations suffering from congestion, pollution and slums (van der Ploeg and Poehlhekke 2008). Urbanization in Africa is characterized by phrases like 'urbanization-without-growth' or 'urbanization-without-industrialization' that emphasize the informal sector and processes of informalization (Fay and Opal 2000). The urbanization of poverty is now a widespread concern for economists and policymakers (Ravallion *et al.* 2007). Similarly, the totality of urban life is widely characterized by poverty and lawlessness, castigated as a crisis that needs to be tamed.[3] As neighbourhoods, they are deemed 'brown areas' where a liberal rule of law is not yet institutionalized (O'Donnell 1993).

Mike Davis popularized this alarmist sentiment in his book and article *Planet of Slums*. Davis argues that the debt crisis of the late 1970s and IMF-led restructuring of Third World economies in the 1980s decreased wages, increased unemployment and led to an urban, informal proletariat (Davis 2004, 9). Davis blames global forces like mechanization, food imports and civil wars that push migrants to cities that cannot accommodate them. These accounts of African urbanization tend to blame neoliberal economic policies for the rising urban crisis. Situating African cities in a broader structural context of 'global neoliberalism', scholars and pundits argue that rising land prices, privatization of subsistence agriculture and declining state and social safety nets have forced rural dwellers to the city to sustain basic livelihoods (Almeida 2012). Mahmud goes as far as to argue that 'the genesis and persistence of slums and slum-dwellers testify to the iron fist of the state working in concert with the hidden hand of the market in the service of accumulation of capital' (2010, 1).

The particulars of neoliberal restructuring include privatization, deregulation, free trade and minimal state interference and regulation (Harvey 2005). The rise of informal self-employment and micro-entrepreneurialism has been attributed to neoliberal adjustment policies (Portes and Hoffman 2003). During Africa's rapid urbanization in the 1990s, its state and civil service was hampered due to neoliberal policies (Rakodi 1997). Specifically, these policies contributed to capital flight, collapse of manufacturing, marginal or negative increases in export incomes, drastic cutbacks in urban public services, soaring prices and a steep decline in real wages (Myers 2005). By the 2000s, many experts and policymakers were already expressing the failures of these policies. The most important report on the growth of slums was published by the UN in 2003, and concluded:

> Instead of being a focus for growth and prosperity, the cities have become a dumping ground for a surplus population working in unskilled, unprotected and low-wage informal service industries and trade ... The rise of [this] informal sector is ... a direct result of liberalization.
>
> *(UN-HABITAT 2003, 76)*

The impact of neoliberal restructuring is believed to have hit African cities particularly hard, where breakdown of state services is more impactful in daily life than in rural areas where traditional and kinship networks play a larger role in providing services and welfare (O'Connor 1993).

Paradoxically, neoliberal policies have served as an impetus for greater political reforms while at the same time exacerbating socio-economic inequalities. Cities serve as a microcosm for broader national politics, and have typically been the main setting for political change in Africa (Chazan and Rothchild 1988). This tension dates back to colonial times where the city acted as both a system of control and the only space to engage in a political struggle against colonial authorities (Austin 1964). When colonialism ended, the city maintained its importance as a site of struggle, but also became a sphere for positive participation and engagement with the state.

During the late 1980s and early 1990s, cities served as important sources for home-grown political opposition that would usher in a new era of democratization (Bratton and van de Walle 1994). The first protests broke out in urbanized countries, mostly in cities (Bratton and van de Walle 1997). Until the wave of democratization that spread across Africa in the early 1990s, there were few institutional mechanisms for Africans to utilize their 'voice' option. Thus, violent protest was the clearest option (Wiseman 1986, 509). The rise of democracy opened new opportunities for political dissent. Perhaps the greatest impact democratization had on African cities was the development of an urban bourgeoisie and a burgeoning civil society.

Political liberalization, supported by international allies and finance institutions like the World Bank, also impacted public policy (Young 2012). For urban planners and development specialists, governance included setting out to 'fix' what went wrong with African cities (Myers 2005). In many ways, this meant taking a 'back to the future strategy' that attempted to go back to the colonial city at independence (Callaghy and Ravenhill 1993). This has limited the role of the state in this process, and ushered in further decentralization and attempted distribution of power to local administrative bodies (Eyoh and Stren 2003).

The dual process of political liberalization and rapid urbanization places intense pressure on urban residents and communities to confront livelihood and welfare challenges without the assistance of the state. Scholars have attempted to give agency to urban dwellers and demonstrate the way that they actively participate in urban life and confront the urban crisis. In this way, scholars emphasize the resilience of urban dwellers and their ability to overcome vulnerabilities (Simone 2004). The ability to cope has been the subject of numerous anthropological and sociological studies (Maylam and Edwards 1996; Ferguson 1999). One strategy is for local community networks to internationalize themselves – termed 'globalization-from-below' – by forming alliances with international NGOs (Appadurai 2001; Grant 2009).

Another common response is to form voluntary associations. These associations are vital for the well-being of urban residents, whether their objective is economic, political, educational, religious, recreational or cultural (Wirth 1938). In Africa, these associations are involved in a range of activities including community management, provision of social services and infrastructure, finance and credit, and religious and social affairs (Tostensen *et al.* 2001). Informal networks can act as useful coping mechanisms for vulnerable populations where the formal structures of the city or the state do not protect them (Tripp 1997; Attahi 1997). Stated simply, the informal economy provides goods, services and jobs that the formal economy cannot provide (Hart 2000). In this way, the informal economy represents societal disengagement from the state and the formal market and offers opportunities and freedom for vulnerable populations (Azarya and Chazan 1987). The conclusion to be drawn from this research is that the success of local communities depends on the strength of its social networks and the underlying networks of civic engagement and social capital (Putnam 1993).

Yet while these attempts to understand community dynamics give agency to local populations, they do so largely by overlooking the institutional context, as well as the linkages with broader society and the state (Meagher 2005). Specifically, they overlook patterns of politics and political behaviour that might shape and condition levels of social capital and types of social and political networks. By examining the dual process of political liberalization alongside rapid urbanization in Ghana, I will show how these two processes interact, support and even shape each other.

80 J. W. Paller

While increasing globalization, neoliberal restructuring and levels of social capital are crucial factors in the growth of slums, these analyses are largely devoid of politics.

Urban Ghana in the age of neoliberalism

The urban challenge is notably severe in Accra, Ghana, where the urban population has grown by 19.5 per cent since 2000 (World Bank 2013a), requiring 5.7 million new households in Ghana to be built by 2020 (UN-HABITAT 2011). The impact of neoliberal restructuring had significant impacts on government policies towards housing the urban poor. These policies shifted the focus of affordable housing from the government to the private sector. The state withdrew from direct housing production and financing and attempted to stimulate the growth of the real estate sector and the indigenous market (Tibaijuka 2009). The 1980s marked the emergence of the new interest group Ghana Real Estate Developers Association (GREDA), who represented private business interests. In effect, quasi-government agencies like Social Security and National Insurance Trust (SSNIT), entrusted with the responsibility of public housing development, have decreased their investment in public housing by 50 per cent over time (Arku 2009).

The government's strategy in 1991 shifted from an emphasis on direct provision to coordination. This shift towards a liberal approach to development included the attempt to regularize land tenure security. According to this perspective, affordable housing in countries like Ghana exists in extralegal environments where housing rights are not secured and owners are unable to produce capital. This informal housing market produces 'dead capital': residents are unable to invest in their homes and leverage their ownership assets into other progressive development (De Soto 2003). The World Bank-supported Land Administration Project was the cornerstone of this agenda, and sought to 'harmonize statutory laws and customary interests bearing on land' (World Bank 2013b).

The ambiguous and insecure land tenure regime has long been recognized as an impediment to economic growth in Ghana (Besley 1995; Goldstein and Udry 2008), and to accessible affordable housing. Nearly a decade ago, the Bank of Ghana found that, along with the rising cost of inputs, land acquisition is the driving force behind the rising price of housing in Ghana (Bank of Ghana 2007). The high costs complement the fact that land transactions are not recorded; titles are not provisioned; and multiple individuals and families claim the same plot of land (Onoma 2009). The government recognized that customary law needed to be better incorporated into the formal state property rights regime (Blocher 2006), and the Land Administration Project attempted to do this. But the project has been for the most part unsatisfactory (World Bank 2013b).

By the end of the twentieth century, the state and formal private enterprises had failed in their attempts to provide sufficient housing to urban residents. In response, the international community stepped in to play a role in facilitating the process of increasing access to housing for poor urban Africans (Arimah 2010). The Ghana

Poverty Reduction Strategy (GPRS) I, implemented in 2001, focused on attracting foreign capital to fund housing development. The GPRS II (2006–09) specifically focused on poor and marginalized populations, detailing a special programme for slum upgrading (Bank of Ghana 2007). Two major initiatives are particularly notable: the Cities without Slums (CWS) action plan, under the auspices of the Cities Alliance and the Slum Upgrading Facility (SUF). These programmes seek to mobilize foreign capital and to link this financial assistance with local actors. While the effectiveness of these policies is still not known, several scholars blame them for contributing to a housing market that privileges the rich over the poor, increasing income inequality and undermining an indigenous housing market that favours the poor (Gruffyd Jones 2012; Obeng-Odoom 2012).

The dual transition of rapid urbanization and political liberalization contributes to the ineffectiveness of these programmes. On the one hand, migrants move to the cities at such rapid rates that the state cannot keep up with a demand for housing and public services. But perhaps more importantly, political liberalization creates a pluralist and open decision-making process where diverse interests coincide and consensus is difficult to reach. The competitive multi-party environment makes confronting these urban challenges even more difficult, and demands inclusion into the study of urban development in Ghana.

This chapter shows how the consolidation of multi-party democracy since 1992 is necessary to understand urban governance in Ghana. Two major political parties, the National Democratic Congress (NDC) and the National Patriotic Party (NPP), dominate the political arena. Today, the NDC is the governing party (2008–present) while the opposition NPP ruled previously (2000–08). The parties have regional and ethnic core areas, and most slums in the Greater Accra Region are NDC strongholds. The struggle for state resources – management of public services like toilets, contracts for infrastructure projects and youth employment opportunities – takes place within the party ranks. The next three sections show how multi-party politics is central to understanding urban development in Ghana.

Political survival calculations

During the 2012 primary election for Minister of Parliament of the Odododiodio Constituency, the campaign organizer for aspirant Edwin Nii Lantey Vanderpuye explained the campaign team's relationship to Old Fadama, Ghana's largest extra-legal settlement: 'In the early 2000s this community was given to us as a gift. People just kept coming and coming. They handed us a victory on a silver platter' (interview, 11 January 2012). The arrival of thousands of migrants from the Northern Regions, loyalists of the NDC party, served as a crucial voting bloc for NDC politicians like Vanderpuye. The NDC continued to mobilize supporters in the slum in order to consolidate power, and it remains an overwhelming base of support for the party. But NDC leaders are in a difficult position: they cannot cater too much to the needs and desires of the slum residents because it will anger the indigenous Ga Mashie community that shares a boundary with Old Fadama. Therefore, politicians like Vanderpuye are hesitant, and unlikely to disturb the status quo – upgrade the slum, demolish the structures or relocate the slum dwellers.

In Ghana's extremely competitive multi-party environment, politicians rely on the support of slum dwellers to gain political support and win elections. Ghana's elections are particularly competitive: in 2012, President John Mahama won the election by less than three percentage points (50.7 per cent to 47.7 per cent). The Greater Accra Region, where many of Ghana's slums are located, is particularly competitive: the NDC gained 52.31 per cent of the presidential vote, compared to 46.92 per cent for the NPP. Elections are most competitive at the constituency level, where MP aspirants are locked into very close elections for their seats. For example, Henry Quartey (NPP) won Ayawaso Central constituency (where slums Alajo, Kotobabi and parts of New Town are located) by 635 votes; Nii Armah Ashietey (NDC) won Korle Klottey constituency (where slums Abuja and Avenor are located) by 1,275 votes. Edwin Nii Lantey Vanderpuye handily won (by 19,698 votes) Odododiodio constituency (where Ga Mashie and Old Fadama are located). But this number far exceeded previous vote margins, largely due to the growing influx of migrants from the Northern Region who live in Old Fadama and vote NDC.

Slum residents are not just prospective voters; they are also valuable 'political muscle'. In new democracies where formal institutions are weak, political parties rely on party activists, 'foot soldiers' and 'macho-men' to patrol polling stations during voting and registration periods, attend rallies and mobilize voters (Bob-Milliar 2012). Slums contain many youths working in the informal sector; they are willing to 'work' for the party on a short-term basis. Political parties view slum settlements as a valuable source of labour. Former Mayor Nat Nunoo Amarteifio explained, 'Political parties find muscle there. We [municipal bureaucrats] also had our own connections with them' (interview, 22 March 2012).

Politicians make strategic calculations in order to gain political support of slum dwellers (Paller 2014). In daily life, politicians visit slums to show sympathy for fire outbreaks and floods; distribute food and clothing to vulnerable populations, like *kayayei* (head porters); attend funerals and weddings of local leaders; and pray with pastors and imams at local churches and mosques. Of course this is not surprising; there is a long history of politicians reaching out to the urban poor for political support (Nelson 1979; Stokes 2007). But what has not been fully theorized is the role of political liberalization in the rapid growth of slums – that is, the liberal political environment creates the opportunity for slum dwellers to demand their democratic dividend, while giving politicians the opportunity for valuable 'political muscle'. This is consistent with recent claims that political liberalization will shift the locus of redistribution from the President to political parties, as well as allow a greater number of people into the redistributive political game (van de Walle 2009).

My survey results confirm that slum residents are important players in the game of multi-party politics. Ninety-four per cent of respondents have a voter's ID card, suggesting that they actively vote in Ghanaian elections. Twenty-six per cent of respondents are card-holding members of a political party. Political parties actively campaign and organize followers in slums. They do this by promising state goods in exchange for votes. Forty-seven per cent of respondents indicate being targeted by political parties with gifts or money; 46 per cent indicate being targeted with social welfare benefits; 47 per cent indicate being targeted with promises of employment; and 31 per cent indicate being targeted with promises of government contracts.

The increasing political liberalization brings the situation of slums into the public purview, while at the same time encouraging the persistence of the status quo. This is because more actors are incorporated into the process, contributing to a political deadlock. International organizations like Slum Dwellers International and Amnesty International encourage slum upgrading 'with a human face', outlawing forced eviction as a possibility; politicians actively politicize the situation in efforts to win votes; community leaders act as brokers between residents and politicians, often being accused of 'selling out' their community; and residents benefit from informal land markets and public services. With a diverse range of interests and de-concentrated power, it is difficult to reach a broad-based consensus. As Parnell and Pieterse sum up succinctly: 'Learning where power lies in the city can be as challenging as persuading those in power of the need for change' (2014, 10). The locus of decision-making is dispersed in the context of liberalization.

These challenges are highlighted by the case of Old Fadama, where there is a vibrant public debate about how to manage the rapid growth of the extralegal settlement. This has contributed to intense political jockeying. Politicians accuse each other of preventing a lasting solution to the Old Fadama crisis because of pandering for votes. While Old Fadama is notable for its size of more than 80,000 residents, its political importance is not unique. The extralegal settlement King Shona is locally understood as a 'fishing village' and central to the livelihoods of the Ga and Fanti people. Therefore, politicians reach out to the 'fisher folk' to show commitment to the indigenes of Accra, as evidenced by the two fishing sheds commissioned by former MPs. Politicians are expected to fill municipal jobs with slum residents from Chorkor and Ga Mashie, indigenous settlements where residents claim ownership of the city. When fire outbreaks spread through Avenor and Abuja, politicians quickly rush to the scene to distribute food and clothing. Zongo settlements like Nima and Maamobi with large Muslim populations have long been a centre of power and patronage (Kobo 2010).[4] Electoral campaigns are particularly intense, and the struggle for political influence dates back to the colonial struggle (Austin 1964). In Tulako and Valco Flat, two slum neighbourhoods in Ashaiman, politicians establish followings to bolster their electoral chances in the NDC primary.

The struggle for political space

Politicians are not the only actors who find political opportunities in slums. They also offer local leaders and their followers the political space to experiment with new modes of governance. They offer political entrepreneurs the opportunity to exploit new opportunities to expand territorial authority and political power. Michael Schatzberg claims that 'much of African history since 1960 [is] a continuation of the pre-colonial struggle for political, cultural, and economic space' (2015, 3). In urban Africa, this includes the expansion of populations to urban slums, where new polities form, marginalized populations seek incorporation into the state and contentious politics emerge between local groups and state actors. In slums, local leaders seek alliances with state actors with the intention of expanding their power and economic bases. In effect, the underlying network of social interactions and exchanges provides an important organizing logic for party politics today.

Party politics in African slums is embedded in forms of patrimonialism and personal rule that is an enduring feature of African politics (Bratton and van de Walle 1997; Paller 2014). 'Big man' rule penetrates all levels of society and has become an institutionalized pattern of expected behaviour and defining feature of daily life (Price 1974, 175). The goal of community leaders is to widen his or her social sphere – to extend local-level politics as much as possible. In other words, community leaders seek a group of followers to grow authority from the ground up.

In urban slums, the struggle for political space hinges on the control of access to housing and the provision of tenure security (Paller 2015). Local leaders establish territorial authority by founding new neighbourhoods, taking in migrant guests and strangers, selling land as *de jure* or de facto landlords, and serving as representatives and spokesmen for social networks and interest groups. In the absence of formal regulation and property rights, residents rely on strong leaders for basic livelihood goods. Further, the underlying land tenure and ownership regimes in West Africa are customary: the state never acquired ownership of land. This gives considerable power to indigenous tribes who are custodians of land, but also places the control of land, territory and housing outside the purview of state and formal jurisdiction. In theory, this means that there is no land in Ghana without an owner (Ollenu 1962; Ollenu and Woodman 1985; cited in Konadu-Agyemang 1991). The land tenure regime therefore privileges legitimacy, or the popular acceptance of authority and ownership, over formal or state rights. It also creates distinctions based on settlement and ownership, as 'a person of a different tribal origin is regarded as a stranger' (Pogucki 1954, 31). The struggle for legitimacy, often played out between groups, is therefore a deeply political struggle.

In Ghanaian slums like Tulako, Ashaiman, the landlord is a personal ruler who is an important father figure in people's daily lives. As one resident explained: 'If you have a problem [you] just go to him. Even if he does not solve [it] he will guide you to solve it' (Focus group, 3 June 2012). Local leaders own businesses like butcher shops, and they will provide stalls to new migrant youth and others in need of work. This gives leaders great political power in the community, and also enhances their wealth.

Community leaders spend many years extending their territorial authority in slums. In today's democratic and decentralized environment, they have stepped

From urban crisis to political opportunity **85**

into formal positions of power after serving their neighbourhoods for many years. They have proven to their constituents that they are viable leaders and hope to upgrade their communities – this gives them legitimacy and the political capital to lead. As one traditional chief says, 'We are all born and bred here. Upon growing to see that the system is not right, we took it upon ourselves to fix things' (interview, 16 February 2012). In slums like Tulako, the elders and leaders are respected and have fostered an environment of innovation and progress.

For early settlers, moving to Ashaiman provided not only opportunities to purchase land and property, but also the chance to found a political community and expand authority. This is consistent with the settlements of zongos across the Greater Accra Region. For example, the origin of Nima is traced to Alhaji Futa's purchase of the land in 1931; Alhaji Seidu Kardi exchanged gifts to customary authorities for Madina in order to 'play a more important role as local leader' (Peil 1976, 163); Malam Nelu purchased a plot of land at Zongo Malam; Malam Bako founded Sabon Zongo (Pellow 1985); and Braimah founded Tudu in in the early 1900s (Ntewusu 2012). Clearly, founding new neighbourhoods provides leaders with the opportunity to expand authority.

Not all slums develop from the legitimate purchase of land, but rather from a desire to seek incorporation into the state after years of political and social marginalization. For example, in the 1980s, people started squatting in Old Fadama illegally. The slum's population exploded due to a few government policies and decisions: the resettling of Northerners fleeing a conflict, the movement of the yam and onion markets and the establishment of Makola Market #2. But because the area was deemed illegal and uninhabitable by the government, the pattern of political development was personal, spontaneous and sporadic. The community grew in a haphazard manner, without proper planning or procedures. The squatters found a way to build a neighbourhood by filling in the swampy area with dirt. But once the community started growing, individuals realized that they could take advantage of the situation for personal gain. A few Ga family heads, members of the indigenous ethnic group, saw the illegal squatting as an opportunity to sell land and make money.

The community grew organically, with the Ga family heads serving as landlords of the community and personally benefiting from the sales. At first, people built their structures from thin wood slabs and cartons. They would use rubber sleeves as windows. People then started using bigger wood slabs. Plywood was used after this. At the early stages of development, the floors were made with wood chips. It was a big step when residents started cementing the floors. Today, many people are building cement structures.

The area grew in accordance with the local leaders who sold the land. These early settlers became influential opinion leaders in the community and still hold symbolic importance: residents are expected to show allegiance to them and occasionally pay tributes. However, the growth of other tribes has shifted the power away from these Ga leaders. Further, other community leaders have taken over the informal land market – mostly because the Ga leaders sold off most of their shares of the land and have since moved out of the community. Ethnic headmen established territorial authority and accumulated wealth by acting as de facto landlords. Migrants from their home town came to them when they needed housing in Accra, providing clustered ethnic social networks within the slum.

In today's multi-party environment, these local leaders establish patron–client relationships with political parties. In some cases, they serve as party representatives, assemblymen or politicians. More commonly, they serve as brokers between politicians and residents on the ground. In Accra, they function through the well-organized 'machine' of the NDC. The politicization of public services is one outcome of multi-party politics and the struggle between community 'brokers'.

In slum neighbourhoods in Ashaiman where governance relies on the municipal assembly, informal power struggles still take place in the party ranks. The case of public toilets illustrates the political struggle. In 2000, after the NPP won the national election, party activists seized the operation of the public toilets. In 2002, after many arguments and complaints, the toilets were officially given back to the Ashaiman Municipal Assembly. However, the Assembly simply awarded the contracts back to the NPP party leaders. In 2008, when the NDC won the election, the NDC youth seized the toilets and took control. After some complaints, the Assembly took them over. But the Assembly is an administrative body of the NDC – the chief executive (or mayor) is appointed by the President. Therefore, the Assembly revoked the contracts (of the NPP) and re-awarded them to the NDC. The toilets are now run by NDC branch leaders and others who 'have done a lot for the party'. These so-called 'toilet wars' have been documented across Accra and Kumasi and have become a source of local tension in many slum areas (Ayee and Crook 2003).

My survey results confirm that community leaders are brokers in the multi-party political game. Eighteen per cent of respondents in my sample have a formal role in the political party, serve as a local branch member (11 per cent), local branch executive (6 per cent) or constituency executive (1 per cent). Nine per cent of respondents indicate having received a contract from the government; 30 per cent indicate that they have been promised a government contract in exchange for votes. Twenty-three per cent of respondents indicate that constituency executive members of one of the major political parties congregate at local community spots where politics and local development are discussed. Community leaders seek links with political parties to bolster their own political power, while parties rely on brokers' support to mobilize followers.

As political liberalization progresses, the consolidation of multi-party politics appears to be giving way to the entrenchment of urban political machines. It is important to note that these patron–client relationships developed well before the age of neoliberalism, and were particularly evident during the national struggle for independence (Austin 1964). Nonetheless, with more resources at the government's disposal and higher capacities of political party operations, these political struggles are increasingly intense and competitive. Yet my data show that the struggle for political space remains a very local story with significant agency by slum leaders themselves. Personal rule has not withered away with the strengthening of Ghana's formal liberal-democratic institutions, but has rather intensified and adapted to the struggle for political space in Ghana.

Insecure land rights

Land rights in Ghanaian slums are insecure at best and non-existent at worst. The most insecure communities are extralegal settlements like Abuja CMB, Old Fadama and King Shona, where the threat of forced eviction by the state is a daily reality. While indigenous settlements and zongo communities are not currently under the threat of eviction from the state, individual land security remains uneven. Property disputes between neighbours and family members continue to shape conflict in these communities. My survey data show that most slum dwellers either do not have formal land rights (20 per cent) or do not know whether they have property title (30 per cent), undermining their formal property security. This means that they rely on informal networks and non-state providers of housing to secure their tenure (Paller 2015). While economists have emphasized the impacts of insecure land rights on economic growth (Besley 1995) and investment in housing (De Soto 2003; Field 2007), less attention has been given to understanding the influence weak property rights has on local authority structures. Insecure property rights provide a small subset of leaders or political entrepreneurs unique opportunities to start businesses, control housing markets and govern resources and services. These opportunities are not equally accessible to everyone, but instead depend on local power dynamics.

Insecure land rights offer varying political opportunities depending on the type of slum. In all slums, leaders can gain legitimacy through resolving property disputes. During these hearings, leaders gain status and prestige, but also are able to extract rents from claimants and defendants. In indigenous settlements, traditional authorities benefit from selling land to the government at inflated prices. The ambiguity of the land tenure regime favours traditional authorities because it allows them to allocate land multiple times, claim legal settlements for misuse of land and demand rents and tributes (Onoma 2009).

Extralegal settlements provide plentiful business opportunities for some slum dwellers. Entrepreneurs in extralegal settlements take advantage of the insecure and informal property rights institutions to enhance their wealth and power through private operations of public services like shower and toilet businesses, scrap recycling and exploiting the informal land market. For example, in Old Fadama, there are approximately 400 shower operators in the community. They form an association that is an important interest group in the community. Shower and toilet operators are some of the wealthiest people in the community – along with scrap dealers and transport operators. Yet extralegal settlements are not entirely 'off the grid' in the way that they are often portrayed. People in government positions own businesses in the community, and residents are often tipped off early when there is a rumour of eviction.

With a population of more than 80,000 people, the business opportunities in Old Fadama are plentiful. Members of the Dagomba ethnic group dominate the informal land market, having taken it over from the early Ga settlers and ruling with force since. The landlords all have various ways that they accumulated power: wealth, early settlement, chieftaincy status, coercion and even spiritual power. These landlords call in 'the Thugs', to come in and 'create the necessary order for the deal to go through'. They make sure that the person moving in will be safe on the ground; they take their cut from the financial deal. Community leaders in extralegal settlements craft creative strategies to take advantage of their informal living environment. In the absence of formal institutions, leaders find informal means to consolidate power through the amassing of wealth, extension of territorial authority and accumulation of followers.

In Tulako in Ashaiman, land disputes have existed since the initial settlement. The neighbourhood was initially designated a 'temporary workplace' by the Tema Development Corporation (TDC), anticipating that it would be a workshop; it did not intend for a human settlement to develop there. But workers from the port of Tema who could not afford housing in the city squatted there and constructed kiosks. The settlement grew rapidly in the 1960s and 1970s. In the 1990s, the assemblyman, known as a kind and gentle man, continued to allow squatters to construct kiosks as long as they paid him and lent their support as followers.

A major problem with the development of Tulako is that the land was not formally allocated. This contributed to poor communication between NGOs, property developers, community leaders and residents on the ground. Today, there is deep distrust among these different actors due to the underlying land insecurity. With new plans for slum upgrading, residents perceive NGOs and developers to be colluding with the chiefs to profit themselves.

Evidence on the ground suggests that ownership and control lies at the heart of property struggles. Building multi-story structures and creating individual title for all residents threatens this control and authority: landlords derive their authority in large part from their landlord status. These issues therefore become politicized, and contribute to political deadlock and the persistence of the status quo. They also divide the community and lead to personal struggles between various residents and leaders. Therefore, overcoming insecure land rights requires a political solution that has winners and losers, rather than merely an administrative or technical one that has been advocated by organizations like UN-HABITAT and other international NGOs. The provision of public services and access to housing remains a central issue dividing groups in slums, and is further politicized in the era of multi-party politics.

Conclusion

African slums in the age of neoliberalism are not best understood as being in crisis. Rather, slums offer significant opportunities for politicians to mobilize electoral support; community leaders to extend their territorial authority and serve as brokers

From urban crisis to political opportunity **89**

between politicians and residents; and some urban residents to claim public goods and services. More importantly, the rise of slums does not take place in a political vacuum, but rather within a context of rapid urbanization and heightened political liberalization. African slums are vibrant political spaces where politicians, leaders and residents are active participants in the construction of their democracies.

While this chapter focuses on urban Ghana, similar patterns of multi-party politics are apparent in democracies across Africa. David Anderson documents the role of vigilante gangs affiliated with political parties in Kenyan slums (2002). Landlords with political connections maintain high rents but low living standards in Kenyan slums (Gulyani and Talukdar 2008). Almost weekly, Kenyan newspapers have headlines like the following: 'Youth storm ODM offices over Mathare seat', demonstrating the importance of party politics to residents' daily life (Daily Nation 2014). Party populism in urban slums is widespread in Zambia and Senegal, as Resnick (2014) documents. Party politics is particularly intense in South Africa, where the struggle for basic goods and services is at the forefront of people's daily lives. Evidence for this is widespread, and includes the rise of Abahlali baseMjondolo, a political and social movement that protests forced evictions and struggles for affordable housing in South African townships. This evidence suggests that there are political actors like landlords and party brokers working in slums to perpetuate the status quo (Klopp 2008; Fox 2014), but also social movements and community organizations attempting to disrupt it. Finally, the success of slum-upgrading interventions has been critiqued from different perspectives, but scholars seem to conclude that local politics and contexts are crucial to their success. Understanding these local power relations in slums is crucial and further requires a research agenda that places African slums in comparative perspective.

Treating slums as political spaces has significant implications for urban development. Confronting urban planning and providing affordable housing requires political solutions. First, this involves creating electoral incentives for politicians to support investments in infrastructure and public goods projects in slums, and also for voters to privilege public goods over club goods. Second, political solutions also necessitate creating incentives for community leaders to serve the broader community interest, rather than a narrow ethnic or family interest. All too often, international NGOs and state bureaucrats seek alliances with community leaders without understanding their role as brokers for particular interests in the community. Broadbased participation at the local level is necessary to organize slum upgrading and urban development. One potential solution is to decentralize decision-making to the community level, as long as there are accountability mechanisms in place to hold leaders to account.

Third, politically connected urban residents benefit from the informal environment by profiting from providing private services and serving as de facto landlords of illegal land. State legal recognition of slum communities will enable municipal services to be distributed to slum communities. But formalization is not merely a technical or administrative problem, but a political one with clear winners and losers. Therefore, a political settlement with broad-based actors at the negotiating table is necessary for overcoming the status quo. While these solutions are not easy and require substantial political will, they provide a pathway for broader socio-economic opportunities for the urban poor in African slums in the age of neoliberalism.

Appendix

The survey entitled *Public Service Provision in Urban Ghana* was conducted in April 2013 in tandem with the Ghana Centre for Democratic Development. The National Science Foundation Award Number 1226588 funded the survey. It is the first comprehensive survey that considers many different types of slum communities in Accra, particularly the extralegal ones. Boundaries of slums are determined by a rich assessment of how residents and officials designate certain neighbourhoods based on insights acquired after qualitative research. The survey asks about political conditions in the slums. The questions are tailored to fit local context and consider dynamics that are specific to slum life.

The survey includes an average of 80 respondents in 15 distinct slum communities in Accra, Ashaiman and Kumasi (1,183 total respondents). Due to lack of adequate baseline data in these communities, the survey utilizes a spatial sampling technique. Using *Google Earth*, the research team constructed maps of all 15 communities. It then constructed a spatial grid of equal geographical units called clusters. Ten clusters were randomly sampled in each slum (150 clusters in total). The cluster is the enumeration area. A starting point was randomly selected using GPS; public service data were collected at each starting point. The enumerators conducted a random walk protocol from each starting point.

Notes

1 UN-HABITAT defines slums by their physical conditions (UN-HABITAT 2003). Slum conditions lack durable housing of a permanent nature that protects against extreme climate conditions; sufficient living space which means not more than three people sharing the same room; easy access to safe water in sufficient amounts at an affordable price; access to adequate sanitation in the form of a private or public toilet shared by a reasonable number of people; and security of tenure that prevents forced evictions. I define slums as neighbourhoods that have these observable conditions.
2 See Appendix for a description of the survey.
3 Murray and Meyers (2006) offer a critique of this perspective.
4 Zongos are 'strangers' quarters' where migrants settled in a host city. The word is a Hausa term that means the camping place of a caravan, or the lodging place of travellers (Abraham 1962, 967). Kobo (2010) calls them 'the generic name for areas inhabited by immigrants in Ghanaian towns'.

References

Abraham, Roy Clive. 1962. *Dictionary of the Hausa Language*. London: University of London Press.
African Development Bank Group. 2012. Urbanization in Africa, 13 December. www.afdb.org/en/blogs/afdb-championing-inclusive-growth-across-africa/post/urbanization-in-africa-10143/.

Almeida, Teresa. 2012. Neoliberal Policy and the Growth of Slums. *The Prospect Journal*, 21 May.

Anderson, David M. 2002. Vigilantes, Violence and the Politics of Public Order in Kenya. *African Affairs* 101: 531–55.

Appadurai, Arjun. 2001. Deep Democracy: Urban Governmentality and the Horizon of Politics. *Environment and Urbanization* 13(23): 23–43.

Arimah, Ben C. 2010. The Face of Urban Poverty: Explaining the Prevalence of Slums in Developing Countries. *UNU-WIDER* Working Paper 2010–30.

Arku, Godwin. 2009. Housing Policy Changes in Ghana in the 1990s. *Housing Studies* 24(2): 261–72.

Attahi, in Swillin, Mark. 1997. *Governing Africa's Cities*. Johannesburg: Witwatersrand University Press.

Austin, Dennis. 1964. *Politics in Ghana: 1946–1960*. Oxford: Oxford University Press.

Ayee, Joseph, and Crook, Richard. 2003. 'Toilet Wars': Urban Sanitation Services and the Politics of Public-Private Partnerships in Ghana. *Institute of Development Studies*, Working Paper.

Azarya, Victor and Chazan, Naomi. 1987. Disengagement from the State in Africa: Reflections on the Experience of Ghana and Guinea. *Comparative Studies in Society and History* 29: 106–31.

Bank of Ghana. 2007. *The Housing Market in Ghana*. www.bog.gov.gh/privatecontent/Research/Research%20Papers/bog%20housing.pdf.

Besley, Timothy. 1995. Property Rights and Investment Incentives: Theory and Evidence from Ghana. *Journal of Political Economy* 103(5): 903–37.

Blocher, Joseph. 2006. Building on Custom: Land Tenure Policy and Economic Development in Ghana. *Yale Human Rights and Development Law Journal* 9: 166–202.

Bob-Milliar, George M. 2012. Political Party Activism in Ghana: Factors Influencing the Decision of the Politically Active to Join a Political Party. *Democratization* 19(4): 668–89.

Bond, Patrick (ed.). 2000. *Cities of Gold, Townships of Coal: Essays on South Africa's New Urban Crisis*. Trenton, NJ: Africa World Press.

Bratton, Michael and van de Walle, Nicolas. 1994. Neopatrimonial Regimes and Political Transitions in Africa. *World Politics* 46(4): 453–89.

Bratton, Michael and van de Walle, Nicolas. 1997. *Democratic Experiments in Africa: Regime Transitions in Comparative Perspective*. New York: Cambridge University Press.

Callaghy, Thomas M. and Ravenhill, John. 1993. *Hemmed in: Responses to Africa's Economic Decline*. New York: Columbia University Press.

Chazan, Naomi and Rothchild, Donald. 1988. *The Precarious Balance: State and Society in Africa*. Boulder and London: Westview Press.

Daily Nation. 2014. Youth Storm ODM Offices Over Mathare Seat, 24 March.

Davis, Mike. 2004. Planet of Slums: Urban Involution and the Informal Proletariat. *New Left Review* 26: 5–26.

De Soto, Hernando. 2003. *The Mystery of Capital: Why Capitalism Triumphs in the West and Fails Everywhere Else*. New York: Basic Books.

Eyoh, Dickson and Stren, Richard (eds). 2003. *Decentralization and the Politics of Urban Development in West Africa*. Washington, DC: Woodrow Wilson International Center for Scholars.

Fay, Marianne and Opal, Charlotte. 2000. Urbanization-Without-Growth: A Not-So-Uncommon Phenomenon. The World Bank Policy Research Working Paper 2412.

Ferguson, James. 1999. *Expectations of Modernity: Myths and Meanings of Urban Life on the Zambian Copperbelt*. Berkeley: University of California Press.

Field, Erica. 2007. Entitled to Work: Urban Tenure Security and Labor Supply in Peru. *Quarterly Journal of Economics* 4(122): 1561–602.

Fox, Sean. 2014. The Political Economy of Slums: Theory and Evidence from Sub-Saharan Africa. *World Development* 54: 191–203.

Goldstein, Markus and Udry, Christopher. 2008. The Profits of Power: Land Rights and Agricultural Investment in Ghana. *Journal of Political Economy* 116(6): 981–1022.

Grant, Richard. 2009. *Globalizing City: The Urban and Economic Transformation of Accra, Ghana* Syracuse, New York: Syracuse University Press.

Gruffyd Jones, Branwen. 2012. 'Bankable Slums': The Global Politics of Slum Upgrading. *Third World Quarterly* 33(5): 769–89.

Gulyani, Sumila and Talukdar, Debabrata. 2008. Slum Real Estate: The Low-Quality High-Price Puzzle in Nairobi's Slum Rental Market and its Implications for Theory and Practice. *World Development* 36(10): 1916–37.

Hart, Keith. 2000. Kinship, Contract, and Trust: The Economic Organization of Migrants in an African City Slum. In Gambetta, Diego (ed.) *Trust: Making and Breaking Cooperative Relations.* Oxford: Oxford University Press.

Harvey, David. 2005. *A Brief History of Neoliberalism.* Oxford: Oxford University Press.

Holston, James. 2008. *Insurgent Citizenship: Disjunctions of Democracy and Modernity in Brazil.* Princeton, NJ: Princeton University Press.

Hove, Mediel, Ngwerume, Emmaculate Tsitsi and Muchemwa, Cyprian. 2013. The Urban Crisis in Sub-Saharan Africa: A Threat to Human Security and Sustainable Development. *Stability* 2(1): 1–14.

Klopp, Jacqueline M. 2008. Remembering the Muoroto Uprising: Slum Demolitions, Land and Democratization in Kenya. *African Studies* 67(3): 295–314.

Kobo, Ousman. 2010. 'We Are Citizens Too': The Politics of Citizenship in Independent Ghana. *The Journal of Modern African Studies* 48(1): 68–94.

Konadu-Agyemang, Kwadwo O. 1991. Reflections on the Absence of Squatter Settlements in West African Cities: The Case of Kumasi, Ghana. *Urban Studies* 28(1): 139–51.

Mahmud, Tayyab. 2010. 'Surplus Humanity' and the Margins of Legality: Slums, Slumdogs, and Accumulation by Dispossession. *Chapman Law Review* 14(1): 1–76.

Maylam, Paul and Edwards, Iain. 1996. *The People's City: African Life in Twentieth Century Durban.* Pietermaritzburg: University of Natal Press.

Meagher, Kate. 2005. Social Capital or Analytical Liability? Social Networks and African Informal Economies. *Global Networks* 5(3): 217–38.

Murray, Martin J. and Meyers, Garth A. (eds). 2006. *Cities in Contemporary Africa.* New York: Palgrave Macmillan.

Myers, Garth A. 2005. *Disposable Cities: Garbage, Governance, and Sustainable Development in Urban Africa.* Aldershot, UK: Ashgate Press.

Nelson, Joan M. 1979. *Access to Power: Politics and the Urban Poor in Developing Nations.* Princeton, NJ: Princeton University Press.

Ntewusu, Samuel A. 2012. *'Settling in and Holding on': A Socio-Historical Study of Northerners in Accra's Tudu: 1908–2008.* Leiden: African Studies Centre.

Obeng-Odoom, Franklin. 2012. Neoliberalism and the Urban Economy in Ghana: Urban Employment, Inequality, and Poverty. *Growth and Change* 43(1): 85–109.

O'Connor, Anthony. 1993. *Poverty in Africa.* Manchester, UK: Wiley.

O'Donnell, Guillermo. 1993. On the State, Democratization and Some Conceptual Problems: A Latin American View with Glances at Some Postcommunist Countries. *World Development* 21(8): 1355–69.

Ollenu, N. A. 1962. *Customary Land Law in Ghana.* London: Sweet and Maxwell.

Ollenu, N. A. and Woodman, G. R. 1985. *Ollenu's Principles of Customary Land Law.* Birmingham: CAL Press.

Onoma, Ato Kwamena. 2009. *The Politics of Property Rights Institutions in Africa*. Cambridge: Cambridge University Press.

Paller, Jeffrey W. 2014. Informal Institutions and Personal Rule in Urban Ghana. *African Studies Review* 57(3): 123–42.

Paller, Jeffrey W. 2015. Informal Networks and Access to Power to Obtain Housing in Urban Slums in Ghana. *Africa Today* 62(1): 31–55.

Parnell, Susan and Pieterse, Edgar (eds). 2014. *Africa's Urban Revolution*. London: Zed Books.

Peil, Margaret. 1976. African Squatter Settlements: A Comparative Study. *Urban Studies* 13: 155–66.

Pellow, Deborah. 1985. Muslim Segmentation: Cohesion and Divisiveness in Accra. *The Journal of Modern African Studies* 23(3): 419–44.

Pogucki, R. J. H. 1954. *Report on Land Tenure in Customary Law of the Non-Akan Areas of the Gold Coast (Now Eastern Region of Ghana)*. Volume II. Accra: Lands Department.

Portes, Alejandro and Hoffman, Kelly. 2003. Latin American Class Structures: Their Composition and Change During the Neoliberal Era. *Latin American Research Review* 38(1): 41–82.

Price, Richard. 1974. Politics and Culture in Contemporary Ghana: The Big-Man Small-Boy Syndrome. *Journal of African Studies* 1(2): 173–204.

Putnam, Robert D. 1993. *Making Democracy Work: Civic Traditions in Modern Italy*. Princeton: Princeton University Press.

Rakodi, Carole. 1997. *The Urban Challenge in Africa: Growth and Management of its Large Cities*. Tokyo, Japan: United Nations University Press.

Ravallion, Martin, Chen, Shaohua and Sangraula, Prem. 2007. New Evidence on the Urbanization of Global Poverty. The World Bank Development Working Group 1–46.

Resnick, Danielle. 2014. *Urban Poverty and Party Populism in African Democracies*. New York: Cambridge University Press.

Schatzberg, Michael G. 2015. Transformation and Struggle: Space in Africa. In Förster, Till and Koechlin, Lucy (eds) *The Politics of Governance*. London: Taylor & Francis.

Simone, Abdou Maliq. 2004. *For the City Yet to Come: Changing African Life in Four Cities*. Durham: Duke University Press.

Stokes, Susan C. 2007. Political Clientelism. In Boix, Carles and Stokes, Susan C. (eds) *Oxford University Press Handbook of Comparative Politics*. Oxford: Oxford University Press.

Tibaijuka, Anna Kajimulo. 2004. *Africa on the Move: An Urban Crisis in the Making. Submission to the Commission for Africa*. Nairobi: UN-HABITAT.

Tibaijuka, Anna Kajimulo. 2009. *Building Prosperity: Housing and Economic Development*. Abingdon: Routledge.

Tostensen, Arne, Tvedten, Inge and Vaa, Mariken. 2001. *Associational Life in African Cities: Popular Responses to the Urban Crisis*. Oslo: Nordiska Afrikainstitutet.

Tripp, Aili. 1997. *Changing the Rules: The Politics of Liberalization and the Urban Informal Economy in Tanzania*. Berkeley: University of California Press.

UN-HABITAT. 2003. *The Challenge of Slums: Global Report on Human Settlements*. Nairobi: UN-HABITAT.

UN-HABITAT. 2010. *State of the World's Cities 2010/11: Cities for All: Bridging the Urban Divide*. Nairobi: UN-HABITAT. https://unhabitat.org/books/state-of-the-worlds-cities-20102011-cities-for-all-bridging-the-urban-divide/.

UN-HABITAT. 2011. *Ghana Housing Profile*. Nairobi: UN-HABITAT. http://mirror.unhabitat.org/pmss/listItemDetails.aspx?publicationID=3258&AspxAutoDetectCookieSupport=1.

94 J. W. Paller

van de Walle, Nicolas. 2009. The Democratization of Political Clientelism in Sub-Saharan Africa. Working Paper, *European Conference on African Studies*. Leipzig, Germany.

van der Ploeg, Frederick and Poehlhekke, Steven. 2008. Globalization and the Rise of Mega Cities in the Developing World. *Cambridge Journal of Regions, Economy and Society* 1: 477–501.

Vidal, John. 2010. 227 Million People Escape World's Slums, UN Report Finds. *Guardian*, 22 March.

Wirth, Louis. 1938. Urbanism as a Way of Life. *American Journal of Sociology* 44: 1–24.

Wiseman, John. 1986. Urban Riots in West Africa, 1977–85. *Journal of Modern African Studies* 24(3): 509–18.

World Bank. 2013a. *World Development Indicators*. http://data.worldbank.org/indicator/SP.URB.TOTL.IN.ZS?page=3.

World Bank. June 2013b. *Project Performance Assessment Report Ghana: Land Administration Project*. http://documents.worldbank.org/curated/en/288501468030342367/pdf/750840PPAR0p0711570Box377346B00OUO090.pdf.

Young, Crawford. 2012. *The Postcolonial State in Africa: Fifty Years of Independence, 1960–2010*. Madison, WI: University of Wisconsin Press.

6

THE POVERTY OF 'POVERTY REDUCTION'

The case of African cotton

Adam Sneyd

African cotton in the age of neoliberalism continues to generate an impoverishing imbalance between risk and reward. The primary producers of cotton in the 30 or so African countries where cotton cultivation is most prominent are small-scale farming families. The millions of families that sow cottonseeds and tend to their thirsty crops hope ultimately to generate an income from sales at the farm gate. Their faith is not necessarily misguided. African farmers that seek to reap cotton's ostensible returns of cash and an improved position in the money economy attempt to emulate the evident economic successes of some of their peers. Many who are induced to go down this path nonetheless fail to realize sustained financial prosperity. The promise of 'white gold' is often not kept.

The idea that cotton in Africa can also be the 'mother of poverty' is not new and was certainly not imposed from abroad (Isaacman and Roberts 1995). According to social historian Allen Isaacman, this perspective was evident in indigenous responses to the imposition by force of colonial cotton schemes in numerous African places. For those who care to look for it, the legacy of Europeans pushing to maximize cotton outputs from Africa to supply textile and garment mills in Europe remains evident today (Roitman 2005, 55). Africa's ongoing role as a supplier of this industrial raw material to processors including yarn and thread spinners, weavers, dyers and wax printers in Europe and in Asia bears upon the potential for African cotton to durably reduce poverty. So too does the reality that cotton production demands that farmers reduce the area of land they devote to growing food crops. Beyond the food security challenge, cotton production often has other social and ecological costs. It can yield gender and intra-household inequities, and return soil exhaustion and groundwater contamination if cultivated using antiquated and unsustainable agrochemicals. The risk that quality issues, adverse weather events, price volatility or foreign exchange movements could undercut farmer margins has also been omnipresent in contexts where farmers remain uninsured (UNCTAD 2011a).

Nonetheless, the fact that tales of cotton farming 'success' are exceptional is not foreordained. While cotton and poverty might have grown up side-by-side across Africa south of the Sahara, there is nothing inevitable about this unenviable condition. The heart of the matter is that over the past decade discussions of Africa's present and future with cotton have taken a distinctly neoliberal turn. Few analysts have been immune from the stagnant viewpoint that more market-friendly policies and more market access will generate poverty reduction. Neoliberal calls for more private competition in input and output markets, deregulated market-based pricing, deeper sub-regional and inter-regional integration, individualized risk management systems, greater reliance on transnational agribusinesses and a 'freer' global cotton trade have resonated. Academics who have sought to identify Africa's domestic cotton 'problem' have propagated these canards as reliably as trade policy reformers. If the efforts of the latter to 'free' trade were ultimately successful, Africa's position as an exporter of the lowest value added cotton product traded internationally – lint with the seeds removed – would be solidified.

Contributors to the policy-oriented academic and professional literature have at best acknowledged and at worst 'disappeared' the history that would put paid to the neoliberal conventional wisdom (Stanfield and Stanfield 2011). They have generally expunged the inconvenient truth that all presently 'developed' or 'emerging' capital-intensive cotton sectors have been governed in ways that cannot be construed as being neoliberal or governed by market fundamentalist principles, regulations, policies or laws. Market-first 'solutions' to Africa's cotton crises now stand in stark contrast to the moves of Asian producers and importers to become price-makers and not price-takers. In the context of enhanced cotton price volatility in 2013, for example, India considered imposing a ban on raw cotton exports. China, the world's biggest importer, for its part, moved in 2014 to end its policy of stocking large quantities of foreign origin cotton as a buffer against shortfalls in its heavily subsidized domestic cotton production system. As the prospects for further demand growth in China subsequently dimmed, African suppliers of raw cotton who had reoriented their sales to Asia had to peddle their stocks elsewhere.

Surveying this scene it can be said with certainty that neoliberal ideas and financial and commercial realities impede the prospects for a Pan African cotton renaissance. African governments have simply been unwilling or unable to provide the levels of support to the sector evident elsewhere. Moreover, African economies are awash in the bitter fruit of trade liberalization: nominally 'cheap' used clothes and Asian-origin knock-off garments. This influx has come at a high real cost: aborted or foregone industrialization, and the relegation of African branded and designed clothing to the racks of high-end boutiques and the associated niche-market status. That being said, export-oriented African enterprises that source and transform cotton with quality characteristics that have been verified or certified by a third party (i.e. fair trade, organic or both) have emerged. Still, few African firms aim to serve the African market through specializing in the transformation of cotton produced, spun and weaved at artisanal scales.

To spin the tale of the poverty of 'poverty reduction' in this context, the article commences with an account of the complex linkages between cotton production and poverty. It then recounts how poverty reduction has been underpinned by or has exuded neoliberalism. To do so, a multi-level analysis of neoliberal poverty reduction is employed. The first level of analysis covered is the multilateral or *international*. Here the article recounts the liberalization proposal of the so-called Cotton-Four (C4) countries (Bénin, Burkina Faso, Tchad and Mali). Officially termed *Poverty Reduction: Sectoral Initiative in Favour of Cotton*, the C4 have pursued this proposal through trade negotiations at the World Trade Organization (WTO). Related to this level but distinct from it is *regional* inter-state cooperation. This section analyses the complex engagements of the European Union (EU) with official public and private sector players involved with African cotton production and trade. The engagements of the EU on cotton have fallen under the auspices of its All African, Caribbean and Pacific Group of States (ACP) agricultural commodities programme (AAACP) and its EU–Africa partnership on cotton. Here particular attention is paid to the EU's engagement with regional economic organizations, including the Communauté Économique des États de l'Afrique Centrale (CEEAC), L'Union Économique et Monétaire Ouest-Africaine (UEMOA) and the Common Market for Eastern and Southern Africa (COMESA). Through this effort, the EU has funded the development of regional cotton strategies that aim to inform the eventual roll out by the African Union (AU) of a *Pan African Cotton Road Map*. An argument is ultimately made that the Pan African appellation in this instance is misleading. The term has been employed as a technical descriptor of integration and, as such, bears no necessary relation to the strategy of collective autonomy or anti-poverty orientation typically denoted by users of the term 'Pan Africanism'.

The final substantive section focuses on the *global* level or transnational phenomena. In particular, it hones in on global private sector-led governance initiatives. An abundance of corporate social responsibility (CSR) principles, norms or standards entailing a range of corporate commitment or adherence has cemented the rule of corporate-driven or controlled regulation in African cotton. While the outcomes from this shift for producers have been mixed, the very real threat associated with multiple overlapping and competing approaches to governance by market players is that lowest common denominator, lowest cost approaches will dominate. More costly CSR approaches with stronger potentials to reduce poverty are at risk if Africans continue to embrace the principle of lowest cost to engage with the global cotton market. Several concluding thoughts on policy and governance alternatives that might alleviate, reduce or ultimately eradicate the poverty of 'poverty reduction' as currently practised in African cotton are offered at the end. The paper's final point implores Africa's leading cotton experts to turn their attention to neoliberalism at the international, regional and global levels, and away from rear-view mirror studies that simply attempt to differentiate the experiences that Africa's cotton producing countries had with liberalization.

Poverty and cotton in Africa

Many experts on African agriculture and trade and members of the informed public generally accept the proposition that cotton's status as a cash crop has necessarily contributed to the fight against poverty in Africa. From the perspective of this conventional wisdom, farmers in remote areas have been able to use cotton to climb out of subsistence agriculture and participate in modern rural economic life. Over the past two centuries, those in domestic capitals and foreign commercial centres with stakes in promoting the crop have played up this notion and the corollary that cotton is a win-win proposition for all involved. According to Matthew Schnurr, for example, interest in cultivating cotton in Natal and Zululand was routinely resurrected in the late 1800s and early 1900s when memories of past failures of this 'calamitous commodity' had faded (Schnurr 2013).

Demand-side voices contributed to other instances of historical amnesia, and also to the propagation of cotton across the continent. Ideological efforts to entrench Africa's status as a cotton producer and trader persisted after formal political independence into the era of structural adjustment and beyond (Gibbon 1999). Employing their visible fists, African governments controlled cotton and bred new constituencies of individuals and organizations with vested interests in growing the economic importance of this crop. The idea that cotton's 'double yield' of a durable foreign exchange boost and a reliable rural income stream continues to have a powerful hold over African policy and decision-makers, businesspeople and entrepreneurs today. The salience of this idea is perhaps most evident in the reality that Africa's share of the world agricultural trade was cut in half between 1980 and 2005, while over the same period the continent's share of world cotton exports more than doubled. Those charged with executing control over cotton have been and continue to be richly rewarded. Less clear are the inflation-adjusted absolute or relative income gains, if any, that average cotton farmers have been able to reap. Statistics on this specific south of the Sahara are entirely lacking in the context of the continent's broader 'poor' numbers problems (Jerven 2013).

Turning to the linkages between cotton and poverty in Africa then, it is understandable that many policy-oriented researchers, research organizations and journalists working on this topic have put international trade at the core of their analyses (Watkins with Sul 2002; Baden 2004; Hazard 2005; Anderson and Valenzuela 2006; WTO 2013; ICTSD 2014). It is also worth noting that particular contributors have emphasized different trade-related challenges. The individual researchers cited above and organizations including the International Centre for Trade and Sustainable Development (ICTSD), for example, have tended to emphasize how policy choices elsewhere undermine cotton in Africa. The ICTSD has produced a voluminous literature on the ways that trade barriers and cotton subsidy systems in the United States (the world's biggest exporter) and Europe impede Africa's competitiveness and work against poverty reduction. As the primary destination of Africa's cotton exports has shifted from Europe to China, the world's biggest cotton producer and also its biggest importer, the ICTSD has also raised questions about China's subsidies and challenged its import regime. Additionally, it has encouraged China to grant African cotton preferential duty-free, quota-free access to the Chinese market.

Other organizations, such as the United Nations Conference on Trade and Development (UNCTAD), frame the trade challenge differently. The imperative as viewed by UNCTAD is to break Africa's 'dependence' on trading this commodity in raw form (Gibbon and Ponte 2005). To best tackle trade-related threats to the 'sustainability' of African cotton such as price volatility, and the reality that Africa produces less than 1 per cent of cotton yarn globally, UNCTAD prescribes more value addition or processing. Turning to financial journalists, beyond the attention writers have paid to the C4's initiative at the WTO, those working on cotton have also highlighted a range of trade-related impediments to African success. Some have investigated reports of Asian buyers reneging on their contracts as the cotton price jumped to a nominal record of US$2.20 a pound in March 2010 and subsequently collapsed to $0.90 later that year. Likewise, journalists covered allegations made by a former cotton trader that the world's biggest private cotton-trading house, Allenberg Cotton, a subsidiary of Louis Dreyfus commodities, exacerbated and profited from extreme price volatility in 2010 through manipulating the market. Journalists, including Gregory Meyer, also drew attention to the risk of excessive African reliance on Chinese demand before China moved to pull back from its aggressive stocking policy in 2014.

Many contributors to these literatures have assuredly paid attention to the need for reforms beyond commerce. Trade watchers have articulated prescriptions for better governance of the sector, and for new service provision and capacity-building systems that would aim to enhance productivity and improve cotton quality (Baffes 2004). Even organizations such as the International Trade Centre in Geneva have produced a considerable volume of literature on the need for attention to other dimensions of the cotton problem, such as gender (ITC 2011). Nonetheless, hardcore free traders consider these innovations and the disbursement of cotton-specific aid to support their realization to be complementary or secondary to the need to eliminate trade barriers and distortionary subsidies (Imboden 2004). This viewpoint on the linkage between the cotton trade and poverty reduction implicitly endorses an income-centric definition of poverty. This problematic assumption can be characterized as the original sin of trade-centric approaches to 'fixing' African cotton. Simply put, it is rooted in an overly economistic understanding of the factors that impoverish cotton farmers. The reality is that many farmers – mostly women – would not reap financial gains from a trade reform 'trickle down', and that there are many other forces beyond those that keep incomes low that disempower farmers and entrench poverty.

Poverty is a condition entailing a multidimensional process of deprivation that can have differential impacts even on members of the same family. The context-specific lived experience of poverty often entails a unique combination of low income, a failure to meet basic needs, the denial of capabilities necessary to lead a qualitatively better life, a lack of happiness and subjection to the disproportionate power of others in ways that undermine life chances and choices (Sneyd 2011). Ideas, institutions and power dynamics within and beyond the African homes, communities and countries where cotton is grown contribute to shaping the depth and breadth of poverty where and when it is experienced. These factors or forces of immiseration establish the ideological and structural contexts within which individual farmers lead their lives and engage with cotton. The notion that the redress of one particular force or factor in this milieu could mechanically produce across the board 'poverty reduction' is nonsensical at best, and at worst, downright dangerous. A heuristic on this point could be instructive.

Take, for example, the 'Big Man' problems that afflicted cotton buying and marketing in Bénin and Cameroon in the aftermath of 'privatization' efforts. In both countries, high-level personalities in cotton were accused of 'détournement' – misappropriation or embezzlement – of funds (*Liberation*, 16 September 2013; *Jeune Afrique*, 16–22 June 2013). And in both countries questions were subsequently raised about the political motivations behind these allegations. As with the subsidy issue, it might be tempting to apply silver bullet 'poverty reduction' logic to these cases. It is probable that compelling evidence to support the notion that the removal of bad governance would reduce poverty could be conjured. Perhaps these 'facts' could be produced as readily as they have been by those who have supported the proposition that subsidy removal necessarily fights poverty. However, in the real world, the poverty fallout from the removal of an allegedly corrupt cotton baron would be as complex and mixed as the after-effects of subsidy elimination. If world prices rose slightly as cotton supplies shrank in response to policy change in the US, for example, there are simply no guarantees that cotton company Big Men or their supplicants would not 'chop' or otherwise disappear most of the ensuing windfall. Similarly, after the arrest of corrupt cotton entrepreneurs and the introduction of 'good' governance, the profit implications for their networks of rural clients specializing in input provision or buying could be varied. On the farm, credit availability could dry up or be enhanced, and timely and well-regulated buying could be expedited or could break down. The 'trickle down' from ostensibly 'better' governance or policy in either instance would be far from universally pro-poor. Those on the margins with the most to lose or gain from a particular policy or governance change would disproportionately bear its risks and potential costs.

In sum, the poverty of poverty reduction efforts for African cotton in the age of neoliberalism has been propped up by the invocation of quick and easy 'fixes' or prescriptions. These alleged solutions have conveniently left unchallenged the ideological context, institutional architecture and distribution of power in the world commodity order (Sneyd 2014). Prominently professed 'remedies' have tended to be reflections of a more market-oriented world where international, regional and nongovernmental organizations facilitate multi-stakeholder coordination to advance the development of markets. Coupled with corporate self-regulation and academic studies that are reflective of and conducive to the maintenance of the status quo, the interactions of these organizations at multiple levels form the core of the space where neoliberal poverty reduction continues to be produced. As will be developed

The poverty of 'poverty reduction' **101**

below, many of the proposals that emanate from institutions in this core do not radiate a multidimensional understanding of poverty. This reality has serious implications for the actual poverty-reducing effectiveness of neoliberal poverty reduction. While the circumscribed initiatives that spring from this governance network or 'assemblage' might technically deliver on their intentions, they offer false hope vis-à-vis the durable realization of substantive poverty reduction.

Neoliberal poverty reduction at the WTO

As the world cotton price bottomed out in 2001, efforts commenced to originate and distribute the idea that poverty could be reduced through freer trade. At that time, cotton producer organizations in West Africa were as vocal as they could be about the lower world price and their fears that this reality had exerted downwards pressure on the prices they were offered by cotton companies at the farm gate. As these voices filtered into the internet-enabled research networks of civil society organizations working on African poverty challenges, the notion that the price decline had fuelled increasing poverty rates in West Africa was quickly popularized. The available evidence suggested that cotton was generally more profitable than alternative crops, and that the drivers of price decline were undermining employment generation and government revenues in cotton specialists, including Bénin, Burkina Faso and Mali (Heinisch 2006; WTO 2003).

Two nongovernmental organizations emerged as thought leaders on this issue as the price problem persisted. The first institution, Oxfam International, took up this issue only after a protracted internal debate. Opponents of the launch of an international awareness-raising campaign on the impact of illiberal trade on poor people had questioned whether or not work on this topic would square with Oxfam's mandate to defend the impoverished. They worried that the campaign's orientation could be construed as a move by Oxfam to endorse a link between more liberal trade and poverty reduction, but were overruled. A second institution, the Ideas Centre, did not think twice about embracing the cotton file. The explicit mandate of this Geneva-based think tank is to provide technical assistance and capacity-building support to developing country members of the WTO in order to *enhance the legitimacy of the world trading system*. While cotton producers – the 'principals' – originated the idea of the cotton price problem, these two institutions became the 'agents' that ultimately packaged, presented and distributed the issue for officials and the global public. In so doing their efforts detracted attention from other poverty challenges that the West African producers themselves had articulated, including deficiencies in training and input provision systems, and the persistence of food insecurity. Moreover, the Ideas Centre contributed to shaping and framing the narrow neoliberal strategy taken by cotton-dependent West African governments to advance their interests on this file at the WTO.

The different approaches of the two main civil society actors on cotton produced distinct impacts. Oxfam's Make Trade Fair campaign mainly raised public awareness in cotton-consuming countries. It drew media attention to the over-production and dumping of agricultural commodities produced by rich countries with lavish subsidy systems onto world markets, and to the implications of this practice for the prices poor people were paid. On cotton, Oxfam did this in spite of a gross and unfortunate oversight. The actress selected to be the 'face' for the campaign, Minnie Driver, was prominently featured in glossy print and TV adverts. In these, Driver was made up to look like she was swimming in a sea of cotton *yarn* rather than drowning in a moat of cotton *lint* (the genuine commodity being 'dumped'). Despite this shortcoming, Oxfam's awareness-raising campaign effectively targeted 'citizen-consumers' and implored them to support trade reform. The external evaluators of this campaign nonetheless noted that its policy implications or impact fell short of its initial ambition to influence trade policy insiders.

The Ideas Centre's much more targeted capacity-building drive to sensitize high-level decision-makers did not aim to generate a more informed public. Rather, the Centre intended to exercise control over official discourses on the cotton problem. It consistently and forcefully advocated the position that cotton-dependent states should pursue trade liberalization and compensation within the ongoing Doha Round of trade negotiations. In so doing, Ideas made use of resources disbursed by European governments. This official backing enabled its leadership to engage in an extended effort to convince four African nations to 'delink' their quest to reform the US subsidy system from the means employed by Brazil to pursue the same end. Brazil had previously launched a trade dispute over the aspects of the US cotton subsidy system that it believed fell most afoul of the WTO statute book. Heeding the advice of Ideas, on 10 June 2003, Blaise Compaoré, the President of Burkina Faso, introduced the C4's cotton initiative as a negotiating issue in the Doha Round. The group's advisors at the Ideas Centre had sold this strategy as a lower cost alternative to joining the potentially drawn-out and expensive Brazilian action as third parties to the dispute (Zunckel 2005). The C4 optimistically assumed that this approach would yield an early harvest of trade reform within the broader agricultural negotiations.

Since its initial launch at Geneva, little progress has been made on *Poverty Reduction: Sectoral Initiative in Favour of Cotton*. As the Doha Round broke down into a protracted dispute over the broader agricultural trade liberalization negotiations, the C4's efforts to exhort wealthy nations to move beyond talking the talk of free trade through actually walking the walk on cotton stalled out. No progress on liberalization or compensation was made whatsoever after a decision of the WTO General Council officially brought cotton into the Doha negotiating agenda on 1 August 2004. This decade-long state of suspended animation occurred in the face of the 2005 declaration of the WTO Ministerial Meeting held at Hong Kong. The Hong Kong Declaration mandated the 'ambitious, expeditious and specific' treatment of cotton in the agriculture negotiations. By 21 June 2013, the C4 expressed 'regret' over the lack of progress on the strategy they had been convinced to pursue (WTO 2013).

This genuine failure stands in stark contrast to the prize that Brazil captured through initiating a trade dispute. Several years after the launch of the action, the

WTO dispute settlement and appellate bodies both ruled that numerous components of US cotton policy contravened WTO rules. Between 2000 and 2010, this system offered US farmers direct payments, export credit guarantees, marketing loan assistance, loan deficiency payments and counter-cyclical payments (ICTSD 2013; Ridley and Devadoss 2012; Baffes 2011). More recent iterations of this scheme have also included subsidized disaster insurance and generous handouts for farmers that could demonstrate their compliance with wetland conservation requirements. According to Ridley and Devadoss, the value of the subsidies extended to US cotton farmers each year over the past decade averaged about 80 per cent (US$3.5 billion) of the total annual average production (market) value (US$4.3 billion) of US cotton output.

The 'real' achievement of the Brazilian action has not been the elimination of offensive subsidies in the world's biggest exporter – many of which have continued in new forms – but the realization of compensation. After Brazil became entitled to enforce US$830 million in retaliatory trade measures in 2010, to ward off their imposition, the US inked a memorandum of understanding with Latin America's biggest cotton exporter. Since that time, amongst other concessions, Brazil has received over US$147.3 million per year in compensatory funds. The disbursement of these hundreds of millions has contributed to funding the development of capital-intensive, high-tech cotton production in Brazil. The grim implications of this deal for Africa are clear enough. The US has directly funded the development of Brazil's capacity to export cotton. In sum, the Brazilian action was successful, but its temporary resolution has generated a perverse outcome: the cross-border subsidization of new export market competition for the C4.

The 2013 WTO Ministerial held at Bali failed to produce any legally binding forward movement on the C4's agenda (Wilkinson *et al.* 2014). Its members were reportedly 'unhappy' that the cotton file had been left largely off the table (*This is Africa*, 22 November 2013). Even so, their delegates vented no rage at the reality that power had been exercised by state and non-state actors to inform, work against and limit the poverty scope of their cotton strategy. One root of this seeming incomprehension could stem from the C4's perpetual status as a WTO 'rule-taker'. As Matthew Eagleton-Pierce has argued, to expedite the initiative or, more cynically, to foster the impression of progress, European and US delegates to the WTO worked to divide the C4's quest for liberalization *and* compensation into 'trade' and 'development'-related discussions (Eagleton-Pierce 2012). Once the C4 acquiesced to this division and issue-specific discussions on liberalization and compensation officially commenced after the 2004 decision of the General Council, a façade of anti-poverty progress was generated on the 'development' aspect.

Discussions on the 'development' aspect were coordinated under the grandly titled 'WTO Director General's consultative framework mechanism on cotton'. This forum for engagement produced a consistent stream of information on the state of the provision of development assistance that could be linked to cotton disbursed by Africa's development 'partners'. However, the approach that the WTO secretariat took to measuring aid for cotton was dubious at best. It employed a very loose approach to identifying cotton-linked assistance. This 'methodology' enabled the collection and re-presentation of data on aid for agriculture more generally to appear side-by-side with cotton-specific aid. As a consequence, the secretariat has consistently produced data that paint an artificially inflated picture of the value of aid targeted directly at the cotton sub-sector. Materials featuring these numbers on the WTO website have conveniently fostered the impression that more aid has flowed to African cotton. While it is probable that the actual stock and flows of aid for cotton have increased over time, questions about their veritable connections to 'poverty reduction' – the concept at the core of the initiative – have been left out of the WTO consultations on cotton and 'development'. Instead, the development aspect has degenerated into an overly economistic euro and dollar-counting exercise. The relevance of these consultations to the real poverty challenges of African cotton cannot be assumed a priori.

Taken together, efforts to reduce poverty through pleading for freer trade and relying on aid to potentially assuage the cotton problem in the interim has produced a flow of information and resources linked to African cotton that did not previously exist. This constitutes the limited anti-poverty silver lining of the cotton initiative at the WTO. That being said, the initiative has thus far failed to achieve its minimalist aims despite their congruence with neoliberal, income-centric approaches to understanding and acting on poverty. The cotton initiative has also entirely failed to generate any sustained international or global attention to how the demonstrably small gains to be had from a more liberal trading order might be distributed in ways that actually help African farmers to lead lives that they would value more. Beyond the WTO, the public has been sensitized about the troubled present of African cotton in a fashion entirely consistent with a neoliberal definition of the problem, and also with a neoliberal remedy.

Integration as cure-all: regionalism and the Pan African Cotton Road Map

The European Union's engagements on cotton in Africa commenced in the aftermath of the WTO Ministerial held at Cancún in September 2003. Negotiations at that Ministerial had broken down in part due to a lack of progress on the C4's initiative. Sensitized to the importance of this commodity, the EU issued two communications in early 2004 linked to African cotton (ICAC 2013). The first was its proposal to establish the EU-Africa cotton 'partnership' in support of the sector. This partnership aimed to inform European donors ('partners') about African priorities for future development assistance flows to cotton and to direct future donor support to the sector. The second communication detailed the All Africa, Caribbean and Pacific Group (ACP) agricultural commodities programme (AAACP). This programme aimed to stabilize and raise the incomes of ACP commodity producers, and also to improve their capacities to endure price volatility resiliently (Berti 2012). One-third of the €45 million budget of the latter programme was allocated to cotton, and was thereby directly linked to the cotton 'partnership'.

The poverty of 'poverty reduction' **105**

At the initial EU–Africa cotton forum held at Paris in July 2004 – one month before the WTO officially brought cotton into the Doha Round – the EU and its partners agreed that the cotton partnership would have two aspects: 'trade' and 'development'. This separation informed the 'action plan' of a steering and monitoring committee – the Comité d'orientation et de suivi du Partenariat UE-Afrique sur le coton (COS-Coton) – and the subsequent development of an 'Action Framework' (ACP 2004). The AAACP programme provided the funds for the operation of COS-Coton and also for the multi-stakeholder consultations necessary to develop the Action Framework.

The steering committee facilitated stakeholder agreement on this Framework in February 2010. It sought in the first instance to strengthen the capacity of Africa's cotton exporters to access and make more use of markets. The partnership endorsed interventions that were considered by its signatories to be essential to making cotton farmers more productive and *competitive*. In particular, it sought to enhance their access to *vulnerability*-reducing risk management 'tools'. It also aspired to strengthen the *institutional* environment within which farmer organizations and those of their buyers operated. Additionally, it endeavoured to open new market opportunities for Africa's exporters through the pursuit of greater *efficiency* at all levels. The primary means employed to serve each of these ends was the disbursement of AAACP funds to develop three regional strategies for cotton in what was termed a 'market-driven value chain' approach. Put another way, the bulk of AAACP funding was devoted to an effort to improve the *capacity* of regional international organizations in Africa to draft cotton action plans and strategies. Moreover, in support of the development and implementation of these strategies, the Framework sought to enhance *coordination* amongst governance and market actors at all levels.

In many ways the cotton partnership's approach to providing support for the development and approval of regional cotton strategies and implementation plans was retrograde. For example, the technical assistance component of the partnership was massive. Rather than relying on existing African capacity at the Council for the Development of Social Science Research in Africa (CODESRIA) or at similar organizations based in Africa to develop these strategies, the Geneva-based International Trade Centre (ITC) took the lead. Updated strategies for West (UEMOA), Central (CEEAC) and Eastern and Southern (COMESA) Africa were 'formulated' and 'validated' at regional workshops held between 2009 and 2011 (Berti 2011, 2012; CEEAC 2011; UEMOA 2011). Even so, each of the final or revised strategy documents prominently featured the ITC logo, and each formulaically included several overarching components related to implementation, objectives and actions. The uniformity of this top-down boilerplate approach was reminiscent of an earlier era of development cooperation and can be readily identified when the strategies are read side-by-side. The similarities between the language used in each strategy on the need to strengthen 'capacities for the access' and use of markets was particularly striking. Marginal differences were nonetheless evident between the levels of emphasis particular strategies placed on issues such as 'seeds' or 'quality'. The strategies also differed in terms of the number of activities they endorsed: 96 in UEMOA, 133 in CEEAC and 219 in COMESA.

The overall integrationist thrust of the cotton strategies developed through the partnership was evident insofar as each supported the creation of regional cotton 'hubs' or poles of excellence. Through explicitly endorsing the development of regional hubs, the strategies tacitly condoned efforts to reap efficiencies through the elimination of public or private activities within each regional cotton economy that could be characterized as needless duplication or overlap (Dagnon 2011). The belief fuelling this push for economies of scale was that synergies and enhanced regional coordination would necessarily result from more rational (i.e. more consolidated or concentrated) centres of cotton production. However, the strategies did not foreground the possible implications of regional cotton 'hubs' for employment generation in the future. The lack of consideration of what might actually happen to the people connected to this crop after the new poles were established was indicative of the neoliberal orientation of the strategies.

Another aspect of the ITC's work in support of African cotton concentrated on an effort to enhance market access elsewhere. This dimension of the EU–ACP partnership executed by the ITC was cost-intensive and entailed the facilitation of an African cotton promotion workshop in China in October 2011. At that event, leaders of the African Cotton Producers Association (AProCA) and members of the African Cotton Association (ACA) of companies met with Chinese buyers of the lowest value added cotton product traded internationally. Attendees discussed market access issues ranging from quality through contracts and inspection to better comprehend the 'needs requirements' of the Chinese market (Ranchon 2011). Without a doubt this expensive undertaking enabled the development of Africa–China cotton connections. However, just two years later its limits were exposed. After China unveiled plans to release (i.e. sell) two of its reported 12.6 million tonne cotton stock on the world market, efforts to entrench Africa's greater reliance on the Chinese market were revealed to be nothing more than pro-market neoliberal utopianism (ICTSD 2014). Through its market access focus, the EU–ACP partnership strived for the expansion of a regressive, immiserizing or asymmetrical trade relationship. The partnership consequently did nothing to correct Africa's poor terms of trade for cotton. In a very neoliberal fashion, it mistakenly assumed away the power of Africa's principal export markets to set their own terms of entry.

To be even-handed, the partnership certainly did not simply support free markets. Through striving to build the capacity of AProCA and the ACA, the partnership's steering group brought together and strengthened the leaders of these associations. The irony here was that these leaders could in no way be characterized as being supportive of thoroughgoing market liberalization. Cameroon's Mohammed Iya, for example, attended numerous partnership meetings in his capacity as President of the ACA prior to his arrest for alleged détournement. Sodecoton, the monopsony Iya managed, controlled a market that was the antithesis of competitiveness and efficiency. AProCA's Francois Traoré, for his part, fully supports the

The poverty of 'poverty reduction' **107**

greater uptake of genetically modified cotton containing *bacillus thuringiensis*, a bacteria that is toxic to insects. Traoré's perspective on Bt cotton is conducive to Monsanto, the oligopolistic transnational agribusinesses that holds the patent, and its interest in exercising more power over the seeds used by African farmers (Clapp and Fuchs 2009; Galbraith 1952). The EU–ACP 'partnership' thereby built the capacity of individuals who were either alleged cotton market manipulators or who were willing to subject Africa's cotton future to the distorting largess of an organization seeking to increase its earnings or sales.

Furthermore, the partnership did not use neoliberal language exclusively. It led to the production of at least one strategy that emphasized the need for more value addition to take place in Africa, and that endorsed a shift towards high-value, third-party certified cottons (Dagnon 2011). These directions had been of particular concern to members of the African Cotton and Textile Industries Federation (ACTIF) in Southern and Eastern Africa. Despite the inclusion of this development language, the partnership did not directly fund the uptake of these desires. It did not enable Africans to engage with China in an effort to expedite the transfer of spinning technologies to the continent. Rather, the Chinese workshop noted above left untouched the continent's impoverishing simultaneous reliance on lint exports and on re-imports of the same raw material after its transformation into yarn by others. Similarly, the partnership did not disburse funds to initiatives linked to research indicating that certified organic cotton cultivation is associated with superior socio-economic and environmental outcomes than conventional production techniques (UNCTAD-UNEP 2008; Sneyd 2012; UNCTAD 2013; Textile Exchange 2013).

The single-minded pursuit of a neoliberal integrationist agenda also brushed aside the partnership's stated aim of facilitating greater coordination. The strategies that it supported were undertaken by a scattershot grouping of regional organizations. The strategy in the West was spearheaded by UEMOA, the economic and monetary union, and not by the Economic Community of West African States (ECOWAS). The latter has a much broader membership that includes non-UEMOA cotton producers such as Ghana, Guinea and Nigeria. Conversely, in Central Africa, the CEEAC was selected rather than the smaller six-country Communauté Économique et Monétaire de l'Afrique Centrale (CEMAC). The choice of the CEEAC, a community that includes countries beyond CEMAC, such as Burundi and the Democratic Republic of Congo, was peculiar. Both of those countries are also members of COMESA. Rather than this mélange, a much more rational approach would have been for the strategies to have been developed by the same type of regional organization. While it is true that an economic community (Central), an economic and monetary union (West) and a common market project (East and South) had previously developed cotton strategies, the partnership could have laid the groundwork for more coherent inter-regional cooperation. It could have unhooked cotton from this ad hoc organization through encouraging the transfer of cotton responsibility to institutions of a similar type.

108   A. Sneyd

In hindsight, this lack of harmonization is especially troubling given that the regional strategies are slated to fall under the proposed Pan African Cotton Road Map (PACRM). This initiative, supported by the partnership and by other organizations, including the UN Conference on Trade and Development, seeks to better define cotton at the level of the African Union. Under the Comprehensive Africa Agriculture Development Programme (CAADP) of the AU's New Economic Partnership for Economic Development (NEPAD), cotton was simply not a focus (UNCTAD 2011b; Berti 2011). After UNCTAD hosted a cotton stakeholder meeting at Geneva in December 2008, the cotton partnership's steering committee initiated plans for a Pan African Cotton Meeting in June 2011. Held at Cotonou, Bénin, participants discussed ways to maximize productivity, improve marketing and add more value on a continental scale. In other words, they focused on economies of scale, poles of excellence and transformation. The 150 stakeholders that attended this meeting put these objectives at the heart of the organizational framework of a proposed ten-year 'road map' for the sector (Gayi 2012). Through 2014, the EU–Africa Partnership on Cotton (PACRM) awaited approval by NEPAD and was generally understood to be a means to enable the development of relationships and synergies between the regional strategies for cotton.

If approved, the road map might not have the means to realize even this seriously circumscribed 'Pan African' vision. The lack of harmonization evident at the regional level and the reality that each strategy requires approval and implementation by individual countries are serious potential constraints. Similarly, the hope that the PACRM could facilitate the development of African industries downstream of ginning rests on the willingness of individual governments to take up this issue and to genuinely pursue it at the regional level. To its credit, the EU–ACP cotton partnership has brought to fruition regional strategies and a Pan African mechanism for dialogue. As such, it has stimulated the production of quite a bit of hot air on cotton and enabled more than a little ink to be spilled on this topic. These materials could be used to make African cotton work better for the people that grow it. However, questions about the effectiveness of this neoliberal aid exercise are obvious: will countries and regions follow through on these initiatives once the aid tap is turned off? If so, what aspects will be prioritized in the absence of 'partner' support? Will quick-win integrationist interventions take priority over potentially costlier efforts to nurture downstream start-ups? The unfortunate rhetorical answer is that the partnership has enabled elite stakeholders to dine out on Africa's cotton problems. This approach to technical assistance has bolstered the poverty of poverty reduction in the present, and in concrete terms, has done little to secure for Africa a cotton future free from poverty.

CSR and African cotton: market-driven social and environmental 'justice'

Over the past 13 years, individuals and organizations with direct interests in the maintenance and growth of cotton cultivation and trade have expressed concern

The poverty of 'poverty reduction' **109**

about the 'sustainability' of African cotton. Independent cotton exporters, big transnational commodity trading houses, textile manufacturers and branded retailers have not simply tried to sweep social and environmental scandals linked to this crop under the proverbial rug. Many have pursued governance initiatives that have aimed to avert a recurrence of negative civil society and media attention to the 'rag trade': a key underpinning of the anti-sweatshop movement. They are aware that ecological disasters linked to cotton – such as the failed cotton irrigation projects that disastrously diverted Aral Sea tributaries – have powered anti-cotton environmental activism in the past. Greater corporate motivation to attend to externalities has in several cases been rooted in efforts to preserve and expand the global cotton market and Africa's place in it. In this context, many big buyers and traders have pursued light-touch and low-cost approaches to CSR.

The turn towards corporate self-regulation has nonetheless been far from uniform. A range of initiatives has emerged. Within this array certain non-state governance approaches have been more attentive to the realization of verifiable on-farm quality of life changes than others. This reality is indicative of the divergent potential of different CSR systems to reduce poverty. In its more minimalist incarnation, CSR has aimed to inform stakeholders at all levels about how to improve production practices. The Better Cotton Initiative (BCI), for instance, has pursued this course of action in the hope that farmer adherence to global norms for the production of 'better' cotton can be scaled up (Sneyd 2011). Another market-driven approach that is specific to the continent – Cotton Made in Africa (CMiA) – has endorsed a system for the oversight of process and production methods that is slightly more comprehensive than the BCI's capacity-building approach (Peltzer and Kaut 2011; BMZ 2013). Cotton products bearing the CMiA label are now marketed in Germany and enjoy the ongoing support of the German federal government.

At the other end of the spectrum, several businesses have worked to convert farmers to the production of cotton bearing verifiable social and environmental qualities. These approaches entail independent oversight of adherence to rigorous internal control systems and global standards by accredited third parties, and include certified organic cotton and certified fair trade cotton (Fridell 2007; Ferrigno and Lizarraga 2009; Balineau 2013). The former relies on the development of strong producer support and training systems that give farmers the skills and resources needed to pursue innovative agro-ecological practices, and to obtain and effectively use botanical alternatives to agrochemical inputs. The latter CSR system entails the organization of producers into cooperatives that are democratic and that empower women. Fair trade projects also aim to re-invest in communities and to pay higher prices at the farm gate.

CSR approaches on this spectrum are variously in tune or at odds with the standard neoliberal notion that Africa could fetch higher world prices through the pursuit of higher yields and the production of higher quality fibre (Poulton *et al.* 2004; Kouloumégué 2012). The BCI is aligned with this viewpoint and has sought to introduce 'better' practices in the service of higher quality and yields. This system's corporate backers have consequently attempted to ensconce Africa as a growing source of supply for the global bulk market and avert potential threats to the continent's status as a lint export platform. Conversely, certified organic and fair trade operators have actively worked against conventional methods for measuring yields and quality. Analysts who have continued to insist on evaluating the 'effectiveness' of organic systems using traditional (single-crop, single-year) understandings of yield, for example, have failed to recognize this distinctiveness. Organic farmers and operators measure 'yield' across total farm systems over time. While their interventions remain market-driven, organic and fair trade systems actively subvert the notion that 'better' cotton should serve to secure demand in the first instance. Rather, they have put verifiable change at the supply (farmer) end at the heart of their systems. These systems have worked to nurture demand for new qualities of cotton within and beyond Africa. In areas where organic and fair trade efforts have been most advanced, social and ecological innovations associated with these systems have stimulated considerable spillovers and demonstration effects (Sneyd 2012).

The increasing reliance of African governments and their official 'partners' on market-driven initiatives to moderate the social and environmental impact of cotton is indicative of the pervasiveness of neoliberalism. As resource-constrained African governments have opened cotton up to greater transnational corporate control, the breadth of corporate approaches to social and environmental sustainability has grown. Non-state control over cotton has expanded to such an extent that the International Cotton Advisory Committee (ICAC) has convened an expert panel to assess the competing approaches (ICAC 2014). This panel seeks to determine global indicators or measures of sustainable cotton production. After the ICAC panel issues its final report, Africans will have a clearer picture of CSR for cotton. That being said, the risk moving forward is clear. The provision of overarching sustainability guidance from ICAC could obscure or make it more difficult to realize the anti-poverty 'wins' associated with the most rigorous market-driven systems. The threat that those with vested interests in lowest common denominator approaches might capture future efforts to harmonize CSR systems with each other or with public legal, policy and regulatory frameworks is real. Were they to do so, the poverty of poverty reduction would be sustained.

Beyond the poverty of poverty reduction

None of the challenges facing African cotton recounted above necessarily render poverty an intractable problem. Cotton and poverty might have grown up together in many African places, but their future together is not inevitable. Evidence from organic cultivation systems in Tanzania, for instance, indicates that innovative food and trap crop rotation systems have in some cases eliminated food security trade-offs and yielded new income-generating opportunities. This approach has the demonstrated capacity to reduce multiple dimensions of poverty with a lower carbon footprint (Ton 2011). Similarly, the executive director of ACTIF and other business-side voices continue to push hard for Africans to add more value to cotton

(Arora 2013). They seek to correct the reality captured by the *New York Times* in one memorable headline that 'Africa's Fabric is Dutch' (14 November 2012). Holland's Vlisco and other European and Asian firms that compete with Africa's capacity to pursue own-design and own-brand success at the industrial or artisanal scale are now firmly in the sights of Africa's cotton and textile entrepreneurs. Moreover, in 2009 the umbrella groups representing cotton producers (AProCA) and traders (ACA) signed a strategic partnership. The future engagements of these groups with ACTIF on the cotton transformation question could develop African cotton systems into engines of employment generation.

The neoliberal infusion of regional, international and global poverty responses is nonetheless troubling. It has circumscribed efforts to reform international trade. It has been built into North–South regional intergovernmental cotton cooperation. Likewise, at the global level, the non-state governance initiatives that enjoy the most transnational corporate support have at best fostered a very neoliberal privatization of governance. In this context, the intent of poverty reduction has necessarily been perverted. Powerful actors at all levels have employed 'poverty reduction' as a technical term, the application of which may or may not actually ameliorate the factors that have entrenched impoverishment.

Perhaps most worryingly, many academic analyses of Africa's domestic cotton 'problems' have paid little attention to the implications of neoliberalism at the regional, international and global levels for poverty (Poulton *et al.* 2004; Tschirley *et al.* 2010). With a few notable exceptions, most economists working on this topic have remained obsessed with detailing minor differences in the decade-old uptake of the neoliberal cotton reform packages (Delpeuch and Leblois 2013; Delpeuch and Vandeplas 2013). While space does not permit full elaboration here, these scholars have generally and problematically assumed the political and cultural contexts where cotton is grown away. In so doing they have often reinforced the conventional wisdom that cotton can work for poverty reduction. Through failing to consider the political economy premise that states and markets are never distinct or separable domains, these authors have offered insights that are of little to no value as regards the imperative of poverty eradication (Krätke and Underhill 2006; Cooksey 2011; Chang 2009; Masuka 2013; Lee 2009).

Taken together, these harsh truths have implications for African cotton in the twenty-first century 'fast fashion' world of firms such as Inditex, Hennes & Mauritz, Li & Fung and Primark. Making African cotton work better for those that grow it will require investments that raise costs. Big branded retailers and turnkey fashion suppliers can easily substitute cotton for cheap and readily available synthetics if their consumers will bear the shift. Beyond this surmountable challenge, who owns Africa's cotton suppliers and what exactly they are supplying to whom matters. Cotton value chains continue to be driven by transnational buyers (Morris and Staritz 2014). A turn inwards to pursue genuine Pan African development, coupled with greater African willingness to directly challenge the neoliberal tendencies recounted above, could build an industry that yields more opportunities for poverty reduction. While there are no guarantees that such an approach would be viable, if cotton is to have a future in Africa, for Africa, there is one certainty. The used and knock-off cheap clothing 'dumping' industry must cease to exist. It is up to Africans themselves to determine whether or not they need to heed these warnings and do away with neoliberal 'solutions' for cotton that have entrenched the poverty of poverty reduction. The writing, so to speak, is very much on the wall.

Acknowledgments

The author extends special thanks to the group of incredibly talented development researchers that was based at the North-South Institute (NSI) in Ottawa for providing early inspiration and guidance. Thanks are also due to Brian Cooksey, Ha-Joon Chang, Eric Hazard, Daniel Drache, William D. Coleman and Lauren Q. Sneyd.

References

ACP. 2004. *EU-Africa Partnership on Cotton*. Geneva: ACP Cotton.
Anderson, K. and Valenzuela, E. 2006. The WTO's Doha Cotton Initiative: A Tale of Two Issues. Policy Research Working Paper WPS 3918. Washington, DC: World Bank.
Arora, R. 2013. Changing Perceptions Toward Modern Africa. *Cotton Africa Magazine* 7.
Baden, S. 2004. 'White Gold' Turns to Dust: Which Way Forward for Cotton in West Africa?' Oxfam Briefing Paper 58. Oxford: Oxfam International.
Baffes, J. 2004. Cotton: Market Setting, Trade Policies and Issues. Policy Research Working Paper WPS 3218. Washington, DC: World Bank.
Baffes, J. 2011. Cotton Subsidies, the WTO, and the 'Cotton Problem'. *The World Economy* 34(9): 1534–56.
Balineau, G. 2013. Disentangling the Effects of Fair Trade on the Quality of Malian Cotton. *World Development* 44: 241–55.
Berti, F. 2011. Des Stratégies Régionales Pour le Coton Africain: Opportunités et Risques. Presentation pour Geocoton Séminaire *Les Atouts du Coton Africain dans une Perspective du Développement Durable*.
Berti, F. 2012. *Synthesis Report on Cotton-Related Activities*. Belgium: All AAACP Coordination Unit.
BMZ. 2013. *Competitive African Cotton Initiative*. Bonn: BMZ.
CEEAC. 2011. *Stratégie de Developpement de la Filière Coton-Textile-Confection en Afrique Centrale*. Genève: ITC.
Chang, H-J. 2009. Rethinking Public Policy in Agriculture: Lessons from History, Distant and Recent. *The Journal of Peasant Studies* 36(3): 477–515.
Clapp, J. and Fuchs, D. (eds). 2009. *Corporate Power in Global Agrifood Governance*. Cambridge, MA: The MIT Press.
Cooksey, B. 2011. Marketing Reform? The Rise and Fall of Agricultural Liberalisation in Tanzania. *Development Policy Review* 29: S57–S81.
Dagnon, G.B. 2011. *Analyse comparée des strategies regionals coton en Afrique Subsaharienne en vue de leur alignement sur les politiques agricoles nationales, regionals et panafricaines*. Cergy, France: CNUCED et Rencontre panafricaine sur le coton.
Delpeuch, C. and Leblois, A. 2013. Sub-Saharan Cotton Policies in Retrospect. *Development Policy Review* 31(5): 617–42.
Delpeuch, C. and Vandeplas, A. 2013. Revisiting the 'Cotton Problem' – A Comparative Analysis of Cotton Reforms in Sub-Saharan Africa. *World Development* 42: 209–21.

The poverty of 'poverty reduction' **113**

Eagleton-Pierce, M. 2012. The Competing Kings of Cotton: (Re)framing the WTO African Cotton Initiative. *New Political Economy* 17(3): 313–37.

Ferrigno, S. and Lizarraga, A. 2009. Components of a Sustainable Cotton Production System: Perspectives From the Organic Cotton Experience. *ICAC Recorder:* 13–23.

Fridell, G. 2007. *Fair Trade Coffee: The Prospects and Pitfalls of Market-Driven Social Justice.* Toronto: University of Toronto Press.

Galbraith, J. K. 1952. *American Capitalism: The Concept of Countervailing Power.* Boston: Houghton Mifflin.

Gayi, S. 2012. ACTIF Partnership in Developing the Pan African Cotton Road Map: Long Road to Travel. *ACTIF Magazine Online Edition*, 29 October.

Gibbon, P. 1999. Free Competition without Sustainable Development? Tanzanian Cotton Sector Liberalization, 1994/95 to 1997/98. *Journal of Development Studies* 36(1): 128–50.

Gibbon, P. and Ponte, S. 2005. *Trading Down: Africa, Value Chains and the Global Economy.* Philadelphia: Temple University Press.

Hazard, E. (ed.). 2005. *Le Livre Blanc sur le Coton: Négociations Commerciales Internationales et Réduction de la Pauvreté*, 2nd edition. Dakar: ENDA Tiers Monde.

Heinisch, E. L. 2006. West Africa Versus the United States on Cotton Subsidies: How, Why and What Next? *Journal of Modern African Studies* 44(2): 251–74.

ICAC. 2013. *Cotton Sector Reform in CFA Zones.* Washington, DC: ICAC Standing Committee.

ICAC. 2014. *Measuring Sustainability in Cotton Farming Systems: Towards a Guidance Framework.* Washington, DC: ICAC Expert Panel on the Social, Environmental, and Economic Performance of Cotton.

ICTSD. 2013. *Cotton: Trends in Global Production, Trade and Policy.* Geneva: ICTSD.

ICTSD. 2014. Cotton Trade: China Shift on Stockpiling Policy Sparks Questions. *Bridges Weekly Trade News Digest* 18(2).

Imboden, N. 2004. *Société Civile et OMC: Rôle et Place des Entités Extra-Gouvernementales dans la Définition des Politiques Commerciales et la Formulation des Positions de Négociations Africaines.* Geneva: ICTSD.

Isaacman, A. F. and Roberts, R (eds). 1995. *Cotton, Colonialism and Social History in Sub-Saharan Africa.* Portsmouth: Heinemann.

ITC. 2011. *Women in Cotton: Results of a Global Survey.* Geneva: ITC.

Jerven, M. 2013. *Poor Numbers: How We Are Misled by African Development Statistics and What to Do About It.* Ithaca: Cornell University Press.

Kouloumégué, D. 2012. *A Potential Alternative to Cotton Production in Africa in the Scope of Sustainable Development? The Case of Organic and Fair Trade Cotton Production in Mali.* PhD Thesis. Belgium: University of Liege.

Krätke, M. R. and Underhill, G. R. D. 2006. Political Economy: The Revival of an 'Interdiscipline'. In Stubbs, R. and Underhill, G. R. D. (eds) *Political Economy and the Changing Global Order.* Oxford: Oxford University Press.

Lee, D. 2009. Bringing an Elephant into the Room: Small African State Diplomacy in the WTO. In Cooper, A. F. and Shaw, T. W. (eds). *The Diplomacies of Small States: Between Vulnerability and Resistance.* Basingstoke: Palgrave Macmillan.

Masuka, G. 2013. Agricultural Liberalization, Cotton Markets and Buyers' Relations in Zimbabwe, 2001–2008. *Singapore Journal of Tropical Geography* 34: 103–19.

Morris, M. and Staritz, C. 2014. Industrialization Trajectories and Madagascar's Export Apparel Industry: Ownership, Embeddedness, Markets, and Upgrading. *World Development* 56: 243–57.

Peltzer, R. and Kaut, C. 2011. Les atouts du Coton Africain dans une perspective de Développement Durable. Séminaire pour Geocoton. Hamburg: Aid by Trade Foundation, 10–14 October.

Poulton, C., Gibbon, P., Hanyani-Mlambo, E., Kydd, J., Maro, W., Nylandsted Larsen, M., Tschirley, D. and Zulu, B. 2004. Competition and Coordination in Liberalized African Cotton Market Systems. *World Development* 32(3): 519–36.

Ranchon, A. 2011. *China-Africa Cooperation: Understanding the Chinese Market and Promoting African Cotton*. Geneva: ITC.

Ridley, W. and Devadoss, S. 2012. Analysis of the Brazil–USA Cotton Dispute. *Journal of International Trade Law and Policy* 11(2): 148–62.

Roitman, J. 2005. *Fiscal Disobedience: An Anthropology of Economic Regulation in Central Africa*. Princeton: Princeton University Press.

Schnurr, M. 2013. Cotton as Calamitous Commodity: The Politics of Agricultural Failure in Natal and Zululand, 1844–1933. *Canadian Journal of African Studies* 47(1): 115–32.

Sneyd, A. 2011. *Governing Cotton: Globalization and Poverty in Africa*. Basingstoke: Palgrave Macmillan.

Sneyd, A. 2012. Governing African Cotton and Timber Through CSR: Competition, Legitimacy and Power. *Canadian Journal of Development Studies* 33(2): 143–63.

Sneyd, A. 2014. When Governance Gets Going: Certifying 'Better Cotton' and 'Better Sugar'. *Development and Change* 45(2): 231–56.

Stanfield, J. R. and Stanfield, J. B. 2011. *John Kenneth Galbraith*. Basingstoke: Palgrave Macmillan.

Textile Exchange. 2013. *Farm & Fiber Report 2011–12*. O'Donnell, TX: Textile Exchange.

Ton, P. 2011. *Cotton and Climate Change: Impacts and Options to Mitigate and Adapt*. Geneva: ITC.

Tschirley, D. L., Poulton, C., Gergely, N., Labaste, P., Baffes, J., Boughton, D. and Estur, G. 2010. Institutional Diversity and Performance in African Cotton Sectors. *Development Policy Review* 28(3): 295–323.

UEMOA. *Stratégie Révisée de Mise en oeuvre de l'Agenda pour la Compétitivité de la Filière Coton-Textiles dans l'UEMOA 2011–2020*. Genève: Le Centre du Commerce International (ITC).

UNCTAD. 2011a. *Commodities at a Glance: Special Issue on Cotton in Africa*. Geneva: United Nations.

UNCTAD. 2011b. *Report of the Pan African Cotton Meeting 2011*. Geneva: United Nations.

UNCTAD. 2013. *Trade and Environment Review 2013: Wake Up Before It is Too Late*. Geneva: UNCTAD.

UNCTAD-UNEP. 2008. *Organic Agriculture and Food Security in Africa*. New York and Geneva: UNCTAD and UNEP.

Watkins, K. with Sul, J-u. 2002. Cultivating Poverty: The Impact of US Cotton Subsidies on Africa. Oxfam Briefing Paper 30. Oxford: Oxfam International.

Wilkinson, R., Hannah, E. and Scott, J. 2014. The WTO in Bali: What MC9 means for the Doha Development Agenda and Why It Matters. *Third World Quarterly* 35(6): 1032–50.

WTO. 2003. *Poverty Reduction: Sectoral Initiative in Favour of Cotton. Joint Proposal by Benin, Burkina Faso, Chad and Mali*, TN/AG/GEN/4. Geneva: World Trade Organization.

WTO. 2013. African Cotton Producers Regret No Progress in Talks, Welcome Improved Aid With More Focus. *WTO News*, Geneva, 21.

Zunckel, H. E. 2005. The African Awakening in the United States – Upland Cotton. *Journal of World Trade* 39(6): 1071–109.

7

WATER, WATER EVERYWHERE BUT NOT A DROP TO DRINK (EXCEPT FOR A PRICE)

Larry A. Swatuk

Introduction

> [T]hose seeking to understand contemporary African politics, in the widest sense, will need new habits of thinking if we are to grasp their true originality and importance.
>
> *(Ferguson 2006, 24)*

The focus of this chapter is on service delivery in sub-Saharan Africa (SSA); not a very 'sexy' topic, it must be said, but one that matters deeply to the more than 700 million people who populate the region. In particular, I focus on water and sanitation services, with data drawn from publicly available sources such as the IMF, United Nations, FAO, World Bank and various SSA organizations and national governments. There is emphasis on nine countries – three from each of West, East and southern African regions – but in an indicative rather than structured, comparative way. I have lived in and/or worked in all nine of these countries, and so bring both anecdotal and empirical evidence to bear in my observations. On occasion, I offer continent-wide data and observations, as well as inter-regional comparison across the Global South. The primary question for investigation centres on the consequences of three and a half decades of structural adjustment conditionalities in the continent: given the neoliberal emphasis on (i) a facilitative rather than determining state form; (ii) privatization of government services; and (iii) self-regulation across private sector systems of delivery, is SSA better off today because of such policies, programmes and approaches? A cursory review of the several tables and graphs presented below would suggest an answer such as 'it depends'. In regard to both potable water supply and sanitation, the data suggest clear improvement. At the same time, the marginal and limited movement away from very low starting points suggests that 'success' is a word one should use with caution in describing service delivery outcomes across the study area. Moreover, it is not clear what has been the role of neoliberalism in these outcomes: would they have been worse without neoliberal policies and programmes, or better? Has neoliberalism been a brake on social progress, or an accelerator held back by persistent problems inherent to African state forms? I will offer my own view on this as we move through the analysis. In line with the epigram from James Ferguson, the argument presented here is that orthodox and predominantly Western markers of 'success' or 'failure' obscure as much as enlighten, thereby creating as many problems as solutions; and so the wheel goes round.

The chapter proceeds as follows: the next section describes 'neoliberalism' in some detail. This is then followed by a discussion of African political economy, particularly in the nine countries under discussion: in West Africa they are Ghana, Senegal and Nigeria; in East Africa they are Ethiopia, Kenya and Tanzania; and in southern Africa, they are Malawi, South Africa and Zambia. The argument made here is that the particularities of African political economies frame the context within which approaches to service delivery take place, marking out the parameters of their possibilities for 'success' or 'failure'. The subsequent section examines the data pertaining to water and sanitation, providing some discussion regarding the role of neoliberalism therein. I place emphasis on two aspects of water: water for agriculture and water for cities. The final section summarizes the argument and reflects on the likelihood of moving 'beyond neoliberalism' in Africa's search for socially equitable, environmentally sustainable and economically viable development.

Neoliberalism and sub-Saharan Africa

As a long-time student of African and global political economy, it was with some amusement, much alarm but no surprise that I watched the world's power brokers force structural adjustment conditionalities upon Greece during the post-2008 fallout from the global financial crisis. It was interesting to see Greece's policymakers take a determined stand against the purveyors of neoliberal shock therapy, hold out for as long as they did, but ultimately succumb – as have all of the world's 'weak states' – and accept the terms and conditions set for them. What was most amusing for me, and for almost everyone I know involved in the teaching and research of 'international development', was how obviously flawed both the diagnosis (a profligate state) and the prescription (classic neoliberal structural adjustment) were. Just as scholars of the intellectual left asked in whose interests were SAPS – the international financiers or citizens of Mexico, Brazil, sub-Saharan Africa – so too were many wondering whose interests were served in the 'bail-out' of Greece. It was the early 1980s all over again.

In relation to Africa, Walter Rodney (1974), among many others, long ago exposed the lie of liberal development strategies. In Jean-François Bayart's (2000) terms, African political economies suffer from extroversion: they have been turned inside-out over centuries of colonial and imperial interests and their post-independence neo-colonial and neo-imperial variants (Bond 2006). Picture a bucket full of water. Now picture that bucket pricked with holes all around its base. This is Africa, the water is the outward flow of its resources and the holes are the coastal port cities that facilitate this leakage. The post-World War II, post-colonial, primarily-Western engagement with Africa preserved this condition. It rewarded the willing and punished those, like Patrice Lumumba, who resisted. It masked its actions in the cloak of the extension and preservation of freedom and democracy and of the elimination of the scourge of communism. This is a common enough story; it does not need to be rehearsed here. However, there are two important points to be made: first, rather than transform African states from *un*developed to developed, three-plus decades (1945–80) of Cold-War-driven engagement reinforced their *under*developed character, the most important aspect of which is perhaps the gulf that exists between a predatory and extroverted state populated by (comprador) elites and a marginalized civil society whose members more resemble 'subjects' than 'citizens', to use Mamdani's terms; second, the subsequent three-plus decades (1980–present) of neoliberal structural adjustment (initially economic and, following the end of the Cold War, also political) conditionalities exacerbated existing pathologies and incubated new ones (e.g. 'shadow states'; 'new wars'; blood diamonds, etc.) of the underdeveloped state form (for the general point, see Ferguson 2006, 11; on specific instances and cases, see Clapham 1996; Bayart *et al.* 1999; Ellis 1999; and Reno 1998). Whereas the Asian tigers built developmental states on the back of post-war American socio-economic, political and military support, no such constellation of social forces emerged in any African state to mimic this process. The nearest to this model was apartheid-oriented South Africa and its race-based neighbour Rhodesia. However, these two state forms spent a disproportionate amount of their wealth on disarticulating their political economies: on building walls between, not bridges across races; on waging regional warfare, not constructing regional economies. It was an expensive undertaking that resulted in a great deal of 'unfinished business' in South Africa and Zimbabwe today.

When the late-1970s' global economic crisis emerged, Africa's economies were doubly disabled: first from a downturn in demand for their commodities; second in their inability to pay for their production inputs, especially oil. SAPs emerged on the back of Reagan's and Thatcher's infatuation with Hayekian 'small state' economics. But slashing state spending, and facilitating freedom for capital and private enterprise was one thing in First World economies – which were badly shaken but not collapsed – and quite another across the Global South. In 1984, while in Lesotho, my colleague at the National Bank informed me that the micro-state, an enclave of South Africa, had only enough foreign exchange in hand to fuel the national airline's Boeing 747 once, and nothing more. He told me this because there were rumours that 'the President will be travelling' and that, if this were to be the case, South African fuel suppliers required payment in forex and up front. At the same time, a colleague in Tanzania lamented that the Central Bank had but two days' worth of forex: how was the state to meet its obligations? The answer, of course, was that it wouldn't, and so the debt crisis began and, in many places across SSA, it has yet to end.

John Clarke (2008) warns us against 'loose claims' regarding neoliberalism. If it is everything, then it is nothing; if it is everywhere, then it is nowhere, to paraphrase a German proverb. Better, he suggests, to understand 'neoliberalism' as a process, as 'the neoliberalization of things' (Clarke 2008, 139), as much as it is also an ideological position:

> Whether we treat neo-liberalism from the standpoint of capitalist regimes of accumulation, or as a version of liberal governmentality, most of its political work involves practices of de- and re-articulation: reorganizing principles, policies, practices, and discourses into new configurations, assemblages, or constellations.

Clarke argues the utility of this perspective because it then encourages us to see beyond the omnipresence of neoliberalism, and draw into focus the myriad ways in which key aspects of neoliberalism are taken on wholesale, or piecemeal, rearticulated in the context of local social processes, so that what ultimately emerges is, to draw on Peck (2004), a sort of hybridity. This is an important but not especially new idea. In the early days of SAP, there was a good deal of writing that highlighted the ways in which local actors played off the purveyors of these global norms and governance systems against each other, while continuing 'business as usual' within their own state forms (see any of the six books I discuss in detail in Swatuk 1995).

Aside from regarding it as a process, how might we define neoliberalism then? Clarke draws on both Harvey (2005) and Ong (2006), and I see no reason to deviate from this approach. Harvey (2005) sees neoliberalism as 'the political/ ideological project of a class seeking to change the balance of power in global capitalism and create new means of capital accumulation' (in Clarke 2008, 136). In this way, Clarke argues, neoliberalism appears omnipresent. However, omnipresence does not equal omnipotence: neoliberalism plays out differently and quite unevenly across the globe. Here he quotes Ong (2006, 13): 'It therefore seems appropriate to study neoliberalism not as a "culture" or a "structure" but as mobile calculative techniques of governing that can be decontextualized from their original sources and recontextualized in constellations of mutually constitutive and contingent relations.' Hence, if we look close enough we will see perhaps a shared core philosophy – small state, privatization, deregulation, liberalization – that plays out in policy and practice quite differently depending on the particular constellation of social forces within any given state form. So, 'privatization' of water services in South Africa, Ghana and Senegal are actually quite different, though bound to the same philosophical core.

Context matters: a political economy of African state forms

Water is everywhere and in everything. As Savenije (2002) ably explains, it is not an ordinary economic good. In some ways admitting of commoditization, water is also a public good, access to which (along with sanitation) was declared a human right by the UN General Assembly in 2010. To understand the impact of neoliberalism on water access, use and management in SSA, it is necessary to understand the socio-economic and socio-political context within which it is found.

Prior to the recent collapse of oil prices, there was a positively frenzied narrative about 'Africa rising'. Little of this narrative was tied to any deep analysis of the character of the political economy of African state forms. So, as oil prices collapsed along with Chinese demand for Africa's raw materials, the 'rising' narrative has once again given way to 'falling', 'failing' and 'collapsing'. From a critical political economy perspective, an astute observer would at best raise his or her eyebrows at all of this ahistorical analysis.

Success in the globalized neoliberal world order is most often defined through statistics, particularly those compiled by organizations such as the World Bank, the IMF and various United Nations agencies, especially but not only the UNDP: GDP per capita; life expectancy at birth; and so on. Consider these a sort of 'league table' where those at the top of the table – the OECD countries – have, in almost every instance, been there since these data were first invented and compiled. It has been an amazing run; and rare is the ability of an outsider to move into the top rank. The so-called Asian tigers have managed it, as has China. No African state even comes close, though Egypt, Ethiopia and South Africa were founding members of the United Nations back in 1945.

The evidence is incontrovertible: both early (UK, France, Germany, USA) and late (Japan, Asian NICs, China) developers did so on the back of a capable, active and often globally or regionally aggressive state (Harris 1986; Deyo 1987; Leftwich 1995; Stubbs 2009). Usually there were other favourable factors involved, such as the United States bankrolling entire defence budgets while setting up preferential trade agreements with strategic partners such as Japan, Taiwan and South Korea. It is not called *political* economy for nothing. Across parts of sub-Saharan Africa and Latin America, particular socio-political factors created the possibility for dramatic economic structural change (Gereffi and Evans 1981; Marais 1998), resulting in, at best, 'dependent development', meaning economic diversification with an often continuing reliance on commodity exports for foreign exchange generation in order to fund the cost of imports for manufacturing. As stated above, however, the ability to get 'out from underdevelopment', to use Jim Mittelman's term (Mittelman and Pasha 1997), was limited to a very few special cases.

As shown in Figure 7.1, sub-Saharan Africa remains comprised, by and large, of basic commodity exporting economies, far more so than any other world region. Granted, the value of services as a proportion of GDP is significant (see Table 7.1). Nowhere is this more so than in South Africa, where agriculture contributes a minor 2.5 per cent to GDP (employing only 4 per cent of the formal labour force), industry (including mining, construction and manufacturing) accounts for about 29 per cent of GDP and services a whopping 68 per cent. But in most cases this masks the fact that raw materials and/or minimally beneficiated exports are the backbone of African political economies (see Figure 7.1) and smallholder agriculture the main employer of

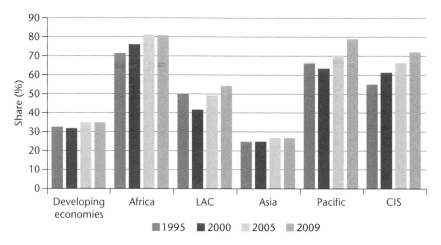

FIGURE 7.1 Share of commodities in total exports

Source: United Nations Development Programme (UNDP) (2011).

labour, especially that which is not captured in GDP statistics, since it is unmeasured and primarily subsistence oriented (Table 7.2). Sure, there is a great deal of internally driven economic activity, as represented through the broad category of 'services'. But most of the inputs into the economy come from outside and must be paid for through commodity exports. When one examines the import and export profiles of select SSA states, it is clear that only South Africa has departed from the classical dependency relationship of raw materials *out* and finished goods *in* (Table 7.2).

Most SSA states are therefore greatly exposed to the vicissitudes of the world economy. As shown in Table 7.3, Malawi, Zambia, Ghana, South Africa and Senegal are greatly dependent on external markets for their GDP growth and

TABLE 7.1 GDP growth per capita (current US$) and change in GDP composition 1996–2014

Country	GDP/cap 1996	GDP/cap 2014	% industry 1996–2014	% agriculture 1996–2014	% services 1996–2014
Ghana	1587.2	1441.6	26.2–27.7	26–22.4	47.7–49.9
Senegal	1081.1	1067.1	24.9–23.5	15.7–15.8	59.5–60.7
Nigeria	2514.1	3203.3	27.8–24.2	22.3–20.2	49.9–55.5
Ethiopia	355.6	573.6	10.5–14.7	44.7–41.9	44.9–43.4
Kenya	1012.9	1358.3	21–19.4	29.3–30.3	49.7–50.4
Tanzania	740.4	955.1	24.3–25	31.3–31.5	43.5–44.4
Malawi	369.6	255	19.2–17	31.1–33.3	49.7–49.6
South Africa	8080.9	6483.9	29.9–29.5	2.5–2.5	67.5–68.1
Zambia	1654.5	1721.6	35.9–33.9	10.2–9.6	53.9–56.5

Source: World Bank: http://data.worldbank.org/indicator/NY.GDP.PCAP.CD.

Water, water everywhere **121**

TABLE 7.2 Percentage of labour force in agriculture and classic dependency X/M profile

Country	% labour force in agriculture	Classic dependency X/M profile: yes (Y) or no (N)
Ethiopia	85	Y
Ghana	44.7	Y
Kenya	75	Y
Malawi	90	Y
Nigeria	70	Y
Senegal	77.5	Y
South Africa	4	N
Tanzania	80	Y
Zambia	85	Y

Source: based on data from the CIA World Factbook: www.cia.gov/library/publications/resources/the-world-factbook/index.html.

stability. Of the other four, only Ethiopia is relatively well insulated from changes in global demand for its commodities. But the Ethiopian economy begins from such a low base (as exhibited in its GDP per capita of $573.60), that events such as the 2008 financial crisis barely register in Addis Ababa's high-density suburbs and across the country's smallholder farms.

When one examines GDP per capita growth in current US dollars (Table 7.1), it is evident that sub-Saharan economies have barely shifted over the last 20 years; and, where they have risen, more often than not they have fallen just as quickly, as they ride the rollercoaster of global commodity prices, currently on the downswing (see Figure 7.2). Table 7.1 also illustrates the relative change in GDP composition over nearly 20 years. What is shown there is a slight shift out of both industry and agriculture and into services, but the change is in no case dramatic. When one considers that the OECD average for GDP per capita in 2014 was nearly US$40,000, one can begin to understand the size of the gap between the 'league leaders' and the 'also rans'.

TABLE 7.3 Exports (X) as a percentage of GDP over time and relative value

Country	X % GDP 1996	X % GDP 2014	2014 X relative value (2000 = 100)
Ethiopia	16.7	11.6	913.7
Ghana	36.9	39.5	791.0
Kenya	21.6	16.4	352.7
Malawi	29.5	45.8	362.3
Nigeria	31.3	18.4	462.5
Senegal	25.2	27.4	305.6
South Africa	30.4	31.3	303.7
Tanzania	20.8	19.5	633.1
Zambia	38.1	40.9	1086.6

Source: World Bank: http://data.worldbank.org/indicator/NE.EXP.GNFS.ZS/countries.

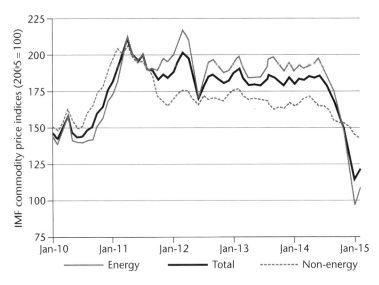

FIGURE 7.2 Global commodity index

Source: IMF: www.imf.org/external/np/res/commod/images/chart_lg.jpg.

So, save for less than a handful of exceptions, seven decades of 'development' have cast SSA in the amber of underdevelopment: as outposts of empire, producing what they do not consume; consuming what they do not produce; with the social relations of production drawing together state power and private/foreign capital to the epicentre of the constellation of social forces, while pushing the vast majority to the margins where they pursue their own livelihoods often beyond either the purview or the interest of the state. While this general observation is an important starting point, one must go deeper to recognize the particular variety of impacts neoliberalism in practice has had upon African state forms. In particular, and as pointed out by van de Walle (2001, 276), the emphasis on 'less state involvement' has resulted in a paradoxical situation where 'many of the states in the region are both more centralized and bigger, and yet they appear to do less development work than they did before adjustment'. This is largely because the shift towards 'privatization' has allowed state actors to cast off extraneous elements – such as service provision – and concentrate on core activities, that is, as nodal points for global capitalism, be it new businesses such as telecoms and financial services or old and dependable ones such as extractives and plantation agriculture. In explication of this point, the essay now turns to an examination of water and sanitation services.

Water, water everywhere but not a drop to drink (except for the right price)

Water is a resource like no other. Most importantly, while it is essential and non-substitutable at the basest level of human survival, it is also needed in vastly different quantities and qualities across a broad spectrum of use profiles, from purely aesthetic and spiritual (non-use values) to household and informal sector (small-scale use) to manufacturing, mining and food production (large, larger and largest use values). Across this vast array of actors come different expectations, partly determined by socio-cultural values, politico-economic considerations, as well as economic needs and abilities to pay.

The large-scale capture of water, beginning especially in the early twentieth century, made industrialization, wealth creation and extensive human settlement possible (Solomon 2010). Leaders of the 'league tables' of development are also the greatest users of water. Even where countries such as the UK, Germany and France do not use water directly, as in local production of food, they nevertheless command the water resources of other parts of the world through their capacity to import it virtually, embedded in food, from all over the world (Allan 2011). What these patterns of world water use demonstrate is the high degree to which water consumption mirrors global social relations of production. Put differently, the world of the 1 per cent is alive and well in the access, use and management of the world's water.

In Africa, the meaning of this should be obvious. The distribution of water resources across the continent reflects the region's abiding conditions of underdevelopment: plenty of water for commodity production, industry (where it exists) and low-density urban areas populated by those closest to the centre of the constellation of social forces within the state (political and economic elites, i.e. the comprador class); and only a little water of the right quantity and quality for everyone else. To better illustrate this claim, take one example from Malawi. In 2014, with a per capita GDP of only US$255, and an HDI ranking of 0.445, Malawi ranked 173rd out of the 188 countries surveyed by the UNDP's Human Development Report for 2015. Typical of other economically poor countries, agriculture accounted for 33.3 per cent of total GDP, much of it coming from a single crop – tobacco (Mandondo and German 2015). About 80 per cent of Malawians live in rural areas, with most engaged in subsistence agriculture. Malawi generates 45.8 per cent of its GDP through exports, almost all of which is agricultural commodities – tea tobacco, groundnuts, sugar, coffee, cotton – with tobacco accounting for 90 per cent of that. Up to the early 1980s, Malawi's agricultural profile mirrored the classic 'dual economy': on the one side, a large-scale, commercial sector owned by the few generating almost all of the farming income through a combination of government subsidies, increasingly mechanized production, large-scale irrigation and seasonal mass employment; and, on the other side, tens of thousands of less than a hectare smallholder, rainfall-dependent, input-starved farms upon which Malawi's millions of peasants resided in subsistence fashion.

In the wake of the debt crisis, significant agricultural sectoral restructuring was undertaken as part of donor-induced structural adjustment. Incentives – for the large producers as well as peasant farmers – were created to encourage and accommodate the inclusion of smallholders into commercial production. Mandondo and German (2015, 33) describe how more than 30,000 small leasehold estates, each 10–20 ha in size, were created by the end of the 1980s. The aim was to help families supplement food crop production with cash crop production. 'Clubs' comprising 10–30 members were supported with government and donor assistance such that, by the end of the 1980s, some 350,000 growers had been brought into commercial tobacco production, selling either to nearby estates or to ADMARC, the Agricultural and Development Marketing Corporation. The impact on poverty alleviation was significant, and is supported by evidence from elsewhere in the African continent regarding the impact of cash crop production on poverty alleviation (Molden 2007). So, some positive impacts, at least as measured in terms of increased income, were realized during the first round of SAP.[1]

Following the end of the Cold War, the entire southern African region witnessed a seismic shift away from authoritarian rule towards multi-party democracy. For Malawi, this resulted in an unfortunate and unanticipated turn of events. With the political toppling of 'Life President' Hastings Kamuzu Banda in 1994 came the unbundling of his economic empire, in particular Press Corporation (a holding company held by the President 'in trust for the nation'). Banda treated the country as a fiefdom and ruled with an iron fist, utilizing para-military groups such as the Young Pioneers to enforce his will. As with the Soviet Union, with Banda out of office (and dead by November 1997) those closest to the centre of political power took advantage of the country's Bank/Fund imposed 'commitment' to privatization to swoop in on the 'commanding heights' of the economy. Indeed, at one point in early 2000, the IMF advised the government to slow down its privatization process, so detrimental was this exercise to the overall stability of the social relations of production, at least from the perspective of the poor. This led to a temporary freeze on privatization in 2001, when parliament, in response to widespread civil society protests, recommended investigation into the impact of having already privatized about one-third of state-owned-enterprises (SOEs) in less than five years (www.africafiles.org/article.asp?ID=192, 1 May 2016).

At the end of the day, however, the result was not only more privatization, but neoliberalism across the board, including the increasing commercialization of communally held rural land through 'customary estates'. At present, only 12 per cent of land in Malawi is privately held, with 20 per cent being state owned and 68 per cent communally held. In terms of agricultural production, this means that of the 7.7m ha of agricultural land, 6.5m ha is in smallholder hands, with the average farm size being less than one-half of a hectare. According to Malawi government estimates, 4.1m ha of the 6.5m ha is 'suitable agricultural land', while 660,000 ha of private land is regarded as suitable for agriculture. Only 1.9m ha of customary land is currently cultivated, with the bulk of activity given over to subsistence food production, in particular maize (Jere 2012). Yields are notoriously poor (the stereotypical 1 tonne/ha for a smallholder farm in Africa being a charitable estimate here).

At the same time, private estates produce tea, tobacco and sugar for export, utilizing extensive systems of irrigation and cheap seasonal labour in the process. Many of Malawi's poor peasant farmers are also seasonal labourers on these estates. Donors have partnered with government, through SAP-linked sectoral reforms, to press for improved agricultural performance on smallholder lands. In part, this involves incentives to shift to cash crops through collective farming enterprises (as described above). It also includes incentives, such as access to fertilizer, technology (e.g. tractors) and markets (through ADMARC), should smallholders shift a percentage of their land over from food crops to cash crops. In the main, however, what we see is more and more people of farming age scratching a livelihood from inadequate land, with inadequate resources, while adjacent to their farms are highly profitable, state-supported, private estates which have captured the best land and blue water (meaning surface water and readily available groundwater) through extensive technology-driven irrigation systems. As the state presses forward with neoliberal policies and programmes, this process, while including many farmers, excludes many more. The durability of the dual economy in agriculture has been made worse by neoliberalism, as holdings are consolidated, and new participants are drawn into the market economy only to be either squeezed out by those with the capital and technical resources to dominate or hemmed in by dependence on limited cash crop income for livelihood security.

This is the invisible side of neoliberalism's impact on water in Africa. It is 'invisible' in the sense that most water is used in agriculture (Falkenmark and Rockstrom 2004), be it green (direct uptake by the plant through moisture in the soil following rainfall) or blue. While water cycles through the atmosphere, the continuing ability of powerful actors to use it for cash crops for export – while generating revenue, taxable income and jobs – means that the opportunity is lost to use that water for another purpose, such as improved production of food crops for rural and urban Malawians. Across the rest of SSA, market liberalization, global demand for biofuels and the commercialization of land has facilitated so-called 'land grabbing', whereby African states enter into land lease agreements with international actors such as other states (e.g. Brazil, China) or private companies, as these actors pursue a combination of food/energy security and profit (Cotula et al. 2009). As pointed out by Ruth Hall (2011), the actual 'land grabbing' is done by the home state, not the foreign actor, because it is the state that must 'legally' shift land classifications from 'communally held' to 'leasehold' before it can 'lease' the land out to someone. While such a phenomenon is yet to be realized in Malawi – at least not on a scale as is underway in places such as Zambia, Ethiopia and Tanzania – land grabs by indigenous state and private sector actors are well underway.[2] In a recent study, Cullis and Van Koppen (2009) showed that Gini coefficients of water inequality, when controlled for residual benefits such as labour income, almost perfectly mirror income inequality in the Olifants River basin of South Africa, so providing empirical evidence of the negative consequences of the capture of invisible water by the region's and the world's most powerful actors.

The most visible entry point of neoliberalism in water resources is through services, where the private sector has ridden into urban Africa on the back of the claim that the state is inefficient, inept and corrupt – a too often accurate assertion (Clapham 1996). In making a generalized claim that bloated bureaucracies and embedded inefficiencies lie at the heart of the 'water crisis' in the continent, neoliberalist interpretations obscure the very productive and profitable ways in which water serves the few at the expense of the many. Put differently, water services work just fine in SSA, just not for almost everybody.

From a capitalist – neoliberal or otherwise – point of view, as a scarce, essential and non-substitutable resource, water cries out for commodification. Granted, the resource is, among other things, bulky, fugitive (adhering to no physical or legal boundaries) and multi-purpose, so over-simplified ideas such as pricing to control demand cannot work across all use categories; in the words of Savenije (2002): 'Water is not an ordinary economic good.' But where a particular type of demand for water can be hived off from all others – such as urban and household water – access, use and management of the resource is amenable to commodification and commercialization: methods of capture and storage; systems of distribution and delivery; methods and systems of treatment; management and maintenance of infrastructure, to name the primary sites of commodification/commercialization.

Urban SSA was opened up to private sector participation in service delivery (water, electricity, transportation, solid waste management, telecommunications, key aspects of the built environment) in the wake of the Thatcherist attack on the state. Unlike the United Kingdom, SSA's infrastructure was not 'mature' in the urban planning sense of being fully rolled out and accessible to all in society. The best example of this is telecommunications where the mobile phone revolution allowed the state to simply abandon land-line development altogether. One would be hard-pressed to claim that telecommunications is a 'human right'; however, the United Nations General Assembly did agree in 2010 that access to adequate and affordable potable water and sanitation is a human right. So, abandoning the development, operation and maintenance of these services to a self-regulating private sector, while attractive to many of Africa's politicians in the early days of SAP, is no longer regarded as an option.

The original argument in support of privatization and, today, of public–private partnerships (PPP) or public–private–community partnerships (PPCP) seems sound: to paraphrase Rhodes (1996), the state should do less rowing and more steering – that is, let those most capable of delivering the service do so, while restricting the state to its core functions of establishing the enabling environment – policies, laws, procedures – to make this happen. With Bank/Fund and donor state support, numerous private sector providers entered the scene in the late 1990s/early 2000s. There is a significant literature chronicling the near-universal disaster that the private sector 'delivered' to urban Africans, so it need not be detailed here (see, for example, Bond 2002; McDonald and Ruiters 2005; Swatuk 2004). There are, however, several important points to make.

Aside from one or two cases, for example, Dakar and Johannesburg, private sector delivery in water services has been rolled back across the continent, with contracts being cancelled in municipalities in Ghana and Tanzania, the latter including a series of court cases to recover lost monies. Several factors led to the rush away from private sector dominance: (i) given the profit motive, companies tended to 'cherry pick', meaning enhancing services only for those able to pay in places where investment in new infrastructure was not needed; (ii) under-performance as per the

Water, water everywhere **127**

terms of contract, meaning, for example, a failure to roll-out systems to the poorer parts of cities and societies; (iii) where the private sector stepped in to take over existing utilities, the combination of price rises for services and job cuts from the utility made the supplier very unpopular among the vast majority of citizens; (iv) a desire on the part of the private company to cut and run, given the complexity of the task across SSA urban landscapes, the expenses to be incurred for new infrastructure and the inability to generate much profit; (v) a desire on the part of the municipal government to regain control of an essential service.

In some ways, this moves many Africans back to square one, where a weak state is either incapable of or uninterested in meeting the basic water and sanitation needs of its citizens. Where the private sector 'experiment' seems to be working – in Dakar and Johannesburg – the reason seems to be a combination of a capable and relatively uncorrupt bureaucracy providing necessary oversight, sufficient finance sourced in a variety of ways (revenues generated through payment for services; state subsidies; inexpensive loans from donor states, IGOs or IFIs) and an engaged citizenry. Yet this is clearly the exception rather than the rule. The scale of the problem is reflected in the data provided in the tables below. Clearly, the problem for most African states is not an absolute physical scarcity of water.[3] As shown in Table 7.4, only Northern Africa and the Sudano-Sahelian regions are water stressed. Indeed, the UNECA and others' *MDG Report 2014* states that SSA withdraws only 3 per cent of the annual renewable freshwater available to it. Table 7.5 highlights the numerous goals set out by the African Union in its Africa Water Vision 2025, while Table 7.7 shows the dismal performance especially in terms of improved sanitation; this despite the fact that World Bank data, in Table 7.6, suggest that Africans spend very little of their incomes on water. Perhaps this is because the service is so poor, and that the data on access (Table 7.7) are badly exaggerated. If so, this is nevertheless an important point: should the service be provided, Africans are willing and able to pay. Studies from Zambia and Zimbabwe have shown that people are willing to pay, but only for a service that is reliable and meets their needs (Ntengwe 2004; Mukheli *et al.* 2002). What most SSA citizens have objected to is the exorbitant cost of water that is

TABLE 7.4 Surface water resources in the sub-regions of Africa

Region	Area (km²)	Runoff km²/year	% of total runoff	Runoff (mm/year)	Water/capita/ year (m³)
Central Africa	5,328,660	1,912	48	359	21,849
Eastern Africa	2,924,970	260	7	89	1,567
Gulf of Guinea	2,119,270	952	24	449	5,388
Indian Ocean Islands	594,270	345	9	581	18,533
Northern Africa	5,752,890	50	1	9	346
Southern Africa	4,738,520	271	7	57	2,653
Sudano-Sahelian	8,587,030	160	4	19	1,609
Africa	30,045,610	3,950	100	131	4,979

Source: FAO (2003).

TABLE 7.5 Milestones and targets of the African Water Vision for 2025

Actions	Targets		
	2005	2015	2025
Improving governing of water resources			
1 Development of national IWRM policies and comprehensive institutional reform			
• In process of development	100% of countries		
• Full implementation		100% of countries	
2 Enabling environment for regional cooperation on shared water			
• Initiated in existing river basin organizations	100% of organizations		
• Implemented in existing river basin organizations	50% of organizations	100% of organizations	
• Initiated in new river basin organizations		100% of organizations	
• Implemented in new river basin organizations		50% of organizations	100% of organizations
Improving water wisdom			
1 Systems for information generation, assessment and dissemination			
• Established at national level	50% of countries	100% of countries	
• Established for international river basins	30% of basins	100% of basins	
• Established at Africa–wide level			100% complete
2 Sustainable financing for information generation and management			
• Review of global experience	100% complete		
• Implementation at national level	50% complete	100% complete	
• Implementation at river basin level	30% complete	100% complete	
• Established at Africa–wide level		30% complete	100% complete
3 IWRM capacity building			
• Create public awareness and consensus	100% of countries		
• Knowledge gaps identified	100% of countries		
• Partnership for strategic assistance	100% of countries		
• National research institutes established	20% of countries	60% of countries	90% of countries
• Regional research institutes established	One established	Two established	Three established
• Gender/youth concerns mainstreamed	30% of countries	100% countries/basins	

Meeting urgent water needs

1 Proportion of people without access:			
• To safe and adequate water supply	Reduce by 25%	Reduce by 75%	Reduce by 95%
• To safe and adequate sanitation	Reduce by 25%	Reduce by 70%	Reduce by 95%
2 Water for achieving food security			
• Water productivity of rain-fed agriculture and irrigation	Increase by 10%	Increase by 30%	Increase by 60%
• Size of irrigated area	Increase by 25%	Increase by 55%	Increase by 100%
3 Development of water for agriculture, hydropower, industry, tourism and transportation at national level	5% of potential	10% of potential	25% of potential
4 Conservation and restoration of environment, biodiversity and life-supporting ecosystems			
• Allocation of sufficient water for environmental sustainability	Implemented in 30% of countries	Implemented in 100% of countries	Implemented in 100% of river basins
• Conserving and restoring watershed ecosystems	Under development	Implemented in 50% of countries	
5 Efffective management of droughts, floods and desertification	Under development	Operational in 50% of countries	Operational in 100% of countries

Strengthening financial base for desired water future

1 Sustainable financing for policy and institutional reform and capacity-building	Operational in 60% of countries		
2 Sustainable financing for information generation and management	Secured in 100% of countries`	Operational in 100% of countries	
3 Financing urgent water needs			
• Implementation of pricing and full cost recovery	Operational in 60% of countries	Operational of 100% of countries	
• Increasing private sector participation	Operational in 30% of countries	Operational in 100% of countries	
• Mobilizing finance from national and international sources	Secured in 50% of countries	Secured in 100% of countries	

Source: UN Water/Africa (2012).

130 L. A. Swatuk

TABLE 7.6 Consumption as percentage of total household income

Country	Water	Energy	Food
Ethiopia	0	9	59
Ghana	1	5	50
Kenya	1	4	55
Malawi	1	3	64
Nigeria	0	2	57
Senegal	1	5	53
South Africa	1	4	15
Tanzania	0	1	67
Zambia	1	4	49

Source: World Bank: http://datatopics.worldbank.org/consumption/detail.

insufficient for their needs and too often detrimental to their health. According to a 2010 African Development Bank report, 60–70 per cent of SSA rural and urban dwellers source their water from what are called 'alternative service providers'. These are small-scale operators servicing not only the poor, but the many who are left outside of the formal sector system of in-house or on-plot delivery. Studies have shown this water to be much more expensive and of lower quality than the water delivered directly into high-income households (Bergkamp and Sadoff 2008).

PPP and PPCP approaches to water services attempt to bring together the necessary combination of actors involved in both 'steering' and 'rowing': state oversight, guidance and finance; private sector finance, management and delivery; and civil society finance, management and delivery. However, it seems to me that widespread civil society involvement generally reinforces the gap between the (extroverted, predatory) state and (marginalized) civil society. Leaving the supply of water

TABLE 7.7 Selected country access to improved sanitation and improved water supply

Country	% access to improved sanitation 2011	% access to improved sanitation 2015	% access to improved water rural 2015	% access to improved water urban 2015
Ethiopia	23	28	49	93
Ghana	14	15	84	93
Kenya	29	30	57	82
Malawi	39	41	89	96
Nigeria	30	29	57	81
Senegal	46	48	67	93
South Africa	64	66	81	100
Tanzania	14	16	46	77
Zambia	43	44	51	86

Source: World Bank: http://data.worldbank.org/indicator/SH.STA.ACSN/countries?display=default and http://wdi.worldbank.org/table/3.5.

to a combination of donors, international NGOs and community-based organizations (CBOs) simply allows the state to ignore the citizenry and concentrate on its 'core' business under neoliberalism: facilitating 'development' or, as critics often say, fashioning a playing field fit for market forces and the commodification of everything. At the same time, it leads to what Xaba (2015) calls 'NGOism' – that is, 'the strategies of NGOs to perpetuate the continual need for their services'. Certainly, this is in line with Fowler's 1991 observation that NGO involvement constitutes a 'new scramble for Africa'.

Civil society has pushed back against privatization of services almost everywhere across the continent, their argument being that access to sufficient water and sanitation is a basic human right. As highlighted above, they are not wrong; indeed, they have widespread support in this claim. Many local governments have supported the people in this cause, clawing back these services from private companies, most recently in Accra, Ghana. But the question should be asked: are Africans any better off with the state?

Beyond neoliberalism?

In a recent essay (Swatuk 2015), I reflected on 20 years of 'integrated water resources management' in SSA, framing it around the central question 'Can you float IWRM in a sea of underdevelopment?' The question, admittedly, was rhetorical, for the answer is a resounding no. However, positive things do happen, sometimes in places you would least expect it. In that essay, I highlighted five situational contexts in which goals such as those articulated in Table 7.5 may be partially or wholly achieved, and I think it is useful to highlight them here: (i) when states themselves are beneficiaries; (ii) when there is pressure from below – that is, from an engaged and active civil society; (iii) when there is peer pressure, with 'peers' meaning mostly donor states and/or intergovernmental organizations; (iv) when actors find themselves in an irresistible setting, often in order to appear like a 'good global citizen'; and (v) when the situational context is neither of interest to the state nor in its general purview (Swatuk 2015, 70–80).

In my view, positive outcomes are limited to these five situational contexts primarily due to the combination – lethal for millions – of a predatory and extroverted state form first fashioned in the interests of colonialism/imperialism, later hobbled by global economic change, and presently shackled to neoliberal globalization. African elites are comfortable with this arrangement, for they profit mightily from the numerous ways, both formal and informal, in which the continent is selectively inserted into the global political economy.[4] Thus we hear about 'Africa rising', but in truth, only insofar as commodity prices are also rising. Neoliberalism has been a two-edged sword: at once facilitating the slicing-up of the magnificent resource cake that is SSA, through participation in the global market; as well as making space for innovative, entrepreneurial capitalists (of all stripes) by rolling back the state. To be sure, opportunities as well as new fortunes are created by these processes. The United Nations (UNDP 2015, 58–9) claims that, through the

132 L. A. Swatuk

Millennium Development Goals process, 30 per cent of sub-Saharan Africa's people now have access to improved sanitation, up from 24 per cent in 2000; and 68 per cent have access to an improved drinking water source, up from 48 per cent 15 years earlier. Given absolute increases in population, the numbers of people here are not insignificant. But one wonders whether this is because of or in spite of neoliberal globalization. We can never know. What we do know is that SSA's people are badly served and where they organize and rise up (à la A. O. Hirschman's [1970] 'voice'), or where they are left alone to their own devices (Hirschman's 'exit'), sometimes good things do happen. Hirschman's third option for the citizenry – loyalty – seems to yield the fewest benefits, a sad fact when you consider that we are talking about the sovereign state. In my view, neoliberalism's persistence, with its insistence on the commodification of everything, widens the gap between the state and civil society: hence the fights over big but largely invisible water across rural areas, and small but clearly visible water in the cities and towns.[5] So, while Africans are still struggling, in Mamdani's words, to become citizens rather than subjects, neoliberalism has crept in and turned us all into individual, isolated consumers. What is needed across SSA is common purpose to put in place infrastructure for all, whatever it takes. The disciplining effect of neoliberal discourse makes this sentence unthinkable without the addendum, 'as long as it pays for itself'. Almost 15 years ago, Patrick Bond and colleagues observed:

> Even before the logic of privatization sets in, the necessary preliminary work by the neoliberal state – commercializing, delinking water from other state functions, raising tariffs, cutting off people who cannot pay their bills – all have the same effect ... The commodification of water causes drought for poor people and floods for rich people and companies.
>
> *(Bond et al. 2002, 260)*

While a few states have learned a few lessons from those early practices, in the main the neoliberal principles underpinning all services have not changed. And so in this neoliberal world we slosh about in a rickety African ship barely afloat on a sea of underdevelopment, some shipmates wondering how to profit from plugging the leaks, some already selling off the planks.

Notes

1 Of course, a whole host of negative aspects also materialized, such as food insecurity, environmental degradation due to increased demand for wood fuel for tobacco curing, and shattered families, communities and villages as communal land was increasingly consolidated into what were called 'small leasehold estates' (Mandondo and German 2015).
2 I am following Hall (2011, 207–8) in my use of 'land grabbing': as a metaphor for resource capture, ecological marginalization and social injustice; and, to quote Hall, as:

> trends that involve not the mere capture of land but the capture of labour, water, and most of all, the adverse incorporation – rather than exclusion – of smallholder agriculture into new value chains, patterns of accumulation, and the wider transformations in agrarian structure and agro-food systems that these precipitate.

Water, water everywhere **133**

3 Mehta (2001, 2007), drawing on the case of India, usefully shows how most scarcity is 'manufactured' by social disparities.

4 In relation to water resources development, I have discussed this in detail as it relates to South Africa (Swatuk 2010) and across the continent with a case study of the Nile River Basin (Swatuk 2012).

5 Tony Allan uses the terms 'big' and 'small' to encourage us to understand water for agriculture's vast order of magnitude beyond that which we need for domestic consumption. Put simply, on average we need $1700\,m^3$ per capita per year (combining water for food, industry and domestic consumption); of this total perhaps $1400\,m^3$ is contained in the food we consume, which compares to the $200\,m^3$ for industry and $100\,m^3$ for personal use. So, water for drinking, bathing and cooking – even for filling swimming pools – is 'small water'.

References

Allan, T. 2011. *Virtual Water*. London: I. B. Taurus.

Bayart, J-F. 2000. Africa in the World: A History of Extraversion. *African Affairs* 99: 217–67.

Bayart, J-F., Ellis, S. and Hibou, B. 1999. *The Criminalization of the State in Africa*. London: James Currey.

Bergkamp, G. and Sadoff, C. W. 2008. Water in a Sustainable Economy. In Worldwatch Institute, *State of the World 2008: Innovations for a Sustainable Economy*. New York and London: W. W. Norton & Co.

Bond, P. 2002. *Unsustainable South Africa: Environment, Development and Social Protest*. Pietermaritzburg: University of Natal Press.

Bond, P. 2006. *Looting Africa: The Economics of Exploitation*. London: Zed.

Bond, P., Ruiters, G. and Steyn, R. 2002. Droughts and Floods: Water Prices and Values in the Time of Cholera. In Bond, P. (ed.) *Unsustainable South Africa: Environment, Development and Social Protest*. Pietermaritzburg: University of Natal Press.

Clapham, C. 1996. *Africa and the International System*. Cambridge: Cambridge University Press.

Clarke, J. 2008. Living With/in and Without Neo-Liberalism. *Focaal – European Journal of Anthropology* 51: 135–47.

Cotula, L., Vermeulen, S., Leonard, R. and Keely, J. 2009. *Land Grab or Development Opportunity? Agricultural Investment and International Land Deals in Africa*. London and Rome: IIED/FAO/IFAD.

Cullis, James and Van Koppen, Barbara. 2009. Applying the Gini Coefficient to Measure Inequality of Water Use in the Olifants River Water Management Area, South Africa. In Swatuk, Larry A. and Wirkus, Lard (eds) *Transboundary Water Governance in Southern Africa: Examining Underexplored Dimensions*. Bonn: Nomos Publishers.

Deyo, F. (ed.). 1987. *The Political Economy of the New Asian Industrialism*. Ithaca: Cornell University Press.

Ellis, S.1999. *The Mask of Anarchy*. New York: New York University Press.

Falkenmark, M. and Rockstrom, J. 2004. *Balancing Water for Humans and Nature*. London: Earthscan.

FAO. 2003. *Review of World Water Resources by Country*. ftp://ftp.fao.org/agl/aglw/docs/wr23e.pdf.

Ferguson, J. 2006. *Global Shadows: Africa in the Neoliberal World Order*. Durham, NC: Duke University Press.

Fowler, A. 1991. The Role of NGOs in Changing State–Society Relations: Perspectives from Eastern and Southern Africa. *Development Policy Review* 9(1): 53–84.

134   L. A. Swatuk

Gereffi, G. and Evans, P. 1981. Transnational Corporations, Dependent Development and State Policy in the Semiperiphery: A Comparison of Brazil and Mexico. *Latin American Research Review* 16(3): 31–64.

Hall, R. 2011. Land Grabbing in Southern Africa: The Many Faces of the Investor Rush. *Review of African Political Economy* 38(128): 193–214.

Harris, N. 1986. *The End of the Third World*. Lanham, MD: Rowman and Littlefield.

Harvey, D. 2005. *A Brief History of Neoliberalism*. Oxford: Oxford University Press.

Hirschman, A. O. 1970. *Exit, Voice and Loyalty: Responses to Decline in Firms, Organisations and States*. Cambridge, MA: Harvard University Press.

Jere, P. 2012. *Improving Land Sector Governance in Malawi: Implementation of the Land Governance Assessment Framework*, draft paper prepared for the Government of Malawi; no imprint.

Leftwich, A. 1995. Bringing Politics Back In: Towards A Model of the Developmental State. *The Journal of Development Studies* 31(3): 400–27.

Mandondo, A. and German, L. 2015. Customary Rights and Societal Stakes of Large Scale Tobacco Cultivation in Malawi. *Agriculture and Human Values* 32: 31–46.

Marais, H. 1998. *South Africa: Limits to Change, the Political Economy of Transformation*. London: Zed Books.

McDonald, David and Ruiters, Greg (eds). 2005. *The Age of Commodity: Water Privatization in Southern Africa*. London: Earthscan.

Mehta, L. 2001. The Manufacture of Popular Perceptions of Scarcity: Dams and Water-Related Narratives in Gujarat, India. *World Development* 29(12): 2025–41.

Mehta, L. 2007. Whose Scarcity? Whose Property? The Case of Water in Western India. *Land Use Policy* 24(4): 654–63.

Mittelman, J. and Pasha, M. 1997. *Out From Underdevelopment Revisited*. Basingstoke: Palgrave.

Molden, D. (ed.). 2007. *Water for Food Water for Life: A Comprehensive Assessment of Water Management in Agriculture*. Abingdon: Routledge.

Mukheli, A., Mosupye, G. and Swatuk, L. A. 2002. Is the Pungwe Water Supply Project a Solution to Water Accessibility and Sanitation Problems for the Households of Sakubva, Zimbabwe? *Physics and Chemistry of the Earth* 27: 723–32.

Ntengwe, F. W. 2004. The Impact of Consumer Awareness of Water Sector Issues on Willingness to Pay and Cost Recovery in Zambia. *Physics and Chemistry of the Earth* 29: 1301–8.

Ong, A. 2006. *Neoliberalism as Exception: Mutations in Citizenship and Sovereignty*. Durham, NC: Duke University Press.

Peck, J. 2004. Geography and Public Policy: Constructions of Neoliberalism. *Progress in Human Geography* 28(3): 392–405.

Reno, W. 1998. *Warlord Politics and African States*. Boulder: Lynne Rienner.

Rhodes, R. 1996. The New Governance: Governing without Government. *Political Studies* 44(4): 652–67.

Rodney, W. 1974. *How Europe Underdeveloped Africa*. Washington, DC: Howard University Press.

Savenije, H. H. G. 2002. Why Water Is Not an Ordinary Economic Good, or Why the Girl Is Special. *Physics and Chemistry of the Earth* 27: 741–4.

Solomon, S. 2010. *Water: the Epic Struggle for Wealth, Power and Civilization*. New York: Harper Collins.

Stubbs, R. 2009. What Ever Happened to the East Asian Developmental State? The Unfolding Debate. *The Pacific Review* 22(1): 1–22.

Swatuk, L. A. 1995. Dead-End to Development? Post-Cold War Africa in the New International Division of Labor. *African Studies Review* 38(1): 103–17.

Swatuk, L. A. 2004. Water Reforms and Privatization Processes in Southern Africa. In Wohlmuth, K. Gutowski, A., Knediuk, T., Meyn, M. and Ngogang, S. (eds) *African Development Perspectives Yearbook 2004: Private and Public Sectors: Towards a Balance*. Münster: Lit Verlag.

Swatuk, L. A. 2010. The State and Water Resources Development through the Lens of History: A South African Case Study. *Water Alternatives* 3(3): 521–36.

Swatuk, L. A. 2012. Water and Security in Africa: State-Centric Narratives, Human Insecurities. In Schnurr, M. and Swatuk, Larry A. (eds) *Natural Resources and Social Conflict: Towards Critical Environmental Security*. Basingstoke: Macmillan.

Swatuk, L. A. 2015. Can IWRM Float on a Sea of Underdevelopment? Reflections on Twenty-Plus Years of 'Reform' in Sub-Saharan Africa. In Munck, R., Asingwire, N., Fagan, H. and Kabonesa, C. (eds) *Water and Development: Good Governance After Neoliberalism*. London: Zed Books.

UN Water/Africa. 2012. *The Africa Water Vision for 2025: Equitable and Sustainable Use of Water for Socioeconomic Development*. www.afdb.org/fileadmin/uploads/afdb/Documents/Generic-Documents/african%20water%20vision%202025%20to%20be%20sent%20to%20wwf5.pdf.

UNDP. 2011. Chapter 2: Commodity Dependence and International Commodity Prices. In *Towards Human Resilience: Sustaining MDG Progress in an Age of Economic Uncertainty*. New York: UNDP.

UNDP. 2015. *Human Development Report*. New York: Oxford University Press.

UNECA, African Union, African Development Bank Group, UNDP. 2014. *MDG Report 2014: Assessing Progress in Africa Toward the Millennium Development Goals*. Addis Ababa: Economic Commission for Africa.

van de Walle, N. 2001. *African Economies and the Politics of Permanent Crisis, 1979–1999*. New York: Cambridge University Press.

Xaba, T. 2015. From Public-Private Partnerships to Private-Public Stick 'Em Ups! NGOism, Neoliberalism, and Social Development in Post-Apartheid South Africa. *International Social Work* 58(2): 309–19.

8

AUTOCRATS AND ACTIVISTS

Human rights, democracy and the neoliberal paradox in Nigeria

Bonny Ibhawoh and Lekan Akinosho

Political, civil and economic rights are integral to the development of democratic societies. Like many African countries, Nigeria suffered from the debilitating effects of military rule which swept across the continent soon after the attainment of political independence from European colonialists. The four decades between independence in 1960 and 2000 were dominated by military dictatorships. Military intervention in politics was sometimes justified as a necessary stage in the nation-building process. It was believed that the fragile post-colonial state inherited at independence sometimes required the strong hand of 'benevolent dictators' to keep it from breaking apart. However, it soon became clear that military involvement in politics did not serve to strengthen national integration or facilitate the transition to full democracy. Successive military regimes provided no coherent master plans to forge unity among the disparate constituents of the nation or to foster democracy. Expropriation and exploitation of human and economic resources became the primary modes of interaction between the ruling military regimes and the general populace. The discontent engendered by repressive governance, corruption and the competition to retain power created political upheavals and social unrests which came to define the decades of military rule in the country.

During the period under review (1980s–1990s), the quest for popular democracy resulted in massive public protests and organized civil society action as Nigerians demanded political reforms and an end to military dictatorship. The primary demand was for the institutionalization of democracy, ending arbitrary rule and a return to the rule of law. These demands were characterized by the catch phrase 'democracy and good governance'. The timing of this pro-democratic fervour coincided with protests in many parts of the Global South against the World Bank and International Monetary Fund (IMF)-backed economic austerity measures also known as Structural Adjustment Programmes (SAP). The World Bank and IMF became increasingly prominent in Africa due to the economic crisis of the early

1980s. In the late 1970s, rising oil prices, rising interest rates and falling prices for other primary commodities left many poor African countries unable to repay mounting foreign debts. In the early 1980s, Africa's debt crisis worsened as the ratio of its foreign debt to its export income grew to 500 per cent (Watkins *et al.* 1995, 74). The decision by African countries to adopt SAPs as part of the conditionalities for securing World Bank and IMF loans, and the economic difficulties that followed, prompted strong public backlash. In Nigeria, the pro-democracy movement was anchored by the Campaign for Democracy, an umbrella of human rights NGOs, which was used to mobilize the masses against the military-backed SAP.

This chapter examines the linkages between military rule, human rights and the Structural Adjustment Programme within the context of the civil society-led pro-democracy movement in Nigeria. It explores the paradoxical place of neoliberal structural adjustment economic policies on human rights in Nigeria in the 1980s and 1990s. It argues that pushing through unpopular austerity measures mandated by the IMF and the World Bank accentuated the authoritarian character of the successive ruling military regimes, resulting in widespread repression and human rights violations. However, the economic difficulties and political uncertainties arising from those neoliberal policies provided a rallying point for civil society and the emergence of vibrant new NGOs such as Campaign for Democracy, which were committed to the human rights and pro-democracy struggles. The chapter also explores how this tension in the neoliberal experiment shaped the human rights and pro-democracy movement under Nigeria's military dictatorships. It concludes, however, that the promising advances made by civil society groups in the struggle to end military dictatorship have not been extended to sustain democratic gains under civilian rule. In order to understand the role of human rights and pro-democracy organizations in the opposition against military-backed neoliberal policies, and the eventual transition to democratic rule, it is necessary to locate these developments in the historical context of military intervention in Nigerian politics.

The politics of military rule in Nigeria

The history of Nigeria since gaining independence from Britain in 1960 has been defined by democratic instability and one of the longest periods of military rule in Africa, characterized by military coups and counter-coups. Besides being Africa's most populous country, Nigeria has been described as one of the world's most deeply divided societies where ethnic identity politics poses a barrier to national integration (Suberu and Diamond 2002, 401). The country's political history since independence may be divided into four broad phases. The first phase began in 1960 when the military overthrew the civilian government under Tafawa Balewa in a bloody coup that ended the first republic. The second period started with another military coup in 1966 and ushered 13 years of the successive military regimes which ended in 1979, when the military handed over power to a civilian government. The Second Republic, which marked the third phase, began with the election of

Shehu Shagari as President in 1979 and was terminated by a military coup in 1983. The third phase, spanning 1984 to 1999, included the military regimes of Generals Ibrahim Babangida and Sanni Abacha, which gained a reputation for their repressive and authoritarian policies. The fourth phase of political development in the country was marked by the return to democratic civilian rule with the election of the former military ruler Olusegun Obasanjo in 1999.

The 1960s in Nigeria was a turbulent period as the country stumbled from one political crisis to another. The country nearly disintegrated as it witnessed an increase in ethnic tension and regional competition which culminated in the Nigeria-Biafra war from 1967 to 1970. The election that heralded independence was defined by the emergence of political parties built around ethnic identities. The three major political parties were dominated and controlled by members of particular ethnic groups. The Action Group (AG) was controlled by the Yoruba of Western Nigeria; the National Council of Nigerian Citizens (NCNC) by the Ibo of Eastern Nigeria; and the Northern People's Congress (NPC) by the Hausa-Fulani of Northern Nigeria. This created a tenuous balance of power between the three major ethnic groups in the country which paved the way for military intervention in national politics (Anifowose 1982, 12–13). In order to justify their intervention in politics and legitimize their rule, successive military regimes declared commitment to political and economic reforms. A recurring theme was the goal of addressing corruption and pursuing economic reforms within the framework of a new politics of national integration.

The military coup of 1979 was framed as a response to the corruption, nepotism, ethnic politics and economic mismanagement of the preceding civilian regime of Shehu Shagari. During Shagari's rule, the country witnessed an unprecedented downturn in its economic fortunes. Mismanagement of the revenues accruing from oil exportation meant that the government was unable to meet basic obligations such as paying the salaries of civil servants. The country also became increasingly unable to meet its external debt-servicing obligations to international lenders. Inflation rose to an all-time high, leading a precipitous decline in the living conditions of ordinary Nigerians. By 1982, signs of an economic crisis were apparent, forcing the government to introduce a series of austerity measures aimed at improving its balance of payments (Aiyede 2003, 5). These measures were part of World Bank/IMF conditions imposed for granting loans to the government. The conditions included a drastic reduction of government spending, privatization of public sector establishments, liberalization of trade through a relaxation of tariffs and a removal of subsidies and government controls on imports (Ahmad 1994, 189). Although these measures were sold as a means of stimulating the moribund economy, they ultimately served to worsen the impact of the economic downturn on the populace and exacerbate a growing rift between the civilian and military elite in the competition for political power. The economic crisis arising from fiscal mismanagement and the effects of World Bank/IMF conditionalities provided the justification for a group of military officers led by General Mohammadu Buhari to overthrow the Shagari government in 1983 (Olorode 2001, 137). In justifying this intervention, the military also pointed to the dysfunctional politics of the Second Republic, electoral fraud by the ruling government and the collapse of the delicate institutional balance of partisan and ethnic interests that had underpinned Nigerian Federalism from the introduction of revised federal constitution in 1979 (Suberu and Diamond 2002, 404).

Economic crisis and military repression

The military regime of General Buhari assumed power in 1983 amidst severe economic and social crises, and an uncertain political situation. Although Buhari's coup was broadly welcomed by most ordinary Nigerians who yearned for change amidst the economic crisis, there was also some scepticism about the role of the military in national politics. Many Nigerians, particularly among the vocal elite class, expressed their anxieties about the authoritarian nature of military rule and demanded a quick return to civilian rule. For instance, when the Buhari government promulgated military decrees restricting the activities of the press soon after it assumed power, the regime was accused of tyranny and neo-fascism. The most draconian of these restrictive laws was Decree No. 2 of 1984, which granted the military the power to detain persons for a period of three months without trial, for any act considered prejudicial to state security. Decree No. 4 of 1984 (The Protection against False Accusation Decree) enabled the government to jail journalists for publishing 'false accusations' against public officials. 'False accusations' in this context came to be interpreted broadly as any information that presented members of the military junta in a negative light. Based on these laws, two journalists, Tunde Thompson and Nduka Irabor of the leading national newspaper, the *Guardian*, were tried and convicted for writing what the government considered embarrassing to its interests.

Other repressive laws introduced by the military regime included Decree No. 13, which effectively placed the government above the law by removing all government actions from the jurisdiction of the courts; and Decree No. 17, which granted immunity to the government against workers even if they had been sacked illegally (Aiyede 2003, 6). Under these and similar laws, several civil society organizations such as the National Association of Nigerian Students (NANS) and the Nigeria Medical Association (NMA) were banned and their leaders detained (Momoh and Adejumobi 1991, 27). These developments were followed by widespread public criticism, demonstrations and workers' strikes aimed at challenging the military regime. The repressive character of the regime heighted political uncertainty and became the cardinal issues of campaigns by civil society against the junta. Concerted public opposition to the excesses of the regime provided the justification for a 'palace coup' which removed General Buhari from power in 1985 and inaugurated the government of General Ibrahim Babangida. The regime of Babangida would come to epitomize the nexus between military authoritarianism and the neoliberal economic restructuring in Nigeria. As Suberu and Diamond have argued (2002, 405), the years between 1984 and 1999 'represented the degeneration of military rule from the regime of hegemonic exchange that was institutionalized for much of the post-civil war period to a system of steep hegemonic repression'. In the Nigerian context, earlier regimes of hegemonic exchange involved practices designed to ensure equitable stabilization and accommodation in state-ethnic and inter-ethnic relations. Later regimes of hegemonic repression came to be characterized by ethnic exclusion, domination and coercion.

Pro-democracy activism and structural adjustment

In the 1980s and 1990s, the African continent witnessed unprecedented public unrest as citizens demanded political reforms, an end to military dictatorship and one-party rule, and the establishment of multi-party democracy. It was a period of transition, which was led by the new social movements under the auspices of organized civil society. As Paul Zeleza has noted (2004, 1), 'This was a period of bewildering extremes, which saw the rise of mass movements and mass revolts driven by democratic and developmentalist ideals, as well as mass murder and mass poverty perpetrated by desperate regimes and discredited global agencies.' Popular struggles in this period have been described as the demand for a 'second independence' for Africa in the sense that they represented a clamour for political freedom and the enforcement of civil rights. In the Nigerian context, such pro-democracy struggles against military rule marked the third phase in a long history of human rights struggles. The first phase hinged on the fight against colonialism and, specifically, the agitation against the abrogation of the rights to self-determination and other civil and economic rights by the British colonialists (Ibhawoh 2003, 18–19). The second phase in the evolution of the human rights movement grew out of the promise of democracy and constitutionalism which independence had ushered in. It reflected the nation-building aspirations of the emergent political elite and its idealism towards forging the structures of the new state. The third phase, characterized by NGO and civil society activism, was a response to the failure of these aspirations; the structural inadequacies of the colonial state; the breakdown of constitutional rule and the authoritarianism and repression that subsequently became associated with military dictatorship in the country.

The crucial link between the neoliberal policies of military government and the rise of NGO human rights activism in Nigeria was the economic austerity programme introduced by the government in the late 1980s. The military government embarked on a Structural Adjustment Programme (SAP), as part of the policies backed by the World Bank and IMF that allowed the government to engage in aggressive privatization and deregulation of the economy, devalue the currency, retrench workers and remove subsidies on social services like health and education. The SAP was designed ostensibly to diversify and reconfigure the Nigerian economy by stimulating domestic production in the agricultural, manufacturing and industrial sectors. It was hoped that by generating internal production through the utilization of local raw materials, the balance of payments deficit would be reduced and a diminution of Nigeria's dependence on Western imports would follow (Walker 2000).

In Nigeria, as elsewhere in Africa, the IMF and World Bank pushed an aggressive policy of trade liberalization and free market fundamentalism. On the one hand, Western powers and international organizations under their control exercised strong pressures to extend neoliberal concepts within the framework of globalization. But, on the other hand, contradictions and symptoms of crisis multiplied as a result of those same policies (González and Baró 2006, 579).

As a result of their reliance on loans and debt relief from bilateral donors and International Financial Institutions such as the World Bank and IMF, many African governments devoted much of their resources to satisfying the interests of the international donor community without reference to the needs of their own economies and people. For this reason, the 1980s and 1990s have been described as Africa's 'lost decades' (Hilary 2010, 79). The IMF eventually admitted that it made serious mistakes in promoting trade liberalization in developing countries. An internal evaluation of adjustment policies in 2009 concluded that the reliance on neoliberal dogma, without reference to the specific national circumstances of each economy, was 'an insufficient basis for a constructive trade policy dialogue between country authorities and the IMF' (IMF 2009a, 2009b).

In Nigeria, SAP not only failed to produce the desired result, it aggravated the economic crisis, triggering a wave of public protests and demonstrations. SAP had a particularly devastating impact on the country's fragile agricultural sector. Increased inflation resulted in a substantial increase in the prices of farm implements, which in turn increased the cost of agricultural production (Walker 2000, 152). The results were food shortages, decreased productivity and industrial unrest. As several studies have shown, women, youth and children bore the brunt of the economic hardships occasioned by structural adjustment and other neoliberal policies in Nigeria (Adeniyi-Ogunyankin 2012). The reduction in state funding for public education and the resulting spike in tuition fees in public institutions galvanized students under the auspices of the National Association of Nigerian Students (NANS) to protest against SAP. Apart from demanding an end to SAP, the students also articulated a pro-democracy agenda that served as an ideological foundation for the human rights organizations that subsequently emerged. At its National Convention held at the University of Ibadan in 1989, NANS demanded that the military government should begin the 'process of instituting a National Constituency Assembly, involving labour, students, professionals, democratic and mass organizations to fashion out a valid and universally acceptable framework for institutionalizing popular democracy' (Ibhawoh 2003, 13). A notable feature during this period was the call for a Sovereign National Conference (SNC), which gained prominence as a symbol of political inclusion and the pro-democracy struggle.

The NANS also engaged in sustained and disruptive public protest against the military government. Undeterred by threats of arrest and violence marshalled by the government to suppress their activities, student leaders mobilized their colleagues and other sectors of the public to protest against SAP while demanding political reforms. The effect of the 1989 NANS protest led to the first concerted effort to coalesce opposition against military governance in Nigeria. In 1990, several civil society and professional organizations such as NANS, the Nigerian Medical Association and the Nigeria Bar Association (NBA) came together to form the coalition known as the National Consultative Forum (NCF) headed by the renowned lawyer and activist Alao Aka-Bashorun. The goal of NCF was to provide a united forum for mass organizations, professionals and individuals to promote the idea of a National Conference that would offer solutions to social, economic and political difficulties confronted by the country (Agenda for Democracy 1990). The NCF defied the military government to organize what it called a 'National Conference' to debate the future of Nigeria and make the country a 'truly free, democratic, self-reliant and just society'. Although the conference was disrupted and NCF leaders arrested by government agents, the work of the NCF set the tone for civil society coalition-building and pro-democracy activism in the country.

Following the aborted National Conference organized by the NCF, the forum transitioned into an organized civil society organization, the Campaign for Democracy (CD) in 1991 under the leadership of Beko Ransome-Kuti, a physician and former President of the Nigerian Medical Association. The CD was a coalition of several affiliate organizations, including the Committee for the Defence of Human Rights (CDHR), Civil Liberties Organization (CLO), National Association of Nigerian Students (NANS), National Consultative Forum (NCF), Nigerian Medical Association (NMA, Lagos Branch), Constitutional Rights Projects (CRP), Women in Nigeria, (WIN), the Nigerian Union of Journalists (NUJ) and the Movement for the Survival of Ogoni People (MOSOP) led by Ken Saro Wiwa (Momoh and Adejumobi 1991, 230). The primary goal that brought these organizations together was their commitment to restoring democratic rule, restoring the right of the people to form their own political parties, establishing impartial electoral bodies and ending military rule. The Campaign for Democracy (CD) also demanded the termination of SAP and other economic policies that had caused the people hardships, poverty, disease, hunger, unemployment, retrenchment and illiteracy (Campaign for Democracy 1991, 1).

'Soldiers must go': confronting military dictatorship

Civil society organizations such as the CD were effective in linking their opposition to neoliberal economic policies with a parallel political campaign for democratic reforms. A defining movement in the challenge to military rule by pro-democratic forces in Nigeria came with the reactions that trailed the nebulous democratic transition programme of the Ibrahim Babangida regime (1986–93) and the annulment of the result of presidential elections held on 12 June 1993. Upon assuming power after a palace coup in 1985, Babangida announced that his government would be anchored on respect for the fundamental rights of all Nigerians. He vowed that, unlike his predecessors, he would not preside over a country where individuals are under the fear of expressing themselves and promised that his government would be open and transparent. As part of the new campaign for human rights, some of the repressive laws promulgated by the ousted Buhari regime were immediately repealed. Babangida also cultivated the support of the political class, holding up the promise of an orderly transition to democratic civil rule. By promising a transition to civilian rule, Babangida's government sought to defuse the most potent source of opposition to the regime. This promise enabled the regime to win public support, especially when contrasted with some of the ruthless and repressive policies of the Buhari dictatorship. However, Babangida soon changed the timetable for the transition to democratic rule from 1990 to 1992, stating that more time was needed to create workable democratic structures (Momoh and Adejumobi 1991, 77).

Sensing the strong public opposition to the government's economic austerity measures and the IMF-mandated SAP, Babangida organized a national debate ostensibly to gauge public mood on the government's loan negotiation with the IMF. Many Nigerians welcomed this consultative approach, which was seen as an attempt to elicit the input of citizens in developing a national economic policy. The IMF debates, which were extensively conducted in the press and other public forums, conveyed an unmistakable public antipathy and rejection of the IMF and World Bank conditionalities. In apparent deference to public opinion, Babangida publicly repudiated the IMF and declared that Nigeria would, instead, opt for a 'home grown solution to her economic difficulties' (Olukoshi 1993, 60). However, less than a month later, the government unveiled an economic package including the deregulation of the exchange rate, higher agricultural prices, financial liberalization and partial privatization. Although this package was presented as 'home grown', it was actually negotiated with World Bank officials and premised on supplementary finance from the World Bank (Mosley 1992). Many within the emergent pro-democracy civil society organizations saw Babangida's economic policies as smuggling in World Bank and IMF SAP conditionalities through the back door.

The Babangida regime also came under increasing pressure from civil society groups for the disruptions, manipulations and lack of transparency that characterized the democratic transition process. It was clear from the onset that the government intended to have full control of the electoral process to ensure that the outcome of the democratic transition programme was favourable to the regime. The regime stipulated which political parties could participate in the process and also determined which politicians could contest elections. The terminal date for military rule, which was initially planned for 1990, was altered four times: from 1990 to October 1992, to January 1993 and later, August 1993. Babangida was accused of pursuing a 'hidden agenda' aimed at perpetuating himself and certainly the military in power. In response to Babangida's vacillations on his promise to hand over power, the National Association of Nigerian Students once again mobilized students from tertiary institutions across the country in protest against continued military rule. The government responded by arresting the student leaders and charging them with treason.

The annulment of the 1993 election provoked reactions from all over Nigeria, resulting in the clearest expression of popular resistance to military dictatorship in Nigeria. With the annulment, it became clear to pro-democracy activists that the military regime was unwilling to relinquish power. The political stalemate was compounded by a protracted economic crisis, making it relatively easy for oppositional civil society groups such as the CD to gain mass support. Many sectors of the public, such as students, market women, artisans, teachers and civil servants, enthusiastically supported the CD in its call for protests and resistance to the military. The media was particularly vehement in its criticism of Babangida's 'hidden agenda' and 'unending transition programme'. In response, the government introduced several new laws aimed at stifling the press. These included Decree No. 43 of 1993, which required media organizations to register with a government-owned media board, and the Offensive Publication (Proscription) Decree No. 35 of 1993, which empowered the President to proscribe any media outlet that published any article or news item disruptive of the process of transition to democratic rule. These decrees were specifically targeted at newspapers that were considered critical of the military regime and supportive of the pro-democracy groups. The media responded creatively to these repressive laws by going underground, publishing secretly and adopting the tactics of 'guerrilla journalism'.

The annulment of the 1998 elections also drew strong international condemnation. Babangida, who had enjoyed some goodwill among international organizations and Western countries for his bold implementation of SAPs, faced mounting criticism of his human rights record. The European Union, Commonwealth and some Western nations, including Britain and the United States, condemned the election annulment and demanded an end to military rule. One implication of these developments was a shift in international support from the government to the organized civil society sector as Western governments and donors pushing a 'good governance and democracy' agenda increased funding to civil society organizations. This was a marked foreign policy departure on the part of some Western governments that had previously prioritized economic reform over good governance or democracy (Tar 2009, 84–6). This shift in support further galvanized the pro-democracy groups.

The campaign against military dictatorship took a dramatic turn in July 1993 when the coalition of civil society groups, the Campaign for Democracy, embarked on a three-day nationwide protest strike involving mass demonstrations and public rallies to mount pressure on the military to validate the results of the annulled presidential elections. As Usman Tar has noted, for the first time since independence, these organizations engaged in massive resistance across ethnic, religious and class lines (Ibid., 83). The protests, which brought social and economic life in the country to a standstill, were perhaps the largest grassroots protests in Nigeria's history. Such sustained domestic and international pressure eventually forced Babangida to leave office and hand over power to a civilian-led Interim National Government (ING) headed by a civilian in 1993.

However, the victory archived by pro-democracy forces with the removal of Babangida turned out to be short-lived. The ING was sacked only three months after its inauguration by General Sanni Abacha and replaced by yet another full-blown military dictatorship. The policies embarked upon by the Abacha regime marked a significant setback for democracy in Nigeria. Seeking to consolidate authority and legitimacy within a fragile political environment, the Abacha regime dismantled all existing democratic structures in the country, including the National Assembly, the state and local government apparatus. The regime also introduced new laws to consolidate its hold on power. These included Decree No. 107, which granted absolute power to the Provisional Ruling Council (PRC), as the highest decision-making body of the regime; Decree No. 112 of 1993, which abolished the National Electoral Commission; and Decree No. 11, which granted the Police Inspector General the power to detain citizens indefinitely without trial (Momoh and Adejumobi 1991, 258.) In effect, the Abacha regime retained all the ills of the Babangida era in arbitrariness, retrospective application of laws and the dismantling of judicial review.

The Campaign for Democracy remained at the forefront of the opposition movement against the Abacha dictatorship and demanding a return to democratic civilian rule (Campaign for Democracy 1994). Two major labour unions in the oil sectors and affiliates of CD played a crucial role in mobilizing workers in the pro-democracy struggle. Leveraging their influence in the key oil sector of the Nigerian economy, the National Union of Petroleum and Natural Gas Workers Union (NUPENG) and the Petroleum and Natural Gas Senior Staff Association (PENGASSAN) embarked on a nationwide strike that paralyzed economic activity of the country for nearly two months. In justifying the strike by his union and its role in the national political crisis, the President of NUPENG, Wariebe Aganeme, remarked:

> It is the duty of all patriots and all forces of progress across the country to join NUPENG in the historic role it finds itself playing. Certainly, the only way forward is to combine all forces of progress to chase away the military in Nigerian politics.
>
> *(Guardian 1994)*

Abacha's reaction to the economic impasse was the dissolution of the unions and the arrest of its leaders.

The period 1995 to 1998 saw a rise in human rights abuses through state terrorism as the Abacha regime sought to suppress the growing pro-democracy movement. Local and international human rights organizations reported assassinations and frequent incidents of attack against pro-democracy activists in the form of arbitrary arrests, detention without trial, prevention from travelling out of the country, seizure of passports or disruption of meetings by security agents. Kudirat Abiola, the wife of Moshood Abiola, the presumed winner of the annulled 1993 elections and one of the leading figures in the pro-democracy movement, was assassinated in 1996. The environmental rights activist Ken Saro Wiwa was executed by the regime in 1995. The insecurity and lack of safety led many pro-democracy activists to flee the country. The sudden death of Abacha eventually paved the way for the end of two decades of military rule and the return to democratic civilian rule in 1999.

Assessing the pro-democracy movement

As in many parts of post-colonial Africa, military intervention in Nigerian politics has impeded the establishment of a stable democracy and has resulted in citizen disengagement from governance. While successive military regimes promised quick transition to democratic civilian rule soon after they assumed power, this was often not the case. Rather, the promise of democratic transition programmes was a means by which military regimes sought to legitimize and extend their rule. By the 1990s, civil society groups had become familiar with this trend and became increasingly impatient with military regimes and promises of democratic transitions. Their concerted efforts not only galvanized popular opposition against military rule but also instituted a tradition of pro-democracy activism that would endure beyond the era of military rule.

The question is often asked why the 1990s marked a defining moment in the emergence of organized civil society opposition to military rule. The reason for the failure of democracy in Nigeria in the immediate post-colonial era was not the absence of a civil society sector but the poor organization of that sector. In the 1990s, civil society was awakened because of several economic and political challenges confronting the state and government policies aimed at addressing them. First among these was the pervasive economic crisis which imposed hardships on the everyday lives of ordinary Nigerians and raised the restiveness of the civil population. A second critical challenge was the weakness of the state arising from pervasive corruption, the failure of development efforts, abuses of power and the use of repression to assert control, which weakened the legitimacy and hold of the state and exposed it to challenges. The third challenge was the imposition of the SAP, which worsened the economic crisis and exacerbated public discontent with the government. The fourth and perhaps most decisive challenge that awakened civil society opposition was the disingenuous democratic transition programme culminating in the annulment of the 1993 presidential elections. This generated a considerable upsurge in civil society activism by radicalizing many civil society groups, including some labour unions that had historically been apolitical.

Scholars of Nigerian politics have offered various readings of the political developments in the country during this period with regard to the increased role that civil society groups came to play in the democratic transition process. Carl Levan argues that these events created a new 'opportunity structure' with sustained and often informal changes to the political environment that generated incentives for collective action. For the rulers of Nigeria's second wave of dictatorships, the cost of coercion increased and public participation became riskier. For civil society organizations, the opportunity structure brought new resources and avenues for activism (Levan 2011, 141). As the government responded with repression, they linked economic grievances to broader political demands. This was when civil society groups articulated their claims, starting from the student protest of 1989, and sought to maintain their autonomy from the state. The developments in Nigeria also appear to follow a pattern which Robert Fatton identifies in his analysis of civil society in African politics in 'the age of democratization'. As Fatton argues:

The state penetrates civil society through multiple economic interventions, its disciplinary regulations of private behaviour and its ideological interpellations. The state aspires to become totalitarian because ruling classes are predators bent on maximizing their supremacy; they seek therefore a complete appropriation of civil society.

(1995, 67)

As in Nigeria, civil society in turn penetrates the state through the erection of protective trenches against coercive abuse and through protest and rejection to challenge the hegemony of power based on government pronouncements and policies.

This relationship between the state and civil society mirrors Gramscian analysis of the relation between power and hegemony. The strength and tenacity of civil society manifested in the organization of widespread protests against structural adjustment policies between 1988 and 1990. The activities of civil society maintained the challenge and pressure for democratization throughout the 1980s and 1990s. The political struggle embarked upon by the pro-democracy civil society organization such as the Campaign for Democracy following the annulment of the 1993 elections questioned the political legitimacy of military rule in Nigeria. Although this struggle did not lead to the reinstatement of the election outcome, it resulted in the removal of Ibrahim Babangida, the dictator behind the cancellation. This unprecedented victory of civil society groups in forcing a dictator out of office shattered the myth of the invincibility Nigeria's Generals had woven around themselves for three decades.

A major factor in the success of the civil society struggle against military dictatorship was the effective organization of the pro-democracy campaign. There was an evident unity of purpose among all the groups that came together to form the CD, which enabled the organization to enhance political mobilization that led to the subsequent termination of military rule. Another factor of success was the commitment of the leadership of the civil society organizations that constituted the CD. These included lawyers, former student leaders and journalists who were well-grounded in the theoretical and practical framework of community activism and popular democratic struggle. Drawing inspiration from the success stories in other parts of the African continent, such as South Africa's African National Congress (ANC) and its anti-apartheid struggle, they were both strategic and uncompromising in their quest to return the country to democratic rule. With the support of Western governments and donors committed to promoting 'democracy and good governance' in a post-Cold War Africa, civil society groups were able to articulate and push a comprehensive agenda which raised broader national questions on federalism, resource control and transparency in governance. The government's attempts to discredit pro-democracy groups by pointing to the Western donor support they received were largely ineffectual.

Despite its successes, however, civil society activism does have some shortcomings. Soon after the return of civilian rule, the civil society organizations seemed to abruptly abandon the struggle to institutionalize democracy in the country, apparently in the mistaken belief that the battle had already been won. These groups have been unwilling or unable to extend their activism beyond opposition to military dictatorship to the civilian dispensation. They have not been effective in raising new issues about democratic reform and social change such as transparency, accountability, participation and responsiveness. Under civilian rule, civil society groups have not played the same critical oppositional and watchdog role that they played so effectively under military rule. If anything, these organizations have become complacent and have tended to associate too closely with the ruling regimes such that crucial civil society constituencies risk being co-opted into the apparatus to state power. Some of the organizations that formed part of the civil society coalition against military rule have become less focused on pro-democracy campaigns. Many of them have transformed into NGOs concerned with self-serving ventures under the slogan of 'democracy and good governance'. This has led to the proliferation of NGOs disconnected from broad-based civil society support. As Falola and Heaton have cautioned:

> the fraternization of state and civil society organizations could lead to complacency on the part of one or both, and the ultimate corruption of civil society organizations, which might over time come to identify more with their partners in government than with their constituent members.
>
> *(1999, 212)*

It is arguable that the Nigerian political space would have witnessed more progress if some of the activists who fought for the termination of military rule had carried on with constructive criticism of civilian leaders. They could have been more effective and responsive to the challenges of good governance and the growing calls for political reforms based on true federalism. One fallout of the diminished pro-democratic role of civil society organization since the country's return to democratic rule in 1999 is that the call for a Sovereign National Conference to address political reforms has waned, as the elected officials in government see a National Conference as a threat to their own legitimacy and claim to power. To this extent, civil society groups have largely failed to act as a conduit for promoting good governance and mobilizing the populace towards a citizen-based democracy. There has been a lack of continuity from grassroots action and coalition-building that characterized the opposition movement against military dictatorship.

Conclusion

The object of this chapter has been to examine the prominent roles played by civil society organizations towards democratization in Nigeria. We have argued that the democratic struggle in Nigeria was influenced by internal and external factors in terms of authoritarian state and the aberration of military rule, IMF and World

Bank-inspired neoliberal economic policies, mass protest engineered by the civil society and, in the long run, external democratic intervention. The growth of civic action can be traced back to the anti-military rule sentiment that grew out of excessive state repression and failed economic policies. This action effectively ended three decades of military rule in Nigeria. In 2009, Nigeria celebrated ten years of uninterrupted civilian rule, marking the longest uninterrupted stretch of civil democratic rule in the country's history. This is the legacy of civil society organizing and action. However, we have also argued that the constructive role of civil society groups in the pro-democracy struggle in Nigerian politics has been intermittent. Once the assumed mission of ending military rule was accomplished, pro-democratic civil society groups disintegrated or retreated into isolation. The consequence is that, although civilian democratic rule has been established in the country, democratic institutions and cultures remain weak as evidenced by the continued lack of transparency in governance, the prevalence of corruption and the persistence of electoral fraud. Under these circumstances, neoliberal economic policies that largely benefit the political elites and their business associates have flourished. Democracy, or at least a semblance of it, has been won, but economic reform aimed at alleviating the living conditions of ordinary Nigerians and protecting their human rights, which the pro-democracy movement promised, remains elusive.

References

Adeniyi-Ogunyankin, Grace. 2012. When Will I Get My Rest? Neo-liberalism, Women, Class and Ageing in Ibadan, Nigeria. *Agenda* 24(6): 29–36.

Agenda for Democracy. 1990. *The National Conference*. Lagos: The National Consultative Forum.

Ahmad, Khan. 1994. *The Political Economy of Oil-Exporting* Countries. Oxford: Oxford University Press.

Aiyede, Remi. 2003. The Dynamics of Civil Society and the Democratization Process in Nigeria. *Canadian Journal of African Studies* 37(1): 1–27.

Anifowose, Remi.1982. *Violence and Politics in Nigeria*. New York: Nok Publishers.

Campaign for Democracy. 1991. Declaration and Objectives, Press Conference, Lagos, 11 November.

Campaign for Democracy. 1994 *Beyond Abacha and the Constitutional Conference*. Lagos: Campaign for Democracy.

Falola, Toyin and Heaton, Matthew. 1999. *History of Nigeria*. Westport: Greenwood Press.

Fatton, Robert 1995. Africa in the Age of Democratization: The Civic Limitations of Civil Society. *African Studies Review* 38(2): 67–99.

González, David and Baró, Silvio. 2006. The Scourge of Neo-Liberalism in Africa and the Middle East. *Review of African Political Economy* 33(109): 577–80.

Guardian. 1994. 11 July, 11.

Hilary, John. 2010. Africa: Dead Aid and the Return of Neoliberalism. *Race & Class* 52(2): 79–84.

Ibhawoh, Bonny. 2003. The Promise of Constitutionalism and the Challenge of Militarism: Constraints and Possibilities of the Human Rights Movement in Nigeria. *Democracy and Development: Journal of West African Affairs*. 3(2): 16–36.

IMF Independent Evaluation Office. 2009a. *IMF Involvement in International Trade Policy Issues*. Washington, DC, International Monetary Fund.

IMF Independent Evaluation Office. 2009b. *IMF Involvement in Trade Policy Issues in Low-Income Countries: Seven Case Studies*. Washington, DC, International Monetary Fund Section E.

Levan, Carl. 2011. Questioning Tocqueville in Africa: Continuity and Change in Civil Society During Nigeria's Democratization. *Democratization* 18(1): 135–59.

Momoh, Abubakar and Adejumobi, Said. 1991. *The Nigerian Military and the Crisis of Democratic Transition: A Study in the Monopoly of Power*. Lagos: Civil Liberties Organization.

Mosley, Paul. 1992. Policy Making Without Facts: A Note on the Assessment of Structural Policies in Nigeria: 1985–1990. *African Affairs* 91(363): 227–40.

Olorode, Toye. 2001. Demilitarization of the Polity: Tactics and Strategies. In CDHR, *State Reconstruction in West Africa*. Lagos: Rights House Publication.

Olukoshi, Adebayo. 1993. *The Politics of Structural Adjustment in Nigeria*. London: James Curry.

Suberu, Rotimi and Diamond, Larry. 2002. Institutional Design, Ethnic Conflict Management and Democracy in Nigeria. In Reynolds, Andrew (ed.) *The Architecture of Democracy: Constitutional Design, Conflict Management, and Democracy*. Oxford: Oxford University Press.

Tar, Usman. 2009. *The Politics of Neoliberal Democracy in Africa: State and Civic Society in Nigeria*. New York: Taurus Academic Studies.

Walker, Ezekiel. 2000. 'Happy Days Are Here Again': Cocoa Farmers, Middlemen Traders and the Structural Adjustment Program in Southwestern Nigeria, 1986–1990s. *Africa Today* 47(2): 151–69.

Watkins, Kevin (ed.). 1995. *The Oxfam Poverty Report*. Oxford: Oxfam Professional.

Zeleza, Paul. 2004. The Struggle for Human Rights. In Zezela, Paul and McConnaughay, Philip J. (eds) *The Rule of Law and Development in Africa*. Philadelphia: University of Pennsylvania Press.

9

NEOLIBERALISM AND ALTERNATIVE FORMS OF CITIZENSHIP

Amy S. Patterson

In the neoliberal era, when the African state has limited social and economic involvement, nongovernmental organizations (NGOs) and donors make and implement policies, and globalization exposes Africans to a variety of cultural, economic and social pressures, what forms does citizenship take on the continent? I define citizenship to be the rights and responsibilities that individuals have in a political community. While the political community has traditionally been understood as the state, in the alternative forms of citizenship examined in this chapter, this community exists at the local, state and international levels. This chapter asserts that neoliberalism contributed to the rise of alternative forms of citizenship which illustrate people's continued disenchantment with the African state and its ability to address the continent's tangible problems of poverty and underdevelopment. These forms include autochthony, Christian citizenship[1] and therapeutic citizenship among people living with HIV/AIDS (PLHIVs). Unlike citizenship rooted in ethnic identity, which has existed throughout the post-colonial period, these alternative citizenship identities have become salient to Africans (and scholars) since the 1980s. These alternative citizenships challenge liberal citizenship with its assumed protection of rights for all citizens and the accountability of government to all community members.

This chapter proceeds in the following manner. First, it outlines two theoretical perspectives on citizenship – liberal and communal citizenship – and highlights major scholarly findings on citizenship in Africa. Next, it investigates how four components of neoliberalism – market economic reforms, democratization, donors' efforts to 'responsibilize' local populations and globalization – have affected citizenship. Third, the chapter analyses the rise of autochthony, Christian citizenship and therapeutic citizenship. These citizenships are rooted in subnational identities (e.g. HIV status or Christianity) that drive participants' sense of responsibility to people similar to themselves. Citizens in these communities possess rights and responsibilities,

152 A. S. Patterson

but their engagement with state institutions and their participation in promoting the rights of all people may be limited. Finally, the chapter questions the effects of alternative citizenships on the continent's long-term democratization.

Defining citizenship

In a narrow sense, citizenship is a bounded and legal category; the state defines who may be called a citizen and the rights and responsibilities of those individuals within the state's territory (Nyamnjoh 2007). For example, one's place of birth might entitle one to state-protected rights or benefits. While such legal criteria have been incorporated into defining the alternative citizenship form of autochthony, I focus on a broader understanding of citizenship. As a set of rights and responsibilities, citizenship is rooted in the expectations that people in the political community have of one another and that they have for the political community itself (Barbalet 1988, 1). A social contract emerges in which citizens acknowledge political authority embedded in the state and they participate in the political community. In turn, state authorities provide economic, social and security benefits. Thus, citizenship varies with the 'degree and realness of people's affiliation to the state' (Bezabeh 2011, 598). Participation is closely linked to citizenship, since it is an outward manifestation of how people view their relationship with the state. Participation includes activities designed to affect public decision-making and allocation of resources. The analysis below will highlight how alternative citizenship forms are manifested in participatory actions.

Scholars have tended to frame citizenship as either liberal or communal, though the line between these two perspectives is not always distinct. Liberal citizenship embodies the idea that people see themselves as part of a larger political entity, which gives them equal access to social, political and civil rights (Marshall 1964, 74). Liberal citizens claim the right to hold government accountable for rights protection and they participate to enhance or protect these rights. The liberal perspective emphasizes the role of the state in rights provision, and it asserts equal protection of all citizens' rights (Dahl 1972). In communal citizenship, individuals participate because they feel a responsibility to society and they want society to achieve common goals (Oldfield 1990). Communal citizens participate in order to garner benefits for their immediate community, which may be defined in terms of subnational or ascriptive identities (Patterson 1999). Through participation, communal citizens do not seek to claim the right of democratic citizenship, but instead bolster their identity and sense of belonging (Ndegwa 1997).

In post-colonial Africa, citizenship reflects a fluid social contract that may be rooted in historical trajectories. The colonial pattern of decentralized despotism prevented Africans from gaining a sense of allegiance to the state (Mamdani 1996), and the insider–outsider nature of nationalism further undermined liberal citizenship (Dorman *et al.* 2007). In Djibouti, for example, the colonial experience of elite domination has hampered the sovereign state's ability to define a community of citizens (Bezabeh 2011). Citizenship fluidity does not mean that individuals have

Neoliberalism and alternative citizenships **153**

no loyalty to the state. Crawford Young writes that there is a 'remarkable contemporary paradox' of the 'persistence of an affective attachment to a territorial nationality ... even when the state institutions are derelict' (Young 2007, 241). Such nationalism may be an instrumental construct, utilized by elites in order to gain private benefits from the state and to make exit from the state territory more difficult. Yet by seeking legal and material benefits from the state, citizens de facto assert state legitimacy and they reinforce social contract expectations (Englebert 2009, 198).

Citizenship rights and responsibilities are dynamic, with citizenship not being a fixed entity but one that is graduated (Migdal 2006). This dynamism may reflect several factors, two of which I explain. First, individuals' incorporation into decision-making processes influences citizenship: if individuals feel that their rights as members of the community have been acknowledged they then continue to participate to meet their responsibilities (Miller 1995). Second, when the social contract between the state and individuals changes due to economic, social or political factors, notions of citizenship may be altered. For example, when the social contract between the state and Senegalese peasants weakened due to the end of state agricultural benefits with market reforms, rural peasants were less likely to give the state and ruling party their loyal participation (Patterson 1999). The analysis below recognizes that citizenship is driven by material, historical and cultural variables, and it does not discount the idea that citizens feel some allegiance to the state. In fact, their participation through alternative citizenships revolves around new visions of the state. If they had no attachment to the state, why would they bother to re-imagine it?

There is very little research on the factors that contribute to a citizenship that respects political equality, protects all individuals' rights and urges participation to foster state accountability. On the one hand, Michael Bratton and Carolyn Logan (2013) find that individuals are more likely to hold leaders accountable if they have knowledge about the political system and their role as citizens within that system. This finding suggests that grassroots citizenship education efforts have an important function. On the other hand, Satu Riutta (2009, 139) discovers that, while voter education programmes in Zambia and Tanzania promote knowledge and interest in politics, particularly among marginalized citizens, they do not boost citizen efficacy, trust in politicians or collective participation. And Robert Mattes and Carlos Shenga (2013) argue that poverty remains an obstacle in the development of an active citizenry. None of these examinations, however, investigates alternative citizenship identities that shape public participation but are not necessarily liberal in orientation. Additionally, none of these studies investigates how neoliberalism might provide openings for alternative citizenship forms.

Neoliberalism and space for alternative forms of citizenship

Neoliberalism encompasses 'techniques of government that work through the creation of responsibilized citizen-subjects' who are mobilized to 'produce

154 A. S. Patterson

governmental results that do not depend on direct state intervention' (Ferguson 2009, 172). As a philosophy, neoliberalism relies on non-state actors – markets, NGOs and individuals – to foster development and good governance. In this section, I focus on four components of neoliberalism – market reforms, democratization, donors' emphasis on the responsibilization of local people and globalization. My goal in this section is not to critique these processes, but rather to demonstrate how they changed the nature of the relationship between citizens and the state and created openings for alternative forms of citizenship.

Market reforms

Despite continent-wide annual growth rates of 2.4 per cent during the 1960s, Africa suffered economic stagnation and decline in the 1970s and 1980s. Growth rates diminished to 0.9 per cent per year during the 1970s, and average incomes declined 1.1 per cent annually during the 1980s (Moss 2007, 89–90). Because of corruption, loose lending policies at the World Bank and International Monetary Fund, and Cold War calculations that led superpowers to loan large sums to their allies, African debt soared. By the mid-1990s, it was nearly $200 billion (Moss 2007, 151). With the election of conservative governments in the United Kingdom and United States in 1979 and 1981 respectively, global lenders began to insist on macroeconomic restructuring in return for loans to African states. These market reforms (or 'structural adjustment policies') included privatization of state-owned enterprises, austerity measures that cut spending on health and education and instituted user fees, trade and investment liberalization, currency devaluation and disinvestment from agriculture.

These policies had many effects, but I will focus on four outcomes that directly relate to citizenship. First, when the state receded from social service provision it left a void that other actors filled. As Nicolas van de Walle (2001) asserts, the post-structural adjustment state resembled the colonial state, with non-state actors such as international and local NGOs and faith-based organizations (FBOs) becoming major social service providers. In Zambia, for example, community schools took the place of government schools, as religious institutions and NGOs constructed classrooms, hired teachers and developed curricula. The new actors competed with the state for resources and legitimacy, as illustrated by the fact that AIDS NGOs and faith-based health associations increasingly competed with the African state for AIDS funding (Patterson 2011). The rise of new service providers led to citizen perceptions that the state was no longer upholding the post-colonial, social contract in which it provided jobs and basic services. The inability of the state to meet these obligations led citizens to re-examine their own role in the social contract (Patterson 1999).

Second, market reforms indirectly contributed to urbanization, since they cut investments in agriculture. This made it more difficult for rural inhabitants to survive. Between 1980 and 2000, global financial assistance to agriculture declined from $6.2 billion to $2.3 billion, leading to a decline in agriculture production.

Despite the fact that agriculture drives 40 per cent of Africa's GDP, agricultural productivity remains low and food insecurity and hunger are huge problems in rural areas (Poku and Mdee 2011, 55–6). In response to these challenges, peasants have flocked to cities; by 2012, 37 per cent of people in sub-Saharan Africa lived in urban areas (World Bank 2014). As scenes of isolation, violence, uncertainty and predation by state and non-state actors, urban environments present challenges to migrants and erode their sense of belonging and obligation to the political community. Without state assistance (or kinship networks found in rural communities), uncertain migrants look for new groups which will provide them with a sense of belonging and material security.

Many urban migrants work in the informal economy, or those income-generating activities outside the realm of state regulation. For example, 70 per cent of people in urban compounds in Lusaka, Zambia work in the informal economy (Resnick 2011). While the informal economy may bring income accumulation and economic inclusion to some individuals, it does not benefit everyone (Kinyanjui 2013; Lyons *et al.* 2013). More broadly, the informal economy further pulls people from the social contract with the state, as the very objective of the informal economy is to operate outside of state control. When the state encroaches in the informal economy, it is often in predatory ways (e.g. demands for bribes from policemen or requirements by health inspectors for food safety certificates from vendors). These actions further push individuals from a citizenship that emphasizes rights and obligations in relation to the state (Englebert 2009).

Finally, the ways in which market reforms were decided and implemented shaped citizens' relationship with the state. African elites, unlike Asian or Latin American elites, never fully accepted structural adjustment. Yet, while these elites publicly blamed donors for painful market policies, they did not engage in inclusive public discussions to generate new visions for development (van de Walle 2001). Such inclusion could have reinforced the relationship between the state and citizens. Instead, citizens perceived that state officials benefited from market reforms such as privatization, and that these reforms have been accompanied by greater economic inequality (Englebert 2009). Market reforms have isolated ordinary citizens from the state and made them disillusioned with the social contract. New actors and identities have emerged in the state's place, shaping alternative visions of citizenship.

Democratization

Over two decades ago, the 'third wave' of democracy swept across Africa (Huntington 1991), pushed by civil society groups such as labour unions and student organizations that pointed out the corruption and illegitimacy of one-party states and donor demands for multi-party elections (Bratton and van de Walle 1997). Between 1989 and 1995, regimes showed rapid democratic improvements; they re-wrote constitutions, instituted multi-party elections and allowed freedom of the press, assembly and speech. In 1990, Freedom House reported that only four

African countries were classified as 'free', while ten were 'partly free' and 32 were 'not free'. By 2011, eight countries were classified as 'free', 22 were 'partly free' and 19 were 'not free' (Harbeson 2013, 90). In these free and partly free states, Africans participate in multi-party elections, and civil society organizations that work on development, human rights, good governance and humanitarian relief emerged. Democracy saw the rise of private media – newspapers, radio and the internet – that debated a host of political, social and economic issues (Gyimah-Boadi 2004). As I illustrate below, alternative citizenships took advantage of these political openings.

Despite this progress, new democracies faced challenges. First, democratization appears to have been a unique moment between 1989 and 1995: of the countries that democratized during that period, 90 per cent remained democratic in 2011 (Peiffer and Englebert 2012), while more recent democratizers have stagnated or reversed their democratic progress. Second, new democracies lacked strong formal institutions to foster political equality and government accountability. For example, multi-party elections were instituted in several countries, but defining who got to participate in these elections was often left up to patrimonial leaders with informal decision-making power (Whitaker 2005). Power centralization and weak rule of law prevent the consolidation of democracy (Diamond 1999; Gyimah-Boadi 2004).

A third limitation is corruption. Afrobarometer (2013) found that 56 per cent of people surveyed in 16 countries said their governments were doing a poor job of fighting corruption. (The country percentages ranged from 82 per cent in Nigeria to 28 per cent in Malawi.) Additionally, 30 per cent of respondents reported having to pay a bribe at least once during the last year, and poor people were more likely than middle- and upper-class individuals to pay a bribe. These statistics illustrate the weak social contract between the state and citizens and the lack of political equality. If some citizens (the poor) must pay a bribe to access education for a child or to receive police protection, then the state is not protecting all citizens' rights. Corruption makes citizens feel limited obligations to the state, decreasing the state's legitimacy. More broadly, since people's sense of citizenship obligations and rights are shaped by their incorporation into political decision-making, ineffective and exclusionary democracy can undermine citizens' affinity to the state.

Responsibilization

With the decline in state-led development and the rise of political liberties, bilateral and multilateral donors have turned to NGOs and FBOs to foster development. The neoliberal logic asserts that these non-state actors are less political, more efficient, more technically competent and less corrupt than African state institutions. For example, the US President's Emergency Plan for AIDS Relief (PEPFAR) has worked primarily through American NGOs and FBOs and their local African partners to implement programmes (Patterson 2006). As a result of donors' shift from the state, there has been an explosion in the number of international and local NGOs and FBOs working in Africa since the 1980s (Hearn 2002; Dorman 2005).

Part of the neoliberal logic has been to emphasize the 'responsibilization' of local people. Responsibilization is defined as empowering local people through training, skill development, knowledge sharing and/or provision of start-up capital for income-generating programmes. Donors assert that responsibilization is essential for sustainability in development, since it enables community members to address local problems using grassroots solutions (Ferguson 2009, 174). Responsibilization is viewed to be a tool through which sustainability can emerge. Scholars have pointed out that responsibilization emphasizes technical solutions which may ignore aspects of power embedded in the development processes. Additionally, these technical approaches may exacerbate power differentials and income inequalities in communities (Ferguson 1990). Training programmes, for example, give some citizens more power and authority, and open up opportunities to gain material resources such as per diems and transport refunds (Smith 2003). More broadly, reliance on local people to solve large structural problems, such as unemployment and poor governance, downplays the complex challenges of underdevelopment (Swidler and Watkins 2009).

The focus on responsibilization has two contradictory effects for citizenship identity and participation. On the one hand, through its focus on the individual, this discourse has the potential to foster liberal citizenship and political equality, or a citizenship that values each person's participation and weighs that participation equally. Through educating citizens, responsibilization also may give citizens the knowledge and skills needed to participate effectively in politics. Many voter education efforts are rooted in this belief. On the other hand, since the framework celebrates individual skill development and empowerment, it contributes to a growing sense among Africans that individualistic goals and actions are eroding community norms. Responsibilization may lead select people to economically benefit while others do not. Resulting income inequalities may erode perceptions of the common good (Smith 2014). As illustrated below, these negative aspects may be observed in some types of Christian citizenship that focus on individual prosperity, not social justice.

Globalization

Neoliberalism is intricately tied to globalization, which I define as the political, economic and social integration of the world's people. Globalization has had several outcomes for citizenship in Africa. First, it opened up African economies to foreign investment and trade, making it difficult for African products (particularly textiles) to compete with Chinese products in either the global or the African market (Taylor 2009). This fact contributed to urban unemployment, heightened personal insecurities and led to the sense that the state did not care about the social contract. Alternative citizenships emerged in response. Second, globalization has brought increased investment to Africa from new sources, such as China, Saudi Arabia, Brazil and diaspora communities (Moss 2013), making Africa host to entrepreneurs and workers from around the world. For example, over one million Chinese now live in Africa (French 2014). As I illustrate with autochthonous citizenship, cross-border migration raises questions about who is a citizen.

Third, the demand for labour (and particularly, skilled workers) in the post-industrial world has pushed Africans to migrate, a phenomenon that has raised dilemmas about legal citizenship requirements for African states. Many African migrants want to exercise participatory rights as dual citizens. In response, many African states have extended citizenship to nationals living abroad, even as they have become more exclusive in their definitions of citizenship at home. States have recognized that migrants bring remittances, skills, ideas and investment to the home country. Emigrants also are increasingly involved in homeland politics, and African politicians may need them in order to generate support and funding for their campaigns (Whitaker 2011). Globalization's opportunities for migration facilitate new ways of understanding the legal boundaries of citizenship.

Fourth, the tools of globalization such as air travel, the internet and social networking sites have facilitated global networks around a host of issues. These networks have contributed to social mobilization and alternative views of citizenship that are not centred on the state. For example, global Pentecostalism and the spread of Prosperity Gospel from African-American churches to Africa shape the political participation and citizenship views of some African Christians (Jenkins 2007). Similarly, rights-based activism among PLHIVs in Africa has been informed by interactions with Western AIDS activists (Nguyen 2010). Global processes may cause individuals to view themselves to be global citizens whose identities are not bounded by territorial lines. In sum, globalization may cause individuals to question their rights and obligations to the state and the ability of the state to meet the social contract. In response, they may embrace new citizenship forms.

Alternative forms of citizenship

In this section, I examine the rise of three citizenship identities and their influences on participation in the public realm. I assert that these have influenced the relationship between the state and individuals, making citizenship less about protecting the rights of all people within a sovereign state territory and more about achieving benefits for a select group in society. In the final section, I will question what these alternative identities and forms of participation mean for the continent's long-term democratization.

Autochthony

Literally meaning 'emerging from the soil' and thus implying local forms of belonging, autochthony refers to the phenomena of individuals who claim an indisputable historical link to a particular territory. As a means of distinguishing those 'who belong' from 'newcomers' or 'outsiders', autochthony has become a crucial form of identity that drives political participation in several African states. Autochthony is socially constructed, with the objective of excluding some while benefiting others.

As a way of defining citizenship, these 'tales of origin' assert that some groups should have inalienable rights to participation and state-provided resources such as land or employment, while others are excluded from these rights and benefits (Boås 2009, 20).

Autochthonous citizens do not ignore the state. Rather, they propose an alternative vision for the state, not as an entity that promotes political equality but as one that upholds the social contract for a select group of individuals, the autochthons (as this group defines the term). As such, they strive to foster state policies to promote this vision. In several African countries, elites have used autochthony to manipulate legal definitions of citizenship for political benefit. In the Democratic Republic of Congo, for example, citizenship rights were extended to Rwandophones (Hutu and Tutsi migrants originally from Rwanda) in eastern Congo in 1964 if they were a member of a tribe or part of a tribe that had been in the Congo territory before 1908. This policy excluded many people from citizenship since a large number of Rwandophones had arrived during the 1930s. In 1971, legislation extended citizenship to people who had been in the Congo since independence in 1960 or who had parents who met this criterion. This inclusive change was resented by many Congolese. In 1981, when then President Mobutu Sese Seko no longer needed Rwandophones' political support, he changed the law so that citizenship required that a person's ancestors had been in the Congolese territory from 1885. At the country's 1991 National Conference, organized ostensibly to guide a democratic transition, Rwandophones were further excluded (Jackson 2007).

Autochthony also was justification for manipulation of citizenship laws in Côte d'Ivoire in the 1990s. At the country's independence, ethnicity was not mentioned in Ivoirian law, and migrants from other West African states were welcomed during the 1960s and 1970s, as their labour was needed in cocoa production. They were allowed to own land, and naturalization into Ivoirian citizenship was relatively easy (Englebert 2009). As the country began to democratize in the early 1990s, and as it faced greater competition for land, jobs and economic resources, autochthony became politically salient. International labour migration contributed to questions about who belongs and who should be given rights. A 1994 legal reform required that the President be born in Côte d'Ivoire to parents who were also born in the country. The law was a direct attempt to exclude the northern presidential candidate Allassane Ouattara, whose father was born in Burkina Faso. A 1998 land law stripped land ownership from anyone who could not prove Ivoirité (autochthony in Ivoirian territory). A 2002 law required identity cards; 'non-citizens', people of foreign descent and urban dwellers who could not demonstrate a village of origin were stripped of economic and political rights.

Autochthony as citizenship, and laws that instituted that narrative, have led to wars and violence, as evidenced by conflicts in Côte d'Ivoire, Democratic Republic of Congo and Liberia. Richard Banégas said the Ivoirian civil war (2002–07) was 'about the rights that are conferred by possession of a national identity document' (Banégas 2006, 537). Yet even in countries without large-scale conflicts, autochthony has driven local-level violence. Scott Straus (2012) reports an increase in the number of low-level conflicts since 1990, many rooted in competition over scarce resources (such as water and fertile land) and divisions about who legitimately can access these limited resources. In Cameroon, Nigeria and Kenya, 'indigeneity' and one's ability to prove a long-time 'rootedness' in a community have led to increased competition over government positions, educational opportunities and land. These identities have also mobilized people to participate in politics, as voters, political party members and/or violence perpetrators (Englebert 2009; Dercon and Gutiérrez-Romero 2012; Geschiere 2009).

Neoliberalism has contributed to autochthonous citizenship. Periods of political and economic transitions have often led to questions about citizenship and the rise of legal measures that exclude some individuals over others (Jackson 2007). In the post-Cold War era when African state leaders have felt internal and external pressures to democratize and adopt market economic reforms, legal efforts to exclude the 'outsider' have become more common (Manby 2009). Economic changes, such as cuts in state services and increased unemployment due to privatization, lessened state legitimacy; in response, state elites used autochthony to galvanize support. Similarly, as countries began to hold multi-party elections, candidates needed ways to distinguish themselves. Incumbents often could not run on records of economic success given their countries' high rates of poverty and unemployment, and market economic reforms often limited access to patronage resources. These constraints led political elites to turn to the politics of identity, heightening autochthonous citizenship. Excluding 'foreigners' from the political process had political benefits, particularly if those foreigners might support the opposition.

Neoliberalism's focus on responsibilized individuals who work at the local level to foster development also provided openings for autochthonous citizenship. Responsibilization did not require community members to work across lines of class, race, ethnicity or historical background. In fact, by ignoring local power dynamics as they implemented technical solutions, donors who 'responsibilize' local populations may empower some people (such as autochthons) over others. Local elites may gain decision-making power and resources, and these elites may manipulate definitions about 'who belongs' to exclude others. In the process, claims to 'indigeneity' trump a liberal citizenship rooted in political equality and rights for all (Geschiere 2009).

Globalization also contributes to autochthony. While autochthony is a return to the local, it is also a global phenomenon. Efforts to exclude the stranger are evident in the rise of the New Right Party in Dutch politics, South African xenophobia against Zimbabwean migrants, US congressional calls to 'build a wall' along the US–Mexico border and violence against ethnic Chinese in Vietnam. Paradoxically, as the world becomes more connected economically, politically and culturally as a result of the neoliberal agenda, 'an obsession with belonging' has emerged (Geschiere 2009, 6). Concerns that globalization, with its accompanying migration and consumerism, will lead to the loss of cultures and languages trickle down to influence local and state policies, as well as citizens' attitudes and participation.

Christian citizenship

Religion is highly salient in Africa. A Gallup poll (2007) found that religious organizations are the most trusted institutions on the continent, with 76 per cent of respondents having confidence in them. Afrobarometer (2009) reported that 93 per cent of Burundians, 94 per cent of Ugandans, 95 per cent of Kenyans and 92 per cent of Namibians said that religion was 'somewhat or very important' to them. In many countries, majorities of Africans also report that they turn to religious leaders for help with a variety of personal, material and political problems. Michael Bratton and Wonbin Cho (2006, 38) write that even decades after independence, 'organized religion looms much larger in the life [*sic*] of ordinary Africans than the apparatus of the state'.

In this section, I focus on Christianity in Africa, since Christianity is the continent's dominant religion. An estimated 57 per cent of Africans are Christian, while 29 per cent are Muslim and 13 per cent practise a traditional religion (Patterson 2011). Christianity has also tended to have a more pronounced public role in politics than Islam or African Traditional Religions (Freston 2001; Gifford 1995). I pay special attention to Pentecostalism, a branch of Christianity in which adherents stress a literal reading of the Bible, emphasize spiritual experiences such as speaking in tongues and highlight their personal conversion experiences. Roughly 12 per cent of Africans identify as Pentecostals, with this Christian grouping having more than 100 million African adherents in 2006 (Pew Forum 2006).

To analyse Christian citizenship in Africa, it is crucial to move beyond what Kevin O'Neill (2009) terms the 'pedagogical paradigm' in which Christianity is viewed as simply a tool in the development of citizenship. The paradigm posits that Christianity is a private force that teaches character, skills and knowledge for liberal citizenship. It is assumed that when Christian organizations act in the public sphere, they resemble any other civil society group, using power rooted in material resources to affect outcomes. In Africa (and much of the Global South), the pedagogical paradigm is incomplete because spiritual power is often viewed as an alternative to political power and because the line between the private and the public realms is murky. In Africa, politics is closely bound with religious beliefs and religious institutions and believers engage the public sphere using moral power, spiritual resources and material tools (Ellis and ter Haar 1998; Jenkins 2007).

Christians have always seen themselves as citizens of the Kingdom of God, with the right to identify with the Kingdom of God being accompanied by responsibilities to uphold Christ's teachings.

This view colours Christian views on citizenship in several ways. First, because all Christians are believed to belong to the Kingdom of God, African Christians look beyond a state-defined citizenship, developing unity with Christians worldwide and a sense of belonging that crosses state borders. Thus, while the vast majority of Christians do not deny state authority, they also see citizenship as multilayered. Second, the fact that they have a common citizenship identity with all Christians may lead African believers to pursue communal citizenship to the

162 A. S. Patterson

exclusion of those who are not like them. They may associate only with Christians (or more specifically, some types of Christians), a phenomenon most apparent among Pentecostals (Gusman 2013), or they may be guided by narrow interests that contribute to structural violence, favouritism and patronage (Gifford 2009; Longman 2010). In the process, protecting the rights of all and promoting political equality may be lost.

Third, when Christians, and particularly Pentecostals, participate in politics, they view their political participation to be an extension of their faith, not separate from it. It is not that faith causes political action; rather, faith and action are inseparable (Gusman 2013). Fourth, when pastors and lay leaders become involved in politics, they stress biblical reasons for their involvement, such as restoring holiness to the nation or extending God's kingdom to earth. These objectives may drive a moralistic focus in politics, particularly for Pentecostals; for example, they may strive to end corruption and impunity for individual politicians and they may seek to elect 'God's people'. These actions are a reaction to the limits of Africa's democratic transitions. These objectives tend to be focused on the individual level, and they do not provide a structural critique of politics (Ranger 2008). Fifth, because the spiritual and material worlds intertwine, actions that some may define as private practices are often considered by Christians to be public acts of participation, intended to influence political outcomes. For example, when Ghana Airways was about to declare bankruptcy, Ghanaian Pentecostal pastors held an all-night prayer vigil in hopes of saving the state-owned enterprise. For them, prayer was a political act (Asamoah-Gyadu 2005).

Aspects of neoliberalism create openings for Christian citizenship. As market reforms led the state to provide fewer services, religious institutions filled this gap. While the mainline Protestant and Catholic churches have provided health and education services since the colonial era, Pentecostal churches have become more active in these areas (Miller and Yamamori 2007). In Zambia, for example, the first support groups for church congregants living with HIV/AIDS emerged in the Northmead Assemblies of God Church in Lusaka in the early 2000s. The church then developed an AIDS treatment clinic, HIV prevention campaigns, a school for AIDS orphans and income generation programmes for women living with HIV (Patterson 2011). These programmes were particularly crucial for urban migrants, who sought a form of belonging in an uncertain environment. Social services have made the church – not the state – a crucial actor in the daily struggles of Africans. Church involvement in service delivery also drew religious individuals and institutions into policymaking (e.g. for many years, the Northmead pastor sat on Zambia's National AIDS Council), a phenomenon that gave believers even more opportunity to shape politics.

Democratization created opportunities for Christian citizenship. Individuals who publicly identify as Christians have founded political parties (e.g. Nevers Mumba and the National Christian's Coalition in Zambia) and competed for electoral office (e.g. Olusegun Obasanjo in Nigeria). Christian organizations have lobbied for specific religious clauses in constitutions (e.g. the Evangelical Fellowship

Neoliberalism and alternative citizenships **163**

of Zambia and the country's 'Christian nation' clause) and advocated for government policies to promote religious education in Ghana and Kenya (Ranger 2008; Freston 2001). Additionally, as democratization brought media freedoms, churches bought radio stations and gained TV access, all arenas in which church leaders could not only share religious messages but also pray for the nation and preach against corruption and public immorality. Pentecostal pastors astutely used these venues, which capitalized on these leaders' charismatic and energetic worship styles (Kalu 2008). More recently, email newsletters, Facebook and Twitter have helped to mobilize congregants to support particular candidates or policy positions. For example, Ugandan Pentecostal pastor Martin Ssempa used television appearances and the internet to mobilize Ugandans to support the country's 2014 anti-homosexuality legislation (Ssempa 2014).

Responsibilization also facilitated Christian citizenship, particularly for Pentecostals whose theology has a more individualistic focus. (Responsibilization aligns less with traditional Catholic and mainline Protestant theologies which have stressed social justice and Christian community. This pattern may be changing, though, as these denominations are influenced by Pentecostalism. See Kalu 2008.) Pentecostals stress the individual believer's religious conversion, his or her relationship with Christ and his or her behaviour, just as responsibilization focuses on empowering the individual for development. As one Pentecostal variant, Prosperity Gospel, a theology predominant in many large urban Pentecostal churches, emphasizes, if individuals have enough faith, God will give them material blessings such as a job, a visa for travel to the United States, a promotion, a spouse, a baby or admission to university (Gifford 2004). Like the discourse of responsibilization, Prosperity Gospel ignores structural variables that may prevent one from gaining these benefits. When material benefits do not appear, it is because the believer lacks sufficient faith, not because of poverty, poor education or the global economic structure. This theology makes it possible for some churches and leaders to ignore growing economic inequality in Africa, since it is assumed that economic benefits have come to some believers (and pastors) because of faith not because of patronage, political connections or economic structures. In reality, some churches may gain state patronage to benefit their members, a process that increases the power of pastors (who are non-elected public figures) and reinforces a narrow and individualistic citizenship identity (Maxwell 2000). The rise of such individualized empowerment and belief may undermine citizenship rights and the state's obligations in the social contract.

Finally, globalization has had two contrasting effects on Christian citizenship. On the one hand, it has enabled African Christians to interact with Christians worldwide. For example, many Pentecostal congregations belong to national-level evangelical councils and the World Evangelical Alliance, both of which provide resources and connections to support local ministries. Large Pentecostal churches also have developed ties to individual congregations in the United States, as well as theological schools such as the Moody Bible Institute in Chicago, Illinois. These connections advance the view that Christian citizenship is global, a perspective which makes individual believers view their rights and responsibilities not solely in relation to the state. On the other hand, globalization has exposed African Christians to Western media images and consumer goods, a fact that threatens some Christians and drives them to increase their participation in politics to promote 'moral virtues' against these Western influences.

Therapeutic citizenship

At the same time that Africa underwent a move to neoliberalism, the HIV/AIDS crisis hit the continent. The first AIDS deaths emerged in the mid-1980s in East Africa, and HIV rates among people 15–49 years old have ranged from less than 1 per cent in Niger to 20 per cent in South Africa. In 2013, 25 million Africans were infected with HIV, and 1.6 million died from AIDS (UNAIDS 2013). As the magnitude of the AIDS pandemic became apparent in the new millennium, and particularly as antiretroviral therapy (ART) was developed to extend the lives of PLHIVs in the West, a transnational activist movement emerged to demand global attention to and funding for AIDS. Such activism was driven by what Vinh-Kim Nguyen (2010) terms 'therapeutic citizens' or people with a health condition who feel entitled to the protection of the right to health and who engage the political process to protect this right.

Therapeutic citizenship comes from the shared experiences of living with HIV/AIDS. Because people with the disease face life-changing circumstances, they develop an 'HIV/AIDS identity' which drives them to help others infected with or affected by HIV/AIDS and which reformulates their citizenship identity vis-à-vis the state. Therapeutic citizens first emerged in the West in the 1980s, with the formation of groups like ACT UP and Gay Men's Health Crisis (Siplon 2002). By the mid-1990s, activists in low and middle income countries also mobilized, and their activities led to the development of global AIDS structures and funding mechanisms (Kenworthy and Parker 2014; Altman 1994; Mbali 2013; Smith and Siplon 2006). For example, the Treatment Action Campaign (TAC) was established in South Africa formed to advocate for state-provided ART access for all eligible South Africans. In Zambia, a country with an HIV rate of roughly 14 per cent, the Network of Zambian People Living with HIV/AIDS (NZP+) was formed in 1996; since then it has developed community-based groups which provide material, social and psychological support to PLHIVs in all of Zambia's districts (Patterson and Stephens 2012).

While the presence of widespread therapeutic citizenship in Africa can be debated (see Whyte *et al.* 2013), for PLHIVs who embraced this citizenship, it has several components. First, it involved rights and responsibilities at all levels of the political community, not just in relation to the state. At the local level, activists viewed citizenship obligations to include caring for other PLHIVs or educating neighbours about HIV. In turn, they believed they had a right to protection from discrimination and inclusion in community decisions (Patterson 2015). At the state level, they asserted a right to medication, health care and non-discrimination; in return, their responsibility was to 'play by the rules' in terms of adhering to medications, attending clinic appointments and practising healthy behaviours. This was seen as their obligation to the social contract (Rasmussen 2013). At the global level, they referred to international human rights documents to lobby donors for medication and funding. Thus, citizenship rights and responsibilities were situated at the local, national and international levels. PLHIV participation reflected this multi-level view of citizenship. In Zambia, NZP+ advocated nationally for the state to provide free ART to all people who needed it, but it also lobbied district officials for local AIDS programmes and donors for funding.

As a second aspect, therapeutic citizenship embraces a relatively narrow understanding of citizenship; citizens are defined based on an individual's health condition. For example, NZP+ was only open to people who were HIV-positive. Therapeutic citizenship has the possibility to exclude some from entitlement to health care (or more broadly, other socio-economic rights). Yet transforming therapeutic citizenship into an identity that seeks to protect the rights of all regardless of health condition can be divisive. For example, TAC has sought to move beyond an AIDS-only agenda to lobby for better health care, education and housing rights in South Africa, but this has created some internal struggles (Friedman and Mottiar 2004). For pragmatic reasons, many other PLHIV organizations in Africa have not sought to broaden their membership. In the process, they promote a communal view of citizenship, as only PLHIVs benefit from participation.

Neoliberalism shapes therapeutic citizenship. Austerity measures caused African states to be ill-prepared to address the pandemic. The initiation of user fees in the 1980s, for example, made it less likely that individuals would seek primary health care treatment for sexually transmitted infections, diseases that can increase vulnerability to HIV (Stillwaggon 2005). Such cuts made it difficult for the state to embody an alternative vision put forward by therapeutic citizens of a state that protects the right to the highest attainable standard of health care (Johnson 2006). Cuts in state spending also meant that bilateral and multilateral donors have provided the vast majority of sums for ART programmes, HIV prevention and support and care for PLHIVs. The Global Fund and PEPFAR, for example, provide roughly 80 per cent of funding for Zambia's AIDS response (Patterson and Stephens 2012). This dynamic necessitated that therapeutic citizens mobilize at the international level to lobby donors, but it also raises questions about how citizens view the state if donors must provide most funding. One possibility is that the state's legitimacy (and thus, the social contract) may be harmed. Another possibility – supported in research by Audrey Sacks (2012) – is that citizens may view the state positively if it can attract donor funding. In the latter view, the state becomes an intermediary or broker. More research is needed to understand the complexities of therapeutic citizenship and state accountability in light of donor projects.

Democratization contributed to the rise of therapeutic citizens in two ways. First, demands for democracy in the early 1990s distracted state elites so that they focused on political survival (or political ascension) rather than AIDS. Few political leaders spoke about the disease, given the AIDS stigma and its connection with sex and death; to do so would not garner votes in multi-party elections. (As an exception, when Ugandan President Yoweri Museveni acted on AIDS, his actions reflected concerns about security and regime survival.) (Patterson 2006). The lack of state attention to AIDS (and democracy's inability to provide a political incentive for state elites to address the disease) led to the rise of therapeutic citizens. Second, democratization provided the space in which therapeutic citizens could emerge, as it allowed civil society organizations to mobilize, access media and use political institutions such as courts and legislatures to push for policy changes.

Responsibilization also provided openings for therapeutic citizenship. Donors wanted local communities to address AIDS, and thus, they sought to empower local people for sustainable solutions to AIDS. For example, donors have worked through AIDS support groups (sometimes even setting up these groups) in order to create 'AIDS competent' individuals who can uphold their responsibilities in the AIDS social contract (Kenworthy 2014). The burden for the AIDS response is thus transferred to local people as therapeutic citizens feel obligations to other PLHIVs and the local community. In the process, donors' empowerment efforts may reinforce therapeutic citizenship identities that potentially exclude other marginalized individuals.

Finally, globalization has facilitated therapeutic citizenship, since it has enabled local activists to make connections to other AIDS organizations. Resources, moral support and ideas have flowed to African AIDS organizations. Therapeutic citizens have particularly benefited from an epistemic community (i.e. groups of health officials and scientists) that demonstrated how access to ART was essential for combating the AIDS stigma, urging HIV testing and lowering the risk of HIV transmission (Patterson 2006). Global norm entrepreneurs framed access to medication as a human right and moral cause, leading wealthy states to accept this norm (Keck and Sikkink 1998; Smith and Siplon 2006). Global tools, resources, norms and entrepreneurs contributed to the rise of therapeutic citizens in Africa.

Alternative citizenships and the continent's democratic future

Autochthony, Christian citizenship and therapeutic citizenship embody notions of communal citizenship in which belonging is defined by participation within a specific community. Communal citizens participate to gain benefits for that community, and citizenship identity is reinforced through such participation. In all political communities, citizens have multiple identities and, in some cases, these identities (such as therapeutic citizenship) have pushed the state to provide important benefits. However, even though all three of the examined citizenships use the language of rights, they do not necessarily urge participation to protect the political, economic and social rights of all individuals within a particular state territory. While these communal citizens do not discount the state, they have alternative visions for its function and their most salient forms of identity may not revolve around the state. For autochthons, the community of origin matters; for Christians, it is the Kingdom of God; and for therapeutic citizens, it is people with the shared health condition of HIV/AIDS.

Neoliberalism has facilitated the rise of these citizenships by decreasing the state's role in service provision and the promotion of order. Why rely on the state when the church or donors can assist? Democratization opens opportunities for new groups to bring their concerns into the public arena. It also threatens elites, who may define citizenship in ways that benefit some (e.g. autochthons) over others. Responsibilization urges local communities to solve their problems, whether those local communities are 'sons of the soil', Pentecostal churches or PLHIVs. And globalization has given autochthons, Christian citizens and therapeutic citizens access to resources and international networks, while sometimes threatening their identities.

These alternative forms of citizenship may potentially affect democracy in two ways. First, they may lead to new types of participation. Research has shown that while voting rates in Africa are relatively high, few individuals contact elected officials about problems or work with other citizens to confront officials on issues. Africans appear to '*prefer* a broadly *delegative* form of democracy' (Bratton and Logan 2013, 203; emphasis in original). Yet, when we include political involvement through alternative citizenship venues (e.g. Pentecostal prayers for the nation, care for PLHIVs or, less positively, autochthonous violence), it is possible to see the depth of Africans' political involvement. Future research should investigate alternative citizenships and the types of participation they embrace.

Second, alternative citizenships may hamper the emergence of liberal citizens who participate in order to hold governments accountable for protecting the rights of all. While individuals in Africa's new democracies have moved from being subjects of authoritarian regimes to voters, democracy ultimately rests on the need for citizens who 'regularly claim accountability from leaders' (O'Donnell 2007, 198). According to Afrobarometer surveys in 18 countries in 2005–06, 56 per cent of adults look to other institutions – the executive or political parties – to hold elected legislators accountable (Bratton and Logan 2013, 203). This finding suggests that individuals often do not 'recognize themselves as legitimate claimants of rights' and, when they do, they tended to claim those rights for a few (autochthons, Christians, PLHIVs or other select groups) instead of all inhabitants of the state's territory (Smulovitz and Peruzzotti 2003, 310). More research is needed to better understand how alternative citizenships may (or may not) draw individuals away from contributing to an inclusive political community.

Stephen Jackson (2007) argues that legal definitions of citizenship are necessary but insufficient for fostering citizenship. Rather, citizenship must include a lived sense of belonging in a community, an embodiment that is ethically vital for a community to function and live in peace. Without a strong sense of this citizenship ethic, manipulation of the legal components of citizenship as occurred in Democratic Republic of Congo or Côte d'Ivoire is possible. A culture of citizenship is one in which the state seeks to protect the rights of all, and citizens hold the state accountable for this protection. Yet neoliberalism, with its push for non-state solutions to community development, its focus on individual advancement and its

168 A. S. Patterson

incorporation of the individual into global markets, has eroded the state's ability to foster such an ethic. As Samson Bezabeh (2011) asserts, the very underdevelopment of the state hampers citizenship, because the state cannot or will not promote a social contract in which both parties – the state and citizen – have rights and responsibilities. As such, the development of liberal citizenship in Africa is inextricably bound to the development of the state. Whether such a transformation is possible in neoliberal Africa is a question for future research.

Note

1 In order to simplify the analysis, I focus on Christianity instead of multiple religious identities in the analysis of religion and citizenship.

References

Afrobarometer. 2009. Are Democratic Citizens Emerging in Africa? http://afrobarometer. org/sites/default/files/publications/Briefing%20paper/AfrobriefNo70.pdf.

Afrobarometer. 2013. Governments Falter in Fight to Curb Corruption. http://afrobarometer. org/sites/default/files/publications/Briefing%20paper/ab_r5_policypaperno4.pdf.

Altman, Dennis. 1994. *Power and Community: Organization and Cultural Responses to AIDS*. Abingdon: Taylor & Francis.

Asamoah-Gyadu, Kwabena. 2005. 'Christ is the Answer': What is the Question? A Ghana Airways Prayer Vigil and Its Implications for Religion, Evil and Public Space. *Journal of Religion in Africa* 35(1): 93–117.

Banégas, Richard. 2006. Côte d'Ivoire: Patriotism, Ethnonationalism and Other African Modes of Self-Writing. *African Affairs* 104(421): 535–52.

Barbalet, J. M. 1988. *Citizenship*. Minneapolis: University of Minnesota Press.

Bezabeh, Samson. 2011. Citizenship and the Logic of Sovereignty in Djibouti. *African Affairs* 110(441): 587–606.

Boâs, Morten. 2009. 'New' Nationalism and Autochthony: Tales of Origin as Political Cleavage. *Africa Spectrum* 44(1): 19–38.

Bratton, Michael and Logan, Carolyn. 2013. Voters But Not Yet Citizens: The Weak Demand for Vertical Accountability. In Bratton, Michael (ed.) *Voting and Democratic Citizenship in Africa*. Boulder: Lynne Rienner Publishers.

Bratton, Michael and van de Walle, Nicolas. 1997. *Democratic Experiments in Africa*. New York: Cambridge University Press.

Bratton, Michael and Wonbin Cho. 2006. Where is Africa Going? Views from Below. http://afrobarometer.org/sites/default/files/publications/Working%20paper/AfropaperNo60.pdf.

Dahl, Robert. 1972. *Polyarchy: Participation and Opposition*. New Haven, CT: Yale University Press.

Dercon, Stefan and Gutiérrez-Romero, Roxana. 2012. Triggers and Characteristics of the 2007 Kenyan Electoral Violence. *World Development* 40(4) 731–44.

Diamond, Larry. 1999. *Developing Democracy: Toward Consolidation*. Baltimore: The Johns Hopkins University Press.

Dorman, Sara Rich. 2005. Studying Democratization in Africa: A Case Study of Human Rights NGOs in Zimbabwe. In Igoe, Jim and Kelsall, Tim (eds) *Between a Rock and a Hard Place: African NGOs, Donors and the State*. Durham: Carolina Academic Press.

Dorman, Sara, Hammett, Daniel and Nugent, Paul. (eds). 2007. *Making Nations, Creating Strangers: States and Citizenship in Africa*. Leiden: Brill Publishers.

Ellis, Stephen and ter Haar, Gerrie. 1998. Religion and Politics in Sub-Saharan Africa. *Journal of Modern African Studies* 36(2): 175–201.

Englebert, Pierre. 2009. *Africa: Unity, Sovereignty, Sorrow*. Boulder, CO: Lynne Rienner.

Ferguson, James. 1990. *The Antipolitics Machine: Development, Depoliticization, and Bureaucratic Power in Lesotho*. New York: Cambridge University Press.

Ferguson, James. 2009. The Uses of Neoliberalism. *Antipode* 41(S1): 166–84.

French, Howard. 2014. *China's Second Continent: How a Million Migrants Are Building a New Empire in Africa*. New York: Knopf.

Freston, Paul. 2001. *Evangelicals and Politics in Asia, Africa and Latin America*. New York: Cambridge University Press.

Friedman, Steven and Mottiar, Shauna. 2004. A Moral to the Tale: The Treatment Action Campaign and the Politics of HIV/AIDS. Paper for the Centre for Policy Studies. Durban, South Africa: University of KwaZulu-Natal. www.escr-net.org/sites/default/files/Friedman_Mottiar_-__A_Moral_to_the_Tale.pdf.

Gallup. 2007. Africans' Confidence in Institutions – Which Country Stands Out? www.gallup.com/poll/26176/africans-confidence-institutions-which-country-stands-out.aspx.

Geschiere, Peter. 2009. *The Perils of Belonging: Autochthony, Citizenship and Exclusion in Africa and Europe*. Chicago: University of Chicago Press.

Gifford, Paul (ed.). 1995. *The Christian Churches and the Democratisation of Africa*. Leiden: Brill.

Gifford, Paul. 2004. *Ghana's New Christianity*. Bloomington, IN: Indiana University Press.

Gifford, Paul. 2009. *Christianity, Politics and Public Life in Kenya*. New York: Columbia University Press.

Gusman, Alessandro. 2013. The Abstinence Campaign and the Construction of the Balokole Identity in the Ugandan Pentecostal Movement. *Canadian Journal of African Studies* 47(3): 273–92.

Gyimah-Boadi, E. 2004. *Democratic Reform in Africa: The Quality of Progress*. Boulder, CO: Lynne Rienner Publishers.

Harbeson, John. 2013. Democracy Autocracy and the Sub-Saharan African State. In Harbeson, John W. and Rothchild, Donald (eds) *Africa in World Politics*, 5th edition. Boulder, CO: Westview Press.

Hearn, Julie. 2002. The 'Invisible' NGO: US Evangelical Missions in Kenya. *Journal of Religion in Africa* 32(1): 32–60.

Huntington, Samuel. 1991. *The Third Wave: Democratization in the Late Twentieth Century*. Norman: University of Oklahoma Press.

Jackson, Stephen. 2007. Of 'Doubtful Nationality': Political Manipulation of Citizenship in the D. R. Congo. *Citizenship Studies* 11(5): 481–500.

Jenkins, Phillip. 2007. *The Next Christendom: The Coming of Global Christianity*. London: Oxford University Press.

Johnson, Krista. 2006. Framing AIDS Mobilization and Human Rights in Post-Apartheid South Africa. *Perspectives on Politics* 4(4): 663–70.

Kalu, Ogbu. 2008. *African Pentecostalism*. New York: Oxford University Press.

Keck, Margaret and Sikkink, Kathryn. 1998. *Activists Beyond Borders: Advocacy Networks in International Politics*. Ithaca, NY: Cornell University Press.

Kenworthy, Nora. 2014. Participation, Decentralization and Déjà Vu: Remaking Democracy in Response to AIDS? *Global Public Health* 9(1–2): 25–41.

Kenworthy, Nora and Parker, Richard. 2014. HIV Scale-Up and the Politics of Global Health. *Global Public Health* 9(1–2): 1–6.

Kinyanjui, Mary Njeri. 2013. Women Informal Garment Traders in Nairobi. *African Studies Review* 56(3): 147–64.

Longman, Timothy. 2010. *Christianity and Genocide in Rwanda*. New York: Cambridge University Press

Lyons, Michal, Brown, Alison and Li, Zhigang. 2013. The China-Africa Value Chain. *African Studies Review* 56(3): 77–100.

Mamdani, Mahmood. 1996. *Citizen and Subject: Contemporary Africa and the Legacy of Late Colonialism*. Princeton, NJ: Princeton University Press.

Manby, Bronwen. 2009. *Struggles for Citizenship in Africa*. London: Zed Books.

Marshall, Thomas H. 1964. *Class, Citizenship and Social Development*. New York: Doubleday.

Mattes, Robert and Shenga, Carlos. 2013. Uncritical Citizenship: Mozambicans in Comparative Perspective. In Bratton, Michael (ed.) *Voting and Democratic Citizenship in Africa*. Boulder: Lynne Rienner Publishers.

Maxwell, David. 2000. 'Catch the Cockerel before Dawn': Pentecostalism and Politics in Post-Colonial Zimbabwe. *Africa: Journal of the International African Institute* 70: 249–77.

Mbali, Mandisa. 2013. *South African AIDS Activism and Global Health Politics*. London: Palgrave Macmillan.

Migdal, Joel. 2006. Whose State Is It, Anyway? Exclusion and the Construction of Graduated Citizenship in Israel. *Israel Studies Forum* 21(2): 3–27.

Miller, David. 1995. Citizenship and Pluralism. *Political Studies* 43: 432–50.

Miller, Donald and Yamamori, Tetsunao. 2007. *Global Pentecostalism: The New Face of Christian Social Engagement*. Los Angeles: University of California Press.

Moss, Todd. 2007. *African Development: Making Sense of the Issues and Actors*. Boulder: Lynne Rienner Publishers.

Moss, Todd. 2013. Reflections on Africa's Rocky Love-Hate Relationship with International Capital. In Harbeson, John and Rothchild, Donald (eds) *Africa in World Politics*, 5th edition. Boulder, CO: Westview Press.

Ndegwa, Stephen. 1997. Citizenship and Ethnicity: An Examination of Two Transition Moments. *American Political Science Review* 91(3): 599–616.

Nguyen, Vinh-Kim. 2010. *The Republic of Therapy: Triage and Sovereignty in West Africa's Time of AIDS*. Raleigh, NC: Duke University Press.

Nyamnjoh, Francis. 2007. From Bounded to Flexible Citizenship: Lessons from Africa. *Citizenship Studies* 11(1): 73–82.

O'Donnell, Guillermo. 2007. The Perpetual Crises of Democracy. *Journal of Democracy* 18(1): 55–69.

O'Neill, Kevin. 2009. But Our Citizenship is in Heaven: A Proposal for the Future Study of Christian Citizenship in the Global South. *Citizenship Studies* 13(4): 333–48.

Oldfield, Adrian. 1990. Citizenship: An Unnatural Practice? *Political Quarterly* 61: 177–87.

Patterson, Amy. 1999. The Dynamic Nature of Citizenship and Participation: Lessons from Three Rural Senegalese Case Studies. *Africa Today* 46(1): 3–27.

Patterson, Amy. 2006. *The Politics of AIDS in Africa*. Boulder, CO: Lynne Rienner Publishers.

Patterson, Amy. 2011. *The Church and AIDS in Africa*. Boulder, CO: FirstForum Press.

Patterson, Amy. 2015. Engaging Therapeutic Citizenship and Clientship: Untangling the Reasons for Therapeutic Pacifism among People Living with HIV in Urban Zambia. *Global Public Health* 10: 1–14.

Patterson, Amy and Stephens, David. 2012. AIDS Mobilisation in Zambia and Vietnam: Explaining the Differences. *Contemporary Politics* 18(2): 213–24.

Peiffer, Caryn and Englebert, Pierre. 2012. Extraversion, Vulnerability to Donors and Political Liberalization in Africa. *African Affairs* 11(444): 355–78.

Pew Forum. 2006. Overview: Pentecostalism in Africa. www.pewforum.org/2006/10/05/overview-pentecostalism-in-africa.

Poku, Nana and Mdee, Anna. 2011. *Politics in Africa: A New Introduction*. London: Zed.

Ranger, Terence (ed.). 2008. *Evangelical Christianity and Democracy in Africa*. New York: Oxford University Press.

Rasmussen, Louise Mubanda. 2013. 'To Donors It's a Program, But to Us It's a Ministry': The Effects of Donor Funding on a Community-Based Catholic HIV/AIDS Initiative in Kampala. *Canadian Journal of African Studies* 47(2): 227–47.

Resnick, Danielle. 2011. In the Shadow of the City: Africa's Urban Poor in Opposition Strongholds. *Journal of Modern African Studies* 49(1): 141–66.

Riutta, Satu. 2009. *Democratic Participation in Rural Tanzania and Zambia: The Impact of Civic Education*. Boulder, CO: Lynne Rienner Publishers.

Sacks, Audrey. 2012. Can Donors and Non-State Actors Undermine Citizens' Legitimating Beliefs? World Bank Report. http://siteresources.worldbank.org/EXTPREMNET/Resources/EP95.pdf.

Siplon, Patricia. 2002. *AIDS and the Policy Struggle in the United States*. Washington, DC: Georgetown University Press.

Smith, Daniel Jordan. 2003. Patronage, Per Diems and the 'Workshop Mentality': The Practice of Family Planning Programs in Southeastern Nigeria. *World Development* 31(4): 703–15.

Smith, Daniel Jordan. 2014. *AIDS Doesn't Show Its Face: Inequality, Morality and Social Change in Nigeria*. Chicago: University of Chicago Press.

Smith, Ray and Siplon, Patricia. 2006. *Drugs into Bodies: Global AIDS Treatment Activism*. Westport, CT: Praeger Publishers.

Smulovitz, Catalina and Peruzzotti, Enrique. 2003. Societal Accountability in Latin America. *Journal of Democracy* 11(4): 147–58.

Ssempa, Martin. 2014. Debate Performance on *Morning @NTV*, 25 February. www.youtube.com/watch?v=LA8nxfRwdKM.

Stillwaggon, Eileen. 2005. *AIDS and the Ecology of Poverty*. New York: Oxford University Press.

Straus, Scott. 2012. Wars Do End! Changing Patterns of Political Violence in Sub-Saharan Africa. *African Affairs* 111(443): 179–201.

Swidler, Ann and Watkins, Susan Cotts. 2009. 'Teach a Man to Fish': The Sustainability Doctrine and Its Social Consequences. *World Development* 37(7): 1182–96.

Taylor, Ian. 2009. *China's New Role in Africa*. Boulder, CO: Lynne Rienner Publishers.

UNAIDS. 2013. Regional Fact Sheet 2013. www.unaids.org/en/resources/campaigns/2014/2014gapreport/factsheet.

van de Walle, Nicolas. 2001. *African Economies and the Politics of Permanent Crisis*. New York: Cambridge University Press.

Whitaker, Beth Elise. 2005. Citizens and Foreigners: Democratization and the Politics of Exclusion in Africa. *African Studies Review* 48(1): 109–26.

Whitaker, Beth Elise. 2011. The Politics of Home: Dual Citizenship and the African Diaspora. *International Migration Review* 45(4): 755–83.

Whyte, Susan, Whyte, Michael, Meinert, Lotte and Twebaze, Jenipher. 2013. Therapeutic Clientship: Belonging in Uganda's Projectified Landscape of AIDS Care. In Biehl, João and Petryana, Adriana (eds) *When People Come First: Critical Studies in Global Health*. Princeton, NJ: Princeton University Press.

World Bank. 2014. *Urban Development Data*. http://data.worldbank.org/topic/urban-development.

Young, Crawford. 2007. Nation, Ethnicity and Citizenship: Dilemmas of Democracy and Civil Order in Africa. In Dorman, Sara, Hammett, Daniel and Nugent, Paul (eds) *Making Nations, Creating Strangers: States and Citizenship in Africa*. Leiden: Brill.

INDEX

Action Group (AG) 138
African, Carribean and Pacific Group of
  States (ACP) 97, 104–8
African Cotton Association (ACA) 106,
  111
African Cotton Producers Association
  (AproCA) 106, 111
African Cotton and Textile Industries
  Federation (ACTIF) 107, 110–11
African Development Bank 48–9, 76
African Economic Research Consortium
  (AERC) 43
African National Congress (ANC) 147
African Union (AU) 24, 51, 97, 108, 127
Agricultural and Development Marketing
  Corporation (ADMARC) 124–5
agriculture 6, 27, 29–31, 58, 78, 102, 104,
  116, 119, 121–5, 154–5
Algeria 26, 48, 52
All African Agricultural Commodities
  Programme (AAACP) 97, 104–5
Angola 11, 12, 48, 52
Arab Spring 7, 9, 48
Asian Infrastructural Development Bank 13
authochthony 151–2, 158–60, 166

Banda, Hastings Kamuzu 124
Bandung Conference 24–5
Bénin 97, 100–1, 108
Berg Report 23, 28–9
Better Cotton Initiative (BCI) 109
Botswana 32, 36, 40, 42
Brazil 16, 54, 102–3, 116, 125, 157

Bretton Woods Institutions 23–4, 30, 38,
  42, 48
BRICS countries 13–16, 54–5
Burkina Faso 36, 48, 97, 101–2, 159

Cameroon 100, 106, 160
Campaign for Democracy (CD) 137, 142,
  144–5, 147
Chad 48, 97
China 13, 16, 26, 54–5, 66, 68, 96, 98–9,
  106–7, 119, 125, 157
civil liberties organization 142
colonialism 8, 25, 78, 131, 140
Comité d'orientation et de suivi du
  Partenariat UE-Afrique sur le coton
  (COS-Coton) 105
Committee for the Defence of Human
  Rights (CDHR) 142
Common Market for Eastern and Southern
  Africa (COMESA) 97
Communauté Économique des États de
  l'Afrique Centrale (CEEAC) 97
Communauté Économique et Monétaire
  de l'Afrique Centrale (CEMAC) 107
community-based organization (CBO)
  131
Comprehensive Africa Agriculture
  Development Programme (CAADP)
  108
Constitutional Rights Projects (CPR) 142
corporate social responsibility (CSR) 97
Côte d'Ivoire 42, 159, 167
Cotton Made in Africa (CmiA) 109

174 Index

Council for the Development of Social Science Research in Africa (CODESRIA) 105

Democratic Republic of Congo 11, 107, 159, 167
Doha Round 102, 105

Economic Commission for Africa (ECA) 24, 26–8
Economic Community of West African States (ECOWAS) 107
economic recovery program 38
Egypt 7–9, 48, 52, 119
Eko Atlantic 66, 69–70
Enhanced Structural Adjustment Facility (ESAF) 4
Ethiopia 12, 36, 55, 116, 119, 121, 125
EU–Africa Partnership on Cotton (PACRM) 97, 104–5, 108
European Union (EU) 97, 104, 144

Final Act of Lagos (FAL) 24, 27–8
Food and Agriculture Organization (FAO) 50, 67, 115
foreign direct investment (FDI) 12

Gabon 48
Ghana 30, 32, 36–42, 76–7, 79–82, 84, 87, 90, 107, 116, 118, 120, 126, 131, 162–3
globalization 2, 6–8, 57, 63, 66–7, 77, 79–80, 131–2, 141, 151, 154, 157–8, 160, 163–4, 177–7
Greece 8, 116
Greek debt crisis 3
gross domestic product (GDP) 5, 12, 16, 31–3, 36, 38–9, 41, 49–50, 52–3, 58, 119–21, 123, 155

heavily indebted poor countries (HIPC) 5
heterotopias 61, 67–8, 71–2
HIV/AIDS 151, 162, 164, 166
Human Development Index (HDI) 12, 38, 123
human rights 136, 140–2, 144–5, 149, 156, 165

illicit financial flows (IFF) 50–1
integrated water resources management 131
Interim National Government 144
International Center for Trade and Sustainable Development (ICTSD) 98–9
International Cotton Advisory Committee (ICAC) 110

International Monetary Fund (IMF) 3–5, 7, 28, 31, 49, 52–3, 77, 115, 119, 124, 136–8, 140–1, 143, 148, 154
International Trade Centre 99, 105

Kenya 12, 42, 55, 68–9, 70–1, 89, 116, 160–1, 163
Keynes, John Maynard 57
Konza Techno City 68, 70

Lagos Plan of Action (LPA) 24, 27–8, 40
land grabs 55, 125
land rights 76, 87–8
Latin America 9–10, 17, 54, 103, 119, 155
Lesotho 36, 42, 117
liberalization 15–16, 23–4, 30, 32, 38–9, 61, 77–9, 81–3, 86, 89, 96–7, 102–3, 106, 118, 125, 138, 141, 143, 154
Liberia 159
licit financial flows 52

Malawi 36, 42, 116, 120, 123–5, 156
Mali 32, 36, 97, 101
Marx, Karl 6
migration 158–60
Morocco 48
Movement for the Survival of Ogoni People (MOSOP) 142
Mozambique 5, 12, 36, 54–5
Mubarak, Hosni 8–9

Nairobi 63, 67, 70–1
National Association of Nigerian Students (NANS) 139, 141–3
National Consultative Forum (NCF) 142
National Council of Nigerian Citizens (NCNC) 138
National Union of Petroleum and Natural Gas Workers Union (NUPENG) 145
New Asian-African Strategic Partnership (NAASP) 26
New Economic Partnership for Economic Development (NEPAD) 108
Nigeria 27, 36, 40, 42, 48, 52, 57, 66, 68–70, 107, 116, 136–8, 140–9, 156, 160, 162
Nigeria Bar Association (NBA) 142
Nigeria Medical Association (NMA) 139
Nigerian Union of Journalists (NUJ) 142
Non-Aligned Movement 25
Northern People's Congress (NPC) 138

Obstfeld, Maurice 3
Organization of African Unity (OAU) 24, 27–8

Index **175**

Organization for Economic Cooperation and Development (OECD) 11, 119, 121

Polanyi, Karl 49
privatization 2–3, 5–8, 23–4, 78, 111, 118, 122, 124, 126, 131–2, 138, 140, 143, 154–5, 160
Program of Action to Mitigate the Social Cost of Adjustment (PAMSCAD) 30
Provisional Ruling Council 145
public–private–community in partnership 126
public–private partnership (PPP) 126

quantitative easing 57

Rwanda 12, 159

Senegal 89, 116, 118, 120, 153
Seychelles 36, 42
Sierra Leone 12, 42
South Africa 12, 48, 50–5, 57, 64, 68, 73, 89, 116–18, 124, 126, 136–7, 140–4, 146
Southern African Development Community (SADC) 14
special economic zone 66
state-owned enterprise124, 154, 162
structural adjustment program (SAP) 4–5, 28, 36, 39, 63, 116–18, 124, 126, 136–7, 140–4, 146
Sustainable Development Goals (SDG) 15–16

syndrome-free 36–42

transnational corporation (TNC) 12, 50, 52–4
terms of trade 23, 29, 32, 36, 106
Togo 36, 42
Tunisia 8–9, 48

Uganda 5, 36, 48
UN-HABITAT 62, 88
L'Union Économique et Monétaire Ouest-Africaine (UEMOA) 97
United Kingdom (UK) 2, 119, 123, 126, 154
United Nations (UN) 115, 119, 126, 131
United Nations Conference on Trade and Development (UNCTAD) 12–13, 52–3, 99
United Nations Development Programme (UNDP) 12, 119, 123
United Nations Economic Commission for Africa (UNECA) 52, 127
United States (US) 25–6, 98, 119, 144, 154, 163

Washington Consensus (WC) 8, 14, 30
World Trade Organization (WTO) 97, 99, 101–5

Zambia 42, 51, 89, 116, 120, 125, 127, 153–5, 162–5
Zimbabwe 4, 117, 127

Taylor & Francis eBooks

Helping you to choose the right eBooks for your Library

Add Routledge titles to your library's digital collection today. Taylor and Francis ebooks contains over 50,000 titles in the Humanities, Social Sciences, Behavioural Sciences, Built Environment and Law.

Choose from a range of subject packages or create your own!

Benefits for you
- Free MARC records
- COUNTER-compliant usage statistics
- Flexible purchase and pricing options
- All titles DRM-free.

Benefits for your user
- Off-site, anytime access via Athens or referring URL
- Print or copy pages or chapters
- Full content search
- Bookmark, highlight and annotate text
- Access to thousands of pages of quality research at the click of a button.

REQUEST YOUR FREE INSTITUTIONAL TRIAL TODAY

Free Trials Available
We offer free trials to qualifying academic, corporate and government customers.

eCollections – Choose from over 30 subject eCollections, including:

Archaeology	Language Learning
Architecture	Law
Asian Studies	Literature
Business & Management	Media & Communication
Classical Studies	Middle East Studies
Construction	Music
Creative & Media Arts	Philosophy
Criminology & Criminal Justice	Planning
Economics	Politics
Education	Psychology & Mental Health
Energy	Religion
Engineering	Security
English Language & Linguistics	Social Work
Environment & Sustainability	Sociology
Geography	Sport
Health Studies	Theatre & Performance
History	Tourism, Hospitality & Events

For more information, pricing enquiries or to order a free trial, please contact your local sales team:
www.tandfebooks.com/page/sales

Routledge
Taylor & Francis Group

The home of Routledge books

www.tandfebooks.com